THE VICTORIAN VISITORS

THE VICTORIAN VISITORS

Culture Shock in Nineteenth-Century Britain

RUPERT CHRISTIANSEN

Atlantic Monthly Press
New York

First published in Great Britain in 2000 by Chatto & Windus, Random House, London, England

Printed in the United States of America

FIRST AMERICAN EDITION

Library of Congress Cataloging-in-Publication Data
Christiansen, Rupert.
    [Visitors]
    The Victorian visitors : culture shock in nineteenth-century Britain / Rupert Christiansen.
        p. cm.
    Originally published: The visitors. London : Chatto & Windus, 2000.
    Includes bibliographical references (p.) and index.
    ISBN 0-87113-790-9
    1. Great Britain—Social life and customs—19th century. 2. Visitors, Foreign—Great Britain—History—19th century. 3. Culture shock—Great Britain—History—19th century. 4. Great Britain—History—Victoria, 1837–1901. I. Title.

DA533 .C57 2001
941.081—dc21   00-065057

Atlantic Monthly Press
841 Broadway
New York, NY 10003

01 02 03 04   10 9 8 7 6 5 4 3 2 1

Contents

List of illustrations

G. M. M.

Die Welt ist lieblich, und nicht fürchterlich dem Mutigen . . .

Those who exchange presents with one another
Remain friends the longest,
If things turn out successfully.

Quoted from the Norse Edda saga by Marcel Mauss in
Essai sur le don (1925)

There is nothing I should care more to do, if it were possible, than to rouse the imagination of men and women to a vision of human claims in those races of their fellow-men who most differ from them in customs and beliefs . . .

George Eliot to Harriet Beecher Stowe, 29 October 1876

A man should know something of his own country, too, before he goes abroad.

Laurence Sterne, Tristram Shandy

Introduction

The visitor travels alone and enters unknown territory. He bears a gift which is symbolic of his benevolent intent and bestows it on a stranger from whom he wants something in return – first, the hospitality of food and shelter; second, some useful or attractive object to take home, as proof of the success of his expedition; third, a bond which will allow continuing trade. This process, a basis of human society, can turn strangers into friends.

But not always. Those we do not understand we fear, and those we fear we banish or destroy. So, in order to communicate, the visitor must learn a culture as well as a language. 'When in Rome, do as the Romans do' was St Ambrose's practical advice to St Augustine. This is not easy, however: different people worship strange gods and, as Jane Austen shrewdly noted, 'One half of the world cannot understand the pleasures of the other.' At every stage there is the possibility of hostility erupting, as people guard the safety and prosperity of their own territory and kind. The visitor may not arrive with the intention of remaining, either as invader or coloniser, but his – or her – motives may be mistrusted.

How can these barriers be broken or surmounted? How do we accommodate and incorporate the foreign and alien? What can visitor and visited learn from their encounters? On these questions, as they apply to visitors to Britain between the Napoleonic and First World Wars, this book is based.

In our sub-conscious, in our dreams, nineteenth-century Britain still appears as 'Victorian England' – a dark and narrow place, dominated by Evangelical Christianity, reeking of drains and hemmed in by corsets: we do not want to linger there. Radiating from the landscape is a lost sense of national self-definition, in which Britannia stands rampantly imperial and confident of her destiny. As we enter the new millennium, this image embarrasses us – shames us even – and whatever our secret heart-swelling at the idea of 'Victorian values' (a phrase of

Margaret Thatcher's, which hit a peculiarly raw nerve in the present panic of our collective psyche)*, all our lives, to some extent, have been spent escaping its deadening influence.

But of course, Britain between the defeat of Napoleon in 1815 and the outbreak of the First World War in 1914 wasn't really 'Victorian' at all (according to the *Oxford English Dictionary*, the prim and fusty connotation of the term dates only from the 1930s). In significant respects it was a society much less neurotic and inhibited than our own: even if it twitched about the matter of sexual intercourse, it was burdened with neither the Freudian scrutiny of the deeper regions of the self, nor the blackest horrors of genocide and totalitarianism. In consequence, it could take a lot of life at face value, in a spirit of cheerfulness, tolerance and good faith – Trollope's novels are a monument to this neglected aspect of the 'Victorian' psyche.

It was also a society shaken by an unprecedented sense of its own volatility. Those who smugly think that ours is the only generation to have lived through the stress and turbulence of constant scientific advance should remind themselves of the climate changes which an 1815-1914 centenarian would have weathered. 'The first of the leading peculiarities of the present age is, that it is an age of transition,' wrote John Stuart Mill in 1831; 'the world moves faster and faster', added James Anthony Froude in 1864. These would become the clichés of every attempt to analyse what was happening to society but, like all the best clichés, they were validated by an undeniable force of truth.

Today, that sense of 'faster and faster' has become primarily a matter of minuscule and invisible increases in speed, calculated by the nanosecond and powered by the megabyte. But in the nineteenth century, alongside the fundamental and visible alteration of pace represented by the passage from travel in horse and carriage to travel in steam-powered trains, people were also confronted by the vast viral growth of cities and what the philosopher Frederic Harrison summarised in 1879 as 'the rattle and restlessness of life which belongs to the industrial maelstrom wherein we ever revolve' Over the last twenty years there has been a lot of talk about an 'information revolution': but is its effect on our daily existence any more radical than

---

*See Raphael Samuel's superb essay 'Mrs Thatcher and Victorian Values' in *Theatre of Memory*, vol. 2 , 'Unravelling Britain' (London, 1998).

that of the advent of telegraph and telephone and the Penny Post? Does the appearance of the latest microchip gizmos make more difference than that of photography, antiseptics, refrigeration and bicycles?*

Probably not: in any case, for all the rearguard fulminations of a section of the intelligentsia – Thomas Carlyle its noisiest and most influential representative – we tend to forget that the great majority of Victorians (the term being used neutrally to signify that notional British 1815–1914 centenarian) bubbled with optimism. They felt that, hand in hand, prosperity increased and enlightenment spread. Society was becoming more policed, documented, classified. Civilisation, like humankind itself, was *evolving*. 'The history of England is emphatically the history of progress,' wrote the first great ideologue of Victorian liberalism, Lord Macaulay. Two great intellectual monuments of the age, now unread and forgotten, H. T. Buckle's *History of Civilisation in England* (1857–61) and William Lecky's *History of Rationalism* (1865), expanded Macaulay's view to an even wider readership. It also fed into mid-century Darwinism and the *fin de siècle* socialism of William Morris's *News from Nowhere*. Even some of the major poets persuaded themselves of the truth of it: 'Progress is the law of life/Man is man not yet,' asserted Robert Browning. Things, in short, were getting better.

Yes, cultured Victorians had doubts. The increasing impossibility of reconciling blind faith in a supernatural God and the truth of the Bible with the laws of reason and science was something they found deeply disturbing: what moral foundations could hold the fabric of society together if the bedrock of Christian mythology crumbled? Intellectual complexities led to more uncertainties, and the constant expansion of the horizons of knowledge led to a yearning for a life that was tranquil, static and unambiguous. Too much was happening.

---

*Geoffrey Best, in *Mid-Victorian Britain* (London, 1971), quotes Frances Cobbe, a feminist and philanthropist, writing in the mid 1860s and looking back to the way the world had changed since the 1840s. 'The steam-engine locomotive by land and sea, steam applied to printing and manufacture, the electric telegraph, photography, cheap newspapers, penny postage, chloroform, gas, the magnesian and electric lights, iron ships, revolvers and breach-loaders of all sorts, sewing-machines, omnibuses and cabs, parcel deliveries, post-office savings banks, working-men's clubs, people's baths and wash-houses, Turkish baths, drinking fountains and a thousand minutiae of daily life, such as matches, Wenham ice, and all the applications of india rubber and gutta-percha' (*Hours of Work and Play*, 1867). See also James Gleick, *Faster: The Acceleration of Just About Everything* (London, 1999).

'Happy the people whose annals are blank in history books!' exclaimed Carlyle.

The Victorians were not so blessed: their pages were crowded and torn. But this never had the effect of turning them blankly conformist or mindlessly insular, and their anxiety never degenerated into cynicism. As Oscar Wilde put it at the end of the century, they understood the importance of being earnest – the importance, in other words, of looking up, believing in something and committing yourself to it, whether it be the Thirty-Nine Articles or Wilde's own 'principle of beauty'.

Such earnestness should not be linked to conservatism, for the Victorians' appetite for novelty was scarcely less insatiable than our own. Nor did they blinker themselves behind xenophobia and racism: on the contrary, Victorians invited, welcomed and appreciated the alien with genuine curiosity and enthusiasm. Even the more violent manifestations of jingoistic patriotism – brilliantly satirised by Dickens in the figure of Mr Podsnap in *Our Mutual Friend* (1864–5) – didn't preclude respect for the foreign. The Empire preached it and popular reaction to the Great Exhibition of 1851 reflects it. There may have been high points of the European artistic avant-garde – Wagner, for example, or the French Impressionists – which met with initial resistance and incomprehension, but in a society as pluralistic as Victorian England they made their way with less trouble than Stockhausen and Jackson Pollock would encounter a hundred years on.

The Visitors aims to illustrate and explore these traits of nineteenth-century Britain, using the stories of an assortment of visitors who arrived with something new to offer.

Why 'visitors'? Because none of them can properly be described as heroic pioneers (such as Marco Polo was in China). Because, equally, they were not émigrés (such as Henry James), political refugees (such as Karl Marx), or sociological observers (such as Prince Hermann von Puckler-Muskau or Hippolyte Taine) and because none of them came with the intention of staying long. Nor were they doctrinaire Anglomaniacs, bruised victims of violent tyranny nursing fantasies of a nation civilised by gentlemanly fair play and tolerance.* These visitors

---

*For which see Ian Buruma's subtle, incisive and entertaining *Voltaire's Coconuts: Anglomania in Europe* (London, 1999)

had no axe to grind, no dream to fulfil. They may have had expectations of the landscape and the manners of the people; they may have hoped to exert an influence over British tastes or morals. But at bottom their purpose for making the trip was the venal one of taking financial advantage of the richest and most powerful nation on earth.

Yet in their different ways all these gentle, friendly, temporary characters carried in their baggage something difficult and dangerous, which dazzled and confused the natives. 'Culture Shock' is another tossed-about phrase, made popular by the alarmist sociology of the 1960s and 1970s: in his book *Future Shock*, Alvin Toffler defined it melodramatically as 'the profound disorientation suffered by the traveller who has plunged without adequate preparation into an alien culture.' Here, however, the shock tends to run the other way, as the British appear more flummoxed by the traveller than vice versa; and rather than being negative or frightening, the effect of the experience is edifying and enriching.

Visiting may not involve the same level of risk that missionaries took to spread the Christian gospel or the hardship that Darwin endured in his scientific quest on HMS *Beagle*. The visit is a finite sort of adventure, in which the path home always remains open. Yet it does require a certain moral courage and imagination – it is not simply a matter of dropping by to leave a card or setting up a stall in the market-place. The visitor struggles to make him- or herself understood; the dialogue does not easily flow. But out of that effort, cultures change and flourish, and men and women learn to recognise new meanings and values in their lives.

CHAPTER I

Théodore Géricault, Painter

Paris, late in 1819. A dull, dishonest time, grey with the defeat of Napoleon and the spirit of revolution.

After the exhibition at the Louvre closed, Théodore Géricault detached the vast canvas from its frame, rolled it up and sent it to the house of his friend Cogniet for storage. The twenty-seven-year-old artist was profoundly depressed, with good reason. His great painting, the result of two years' labour, had failed to bring him the decisive public success he craved – its grandeur had been slighted, its theme misunderstood – and the twists of his emotional life could not be unknotted.

Cogniet had not visited the exhibition to see *Scène de Naufrage* ('scene of shipwreck'), as the masterpiece now known to the world as *The Raft of the 'Medusa'* was first anonymously labelled, so he unrolled the canvas on the floor to see it for himself.

Looking over his friend's shoulder, Géricault was dismayed. 'It's not worth looking at,' he muttered. 'I shall do better.'

If not better, then at least differently. Géricault was as restless an artist as he was a man – a forceful and angry one too. Easy, decorative grace and smoothly elegant composition were no part of his aesthetic. He struggled to bring to the Western tradition of art a sense of energy, of pushing and pulling, of the surge of the wind and the clash of living forms against the elements – powers which could infuse the inert symmetries of the neoclassical rule book. He sweated to infuse a whiff of contemporary reality and physical excitement into the meticulously staged tableaux of his seniors David and Ingres. But he was never satisfied, never still. All he could think was, 'I shall do better.'

Théodore Géricault was born in 1791, into a family that was prosperous, enterprising and middle class – his father was a lawyer turned accountant, of a moderately royalist persuasion. Most of Géricault's childhood was spent in Paris. He seems to have been an unremarkable schoolboy, mad about horses but not otherwise notably gifted. As a young man he emerged tall and poised, with a touch of the dandy, his manner either gently affectionate or stand-offish and insouciant. In 1808 his mother died, bequeathing him an annuity. Around this time he first expressed the wish to become an artist. Perhaps the cushion of financial independence encouraged such an ambition; perhaps it was initially a mere teenage dilettante's whim. In either case, such a thing was unprecedented in his parents' solidly professional dynasties, so, to avoid a painful rift with his elderly and conventional father, Géricault enlisted his late mother's brother, Uncle Caruel, in the fiction that he was undergoing an apprenticeship in the family business, a tobacco manufactory. Under this cover he began to attend the studio of Carle Vernet, a sophisticated painter of sporting scenes in a pseudo-English manner, under whose aegis he was soon tossing off copies and imitations. In a quest for more challenge, he then left Vernet for the more exigent Pierre Guérin, a follower of David, who could systematically teach him the science and theory of academic painting and construct his technique.

The complication was one at which even Géricault's contemporary Stendhal would have baulked. His sponsor, Uncle Caruel, was married to Alexandrine-Modeste, a beautiful and artistically sensitive young woman twenty-seven years his junior, by whom he had two small children. To Géricault, an only child saddened by the loss of his mother, she was at first more sister than aunt. Then, slowly but inexorably, their *tendresse* grew into desperate and incestuous sexual love. The situation, let alone the emotion, could never resolve itself.

The drama of Napoleon's downfall made little apparent impact on Géricault, who seems to have taken no side in the party political issues of the day. What now fulfilled him was a consuming sense of his destiny as an artist, and his sketches of these years show him excitedly exploring the lessons of Rubens, Titian and Caravaggio. Too soon for his abilities and experience, he began painting on an epic scale: his first significant work, dating from 1812, was three metres high and two metres wide. *The Charging Chasseur* depicts a horse rearing up in the thick of battle as its rider turns round and brandishes his sword – the composition is instantly arresting, if clumsy in detail. (The great master David was struck by its originality: as he walked through an exhibition, he stopped and stared at the canvas. 'Where does that come from?' he asked. 'I don't recognise the touch.')

Horses obsessed Géricault, despite (or because of) the fact that there was no tradition of portraying them in French art. It wasn't so much their speed and grace that gripped his imagination as the charged thrust of their rumps, their whinnying fury, the brutality restive within their beauty – so wildly unlike the poised and disciplined beasts meticulously depicted by his British predecessor George Stubbs. He painted and drew his passion in all weathers, from all angles: in the National Gallery in London, *A Horse Frightened by Thunder* stands obediently in Stubbsian profile, but rigid in terror, every sinew stiffened as if electrified; in the Louvre, the *Head of a White Horse*, its forelock brushed gently to one side, suggests a note of vulnerable quivering sensibility otherwise absent from Géricault's art.

To make up for the time he had idled away in adolescence, Géricault resolved on a vigorous programme of self-education:

> Draw and paint the great masters of the ancient world.
> Read and compose. Anatomy. Antiquity. Music. Italian.
> Follow a course in the ancient world, every Tuesday and Saturday at 2 p.m.
> December, figure painting at Dorcy's. In the evenings, draw in the classical style and compose on some themes. Busy myself with music.
> January, go to Guérin's to learn how to follow nature in painting.
> February, busy myself solely with the style of the Old Masters and compose without going out and remaining alone.

While he wrote out such curricula (the musical aspirations came to nothing), he may also have been trying to banish thoughts of Alexandrine. In 1816, as Europe opened its shutters for post-Napoleonic business, he decided to put a firm barrier between himself and his forbidden lover by travelling to Italy for two years. There, enlightened by the actual presence of the antiquities and Old Masters, he believed he could broaden his sensibility and escape his Parisian frustrations.

Leaving his affairs in immaculate order – Géricault was his father's son, no slovenly Bohemian – he passed from Florence to Rome, where he was overwhelmed by the grandeur of Michelangelo's Sistine Chapel. But within months he was scratchy with impatience. 'Italy is a wonderful country to know,' he wrote, 'but it is not necessary to spend so much time there as is sometimes claimed: a single year, well employed, seems quite enough.' He was lonely, homesick and unsure of himself, dwarfed and intimidated by the massive splendours of Rome.

To a friend in France he wrote gloomily: 'I am disorientated and confused. I try in vain to find something steady; nothing seems solid, everything eludes me, deceives me. Our earthly hopes and desires are only idle fancies, our successes mere illusions that we try to grasp. If there is one thing certain in this world, it is pain. Suffering is real, pleasure only imaginary.' A telling anecdote survives from this period. The sculptor Pradier visited Géricault's studio and praised one of his drawings. 'You are a great artist and will be a master!' he exclaimed. Géricault was unnerved by the compliment: after Pradier had left, he stared and stared at the drawing until he became paranoically convinced that it was full of faults and that Pradier had been merely sarcastic. He sent a furious message to the sculptor demanding an apology or a duel. But Pradier hastened over to reassure him of his sincerity. 'Is it really true then that I have talent?' Géricault pathetically asked him.

Yet his year in Italy was not unproductive, for he sketched and drew with brilliance and energy: not just copies of antiquities and Old Masters but landscapes, peasants, little scenes of local life. A larger project, which never came to fruition, was an epic treatment of the carnival race of the Barberi, in which riderless horses, cruelly provoked and goaded, would gallop panic-stricken down the Corso to the delight of hysterical crowds. Géricault planned a vast canvas, ten metres wide, of this barbaric spectacle, but after many detailed compositional studies he suddenly lost confidence, abandoned the idea and returned to France. Why? He seems to have told friends that his father, still unhappy at what he knew of his son's artistic leanings, had summoned him back, but it is more likely that some crisis in his relationship with Alexandrine was the prime cause and, shortly after his return to Paris in November 1817, she became pregnant by him.

In that same month a small volume entitled *The Shipwreck of the 'Medusa'* was published. Written collaboratively by Alexandre Corréard and Henri Savigny, it made a sensational impact throughout Europe with its account of an atrocious episode in which both authors had been participants. In July 1816 *La Méduse*, a French government frigate, part of a convoy carrying soldiers and emigrants to the colony of Senegal, made a foolish navigational error and ran aground in shallows off the West African coast. The fault clearly lay with the captain, a lackey of an aristocrat, with chums in the strongly royalist maritime ministry, whose appointment had clearly been a matter of unwarranted preferment. He failed to refloat the ship (largely because he refused to jettison its twenty-four-pounder guns) and after several days, as it began to break up, he ordered it to be abandoned. Six creaking lifeboats proved inadequate to accommodate all the passengers and crew, so a raft was constructed from planks lashed together with ropes. In the panic, the captain and senior officers took to the stronger boats, promising to tow the raft, but (whether by accident or design it was never established) the cables were lost, leaving it unnavigable in high and heavy seas.

A hundred and fifty people, including one woman inseparable from her husband, had been forced on to the raft, which measured just over twenty metres by seven. Nobody was put in command and no chart of the sea provided. There were no oars or rudder. Masts and sails were improvised, but to little effect. Under the weight of its load, the vessel did not float properly – fore and aft, the timbers were often submerged under as much as a metre of water – and a tiny supply of damp ship's biscuit was exhausted within hours. Crowding made it difficult to move and impossible to sleep. On the first night, adrift in furious seas, twenty of those confined to the edges of the raft were lost – some swept into the shark-infested sea, some drowned as their legs became inextricably caught between the beams. On the second night there were two drunken mutinies against those officers, Savigny and Corréard among them, who attempted to control the raft from a raised platform at its centre and dole out rations: the ensuing battles caused another sixty-five deaths. On the third day, amid hallucinations and delirium, cannibalism began: those with the forbearance to resist the temptation to dine on their fellow sufferers were granted an extra ration of wine. By the seventh day, only twenty-seven remained living, of whom thirteen were totally insane or severely wounded or sick. The only ordinary food was provided by one small catch of flying fish. This could not be reasonably distributed, so it was decided that those with a fair chance of survival should be given priority. Because it was useless to waste food on those who were inevitably dying, the incapacitated were therefore executed – the woman, crippled by a broken thigh, among them. The horror of this cold-blooded slaughter of the innocent seems to have been purgatory. To symbolise the revulsion against any further violence, all weapons except for one sabre of last resort were thrown into the sea after the corpses.

For a further unimaginable six days, the remaining fifteen managed to stay alive and relatively calm, sheltering under a canopy from the relentless daytime heat, with only wine, excrement ('the urine of some of us was more agreeable than that of others'), sea water, human flesh, one lemon and thirty cloves of garlic as their nourishment. The sole ground for hope was a visit from a white butterfly, fluttering about the raft like Noah's dove, a sign that land must be near. But no land was sighted. Finally, on the morning of 17 July, a ship appeared on the horizon.

> The sight of this vessel spread among us a joy which it would be difficult to describe. Fears, however, soon mixed with our hopes; we began to perceive that our raft, having very little elevation above the water, it was impossible to distinguish it at such a distance. We did all we could to make ourselves observed; we piled up our casks, at the top of which we fixed handkerchiefs of different colours. Unfortunately, in spite of all these signals, the brig disappeared. From the delirium of joy, we passed to that of dejection and grief.

Later in the day, however, the same ship – the *Argus*, part of the convoy in which the *Medusa* had originally been sailing – suddenly returned. It had been sent out to hunt for the raft and found fifteen living souls, of whom five died almost immediately.

One of the ten who survived to tell the tale was the ship's surgeon, Henri Savigny, who made it his mission to record the truth of the terrible events, secure compensation for the survivors and bring the captain to justice for his gross dereliction of duty. On his return to France, Savigny submitted a report to the ministry. To the deep embarrassment of the government, this incriminating document was leaked to the press and caused an international sensation – four days after being published in the *Journal des Débats*, it appeared in translation in *The Times*. Meanwhile a naval court quietly punished the *Medusa*'s captain with an absurdly lenient sentence, and the crony-stuffed ministry made clumsy and counter-productive attempts to cover up and damp down the affair. But Savigny joined with another survivor, the naval engineer Alexandre Corréard, and fought valiantly on. As a result of their campaign, both were dismissed from their government positions and harassed to the point of persecution. To further their cause and fan public support, they then wrote their book about the whole affair. It sold sensationally well in both France and England.

The ghastliness of this story haunted and inflamed Géricault's violent and morbid fancy. It also gave him an idea for a painting: Géricault wanted public success, but he was never prepared to win it by flattering society ladies in their best frocks (as Ingres did) or churning out classical or mythical scenes to please the academicians (as Guérin did). His artistic vision – later generations would meaninglessly label it 'Romantic' – demanded matter more vital, dramatic and intense. He was searching for a subject which entailed the actualities of the age. Such art could sell: the pompous and inert canvases of Antoine-Jean Gros, Napoleon's official war artist, were hugely successful, and the fashionable and worldly Horace Vernet, Géricault's neighbour and son of his teacher Carle, made easy money out of pictures of military, humorous, sentimental and picturesque aspects of modern life. Géricault knew himself to be a better, stronger artist than either of these – in order that the rest of the world should know that too, all he needed was the right scene. He had toyed with the depiction of the race of the Barberi horses and sketches also show him exploring the possibilities latent in another current newspaper story, the mysteriously motivated ritual disembowelling and murder of a retired magistrate in the Aveyron region. But Géricault's aim was not mere sensationalising illustration nor political agitprop. Unlike the facile Horace Vernet, he yearned to paint such events in the highest style, composing them as magnificently as the noblest of the Old Masters might have done: he wanted to elevate reality, not reproduce it. Somewhere in the turbulent story of the raft of the *Medusa* was the image that he required.

To help him find it, he turned to memories of Michelangelo's apocalyptic Sistine Chapel, with its masses of terrified struggling figures; another inspiration must have been the popular genre of shipwreck painting, in particular the spectacular rescue scenes dreamed up by the expatriate American John Singleton Copley and much reproduced in engravings. But the more immediate influences were Corréard and Savigny themselves. Géricault became friendly with the two men and through the early months of 1818, they helped him sketch his way through the entire saga – the mutiny, the eruption of cannibalism, the rescue – until he had explored every narrative and pictorial angle on the subject. In his studio he had Corréard, Savigny and the raft's carpenter help him build a scale model of the vessel: the final canvas reproduces it in precise detail, down to the gaps between some of the timbers.

The detail of the painting was exhaustively researched: in the words of his biographer and cataloguer Charles Clément, Géricault compiled 'a veritable dossier crammed with authentic proofs and documents'. He posed live models and copied relevant Old Masters; he travelled to Le Havre to observe marine skies and seascapes; he interviewed the other survivors of the raft; he visited hospitals to understand the faces of the dying and the dead; he even borrowed a severed head from the lunatic asylum and kept it on the roof of his studio for two weeks so that he could draw its features. Nothing was left to chance or fantasy: Géricault was no dreamer. Yet what finally emerged in the completed painting is truer to art than it is to nature. The raft itself may be represented with literal photographic accuracy, but those on board are less the naked, pustulous, bearded, bruised, starved, sunburnt, demented men of the morning of 17 July 1817 than figures posed to fulfil the traditional canons of composition within which Géricault worked – figures which Michelangelo, Rubens or Caravaggio would have recognised and admired for their muscularity and sensuality.

In August 1818 this laboured process of preparation was interrupted when Géricault was obliged to deal with the tragedy surrounding the birth of his son by Alexandrine. We do not know what names were called or what emotion boiled up in the scandal, but its consequences were clearly devastating. Uncle Caruel knew full well that he was not the father of his wife's child and an irreparable rift erupted between his side of the family and the Géricaults. The affair was hushed up – even the birth certificate registers the boy's parents as unknown.

Georges-Hippolyte Géricault was put into care and died in 1882, a pathetic solitary nonentity who did, however, venerate his father's memory. Alexandrine was confined to nun-like seclusion in the country, where she seems to have remained for the rest of her days –

she lived until she was ninety – and became deeply pious. It is doubtful that Géricault saw her again.

Was it out of a sense of mortified penitence for his illicit incest that he shaved his head and shut the door on ordinary life before dedicating himself to his great self-imposed challenge? (Remember, too, that *The Raft of the 'Medusa'* was a commercial speculation: there was no patron underpinning it, no commission or even promise of a sale.) Géricault was at one level a convivial, pleasure-loving man, but from November 1818 to July 1819 his existence became one of rigorous monastic simplicity. The concierge brought him food; occasionally, to keep his sanity, he might venture out for an evening, and a few friends and models dropped by to watch or to pose, but otherwise he was all artist, locked into his studio in the Faubourg du Roule and functioning at the absolute limit of his concentration, so long as daylight allowed.

In every respect he was orderly and methodical, keeping the colours of his palette (vermilion, white, Naples yellow, two yellow ochres, two red ochres, raw Sienna, light red, burnt Sienna, crimson lake, Prussian blue, peach black, ivory black, Cassel earth, bitumen) carefully separate and the studio clean and tidy. Complete silence was an absolute prerequisite and he told one friend that even the scuffling of a mouse could stop him working. He used small brushes and particularly thick, sticky oils, which dried overnight and left little opportunity for second thoughts. The models were posed singly, each figure painted to the finish over a vast outline sketch. This jigsaw procedure, focused exclusively on specific elements of the composition at the expense of its totality, was considered strange by observers and the consequent sense of groups of characters deliberately and theatrically posed for maximum effect is thought by some critics to mar the genius of the painting.

'His manner of working was quite new to me,' recalled his friend Montfort over thirty years later.

> It astonished me as much as his intense industry. He painted directly on the white canvas, without rough sketch or any preparation of any sort, except for the firmly traced contours, and yet the solidity of the work was none the worse for it. I was struck by the keen attention with which he examined the model before touching brush to canvas. He seemed to proceed slowly, when in reality he executed very rapidly, placing one touch after the other in its place, rarely having to go over his work more

than once. There was very little perceptible movement of his body or arms. His expression was perfectly calm . . .

The image which he finally selected eschews the melodramatic excess of the cannibalism, the overcrowded violence of the mutiny or the relief of the rescue. Instead, Géricault chose something less emotionally clear-cut – the point of unbearably intense excitement at which the *Argus* was first sighted on the far horizon. Barely visible, a mere dot of hope (in Géricault's early sketches, the brig looms much larger and clearer), it provokes a massive surge of heroic last-ditch optimism to the north-east of the canvas, counterpointed by the death-marked despair slumped over its south-west. To emphasize the bleakness of the false dawn, Géricault darkened the weather from the blazing blue sunshine of the actual morning to a louring storm and added two historically incorrect corpses. A total of twenty figures occupy Géricault's raft, five more than reality's; three of them – Savigny, Corréard and the ship's carpenter – are depicted from life. The picture which results is an image of tragedy, not triumph. It seems to tear itself in half.

Throughout this period of self-incarceration Géricault's closest companion was a handsome eighteen-year-old student who worked as his assistant. We know almost nothing of Louis-Alexis Jamar, who for some reason proved unforthcoming when interviewed, many years later, for Clément's biography. Apprentice and master slept in the same small room off the studio, and their relationship was at the very least stormy and emotional. One memoir later recorded how Géricault took a rare evening off with some friends, returning home at 2 a.m. drunk 'and in such a state of exaltation that he started to embrace M. Jamar – who had waited up for him – and did not want to let him go'. They quarrelled too. One afternoon, Jamar stormed out after Géricault had casually criticised him in front of some visitors. Having sulked at his parents' house for two days, he was awoken at 6 a.m. by a tap on the door of his attic bedroom. It was Géricault, who had slipped past the concierge and Jamar's sleeping parents to apologise and ask him to return. '*Mon petit Jamar*, you misinterpreted a remark which I made in your best interests,' he pleaded. So Jamar went back with him.

Géricault often sketched his apprentice, his thick black hair, pouting mouth and long nose lending themselves easily to affectionate caricature. He also painted his portrait twice* and posed him nude for the dead youth, sliding out of the grip of the Job-like elder in the foreground of *The Raft of the 'Medusa'*, as well as for two less prominent figures in the painting. No human being in Géricault's oeuvre is afforded the tenderness of expression and delicacy of touch that Jamar is. Why? Of what did their relationship consist? There is no answer. Other painters could dwell on the features of their wives or lovers: Géricault was forbidden Alexandrine, and for a year or so only Jamar was physically close to him – who else was there to hug when he was drunk?

Yet it could have been otherwise, had he wished it so, and what is striking is how little women interest him as an artist, how rarely and peripherally they feature in his work and how entirely absent they are as conventional erotic figures: *'Je commence une femme et ça devient un lion'* ('I begin [to draw] a woman and it becomes a lion'), he is reported to have explained lamely. He did sketch a few frank images of sexual congress, but the female nude – rounded, fleshy, and passive – which had been one of the great obsessions of painting in the 300 years since the Renaissance, did not engage him; the male nude – tense, sinewy and active – clearly did.

After eighteen months of gestation, *The Raft of the 'Medusa'* was finished in July 1819 and hung alongside 1300 other canvases in the Louvre's competitive annual exhibition of new French art known as the 'Salon'. Because the *Medusa* remained such a politically sensitive matter, Géricault inexplicitly entitled the painting *Scène de Naufrage*, although its precise subject would have been as obvious to anyone as a picture called *Car Crash* depicting a smashed-up Mercedes in a tunnel would be to us today. Its dimensions alone ensured that it made an impact, but the image was too original, too powerful and disconcerting to win the sort of instant popular acclaim that Géricault seems to have been hoping for. In the words of Lorenz Eitner, 'surrounded by altarpieces and pallid histories, this scene of a modern martyrdom violated

---

*One of these portraits was destroyed in the Second World War; the other hangs in the Louvre as *Portrait d'un jeune artiste dans un atelier*. The identity of the sitter has not been incontrovertibly established, but the present writer sees no need to doubt it. See *Géricault*, Galeries Nationales du Grand Palais (Paris, 1991), pp. 366–7 and Lorenz Eitner, *Géricault: His Life and Work* (London, 1983), pp. 203–5.

all the rules . . . it affronted authority, spurned official piety and popular taste and offered nothing to national pride.' It was neither Christian nor classical, neither edifying nor elegant. It seems that the majority of visitors to the Salon were impressed but also repelled, and the critics didn't quite know what to make of it either. There was confusion as to whether the scene was meant to serve as a piece of literal historical realism or a political allegory. What was its purpose, what was its message? Some found it too dark, too monochrome; some felt its violence to be distasteful. This ambitious unknown was talented, but he should try harder to conform to the good form of the modern masters. 'Courage, Monsieur Géricault! Try to moderate an enthusiasm that might carry you too far. Being a colourist by instinct, try to become one in practice; being still an imperfect draughtsman, study the art of David . . .' exhorted one reviewer.

At the close of the exhibition the judging panel awarded *Scène de Naufrage* a gold medal, but denied it the supreme honour of purchase for the national collection for the Louvre. Instead, Géricault was offered another consolation prize, in the form of an official commission to paint something on the theme of the Sacred Heart of Jesus. It wasn't a subject calculated to inspire him, but he accepted the compliment and, with characteristically cavalier generosity, secretly passed the job and the fee to the struggling young Eugène Delacroix, who knocked off something that Géricault then signed. Who would care? Or know the difference? Any jobbing artist might have been pleased by these attentions, but the reception of *The Raft of the 'Medusa'* had fallen short of Géricault's dreams and he was becoming thoroughly dis-enchanted with the French art world. His depressed cynicism plummeted towards exhausted nervous collapse.

Listless, morose and occasionally paranoid, tormented by who knows what emotional hell over his forbidden mistress and their baby, he lost his sense of direction. In early 1820 he toyed with the idea of embarking on another grand history painting – sketches survive of two sensational contemporary events, the Greek War of Independence and the murder of the Duc de Berry – but to replicate the Herculean effort of concentration that *The Raft of the 'Medusa'* had required would have been beyond his fragile mental equilibrium. A series of strange portraits of blankly staring, podgy-cheeked children also dates from this period: perhaps the explanation for their charmlessness relates to

Géricault's blocked feelings about his own little son, whom he may never have seen.

In any case, he needed something else to focus on. A long Byronic trip to the East would have been the obvious therapy, the easy route of escape from Parisian gossip, his family's disapproval, and the unequal struggle to make great art. But Gericault was always cussedly reluctant to do the obvious. 'What is it you think you lack here?' the painter François Gérard asked him. 'You have wealth and talent, your first efforts have been crowned by success. Why take the risk of travel in virtually unexplored countries? Don't you have an almost inexhaustible source of inspiration here at home? What more do you want?' To which reasonable questions the self-doubting, self-punishing Géricault replied solemnly, 'What I want is the trial of misfortune.'

So instead of taking the conventional grand tour, he decided to go to London, where a showman by the name of William Bullock had offered to display *The Raft of the 'Medusa'* in the Egyptian Hall, his premises in Piccadilly. It looks like a crudely commercial venture, but Géricault's time in England would constitute one of the most intriguing and productive episodes of his brief, troubled and ultimately mysterious life.

London, 1820. A city of creative vitality and big money. Foreign visitors were exhilarated and intimidated by its pace, bustle and dynamism – one guesses they sensed something of the buzz of present-day New York, something of the hysteria of modern Bombay. 'London was two things at once,' the historian Roy Porter explains. 'It was super-smart wealth, fashion, elegance; perhaps the best place on earth for males with money to enjoy an inexhaustible round of pleasures. Yet as well as being the playground of the rich, it possessed a special demotic energy.'

That energy wasn't entirely benign. Politically the atmosphere in Britain was volatile, particularly in the North, where the simmering problems of industrialisation threatened to turn peasants and labourers into a working class prepared for organised violence. The end of the Napoleonic Wars disrupted trade and a series of bad harvests pushed up food prices. The bitter and disenfranchised joined with radicals to stage strikes and demonstrations. 'Foreign nations regarded us as on the eve of a revolution,' recorded the chronicler of *The Annual Register for the Year 1820*, 'and even the wise and experienced among ourselves were not without apprehension with respect to the possible result.'

Against such agitation the Tory government took a hard line and parried with emergency 'gagging' legislation, suspending ancient liberties and intensifying censorship. In 1819 a peaceful rally in St Peter's Fields in Manchester was violently broken up by a cavalry charge – eleven died and hundreds were injured in what came to be known as the massacre of Peterloo. London was primarily a trading city and therefore less exposed to the conflicts that large-scale manufacture precipitated, but it too had occasion to shudder. In 1820 a serious conspiracy to assassinate the entire cabinet was foiled in a backstreet and there were ugly public scenes as the unpopular Prince Regent succeeded to the throne as George IV on the death of his poor mad father George III. The shabbily vicious manner in which the new king attempted to divest himself of his wretched estranged wife, Queen Caroline, fomented a further wave of hostility against the ruling class.

Yet there was no mistaking the deeper current of confidence flowing through the nation. It forcibly struck visitors from a Europe still struggling out of the post-Napoleonic slump. 'The happy effects of your admirable constitution may, indeed, be traced in all we see in England,' claimed the Marquis de Vermont in a book of the time. 'While every thing on the Continent is growing rather worse than better; while the chateaux, which escaped the united evils of war and revolution, are rapidly falling to decay; while our villages are deserted and our towns dilapidated; England seems, in spite of the complaints of her own politicians, to be rapidly advancing in her proud career of wealth and prosperity.'

Such a view was not an illusion. The government's repressions were effective and widely approved by those in work: 'With what hope could the ill-disposed prosecute machinations, which met with countenance from only the lowest order of people, which were regarded with abhorrence by all the respectable classes, and which the whole power of the state was arrayed to resist?' *The Annual Register* smugly inquired. The landed aristocracy had made handsome profits out of the Napoleonic Wars; new waves of industrialists and entrepreneurs made their fortunes fast, unhampered by the tolls and taxes and red tape which inhibited the rest of Europe. London swaggered with success and busily remapped itself. The architect John Nash was in the middle of his audacious scheme to replace higgledy-piggledy streets of brick and timber with a mile of gleaming imperial stucco, sweeping in one triumphalist curve from the Prince Regent's extravagant new palace of Carlton House up to Regent's Park. Further from the centre, rows and squares of town houses, designed to meet the requirements of the burgeoning middle classes, sprung up in suburbs and villages like Bloomsbury, Stoke Newington, Camden and Highbury.

Other areas remained miserably poor, dangerously filthy and overwhelmingly stinking. A generation before the triumph of the Victorian Utilitarian obsession with putting everything in order, there was no overall strategy of urban development or governance: the capital's growth was anarchic, its mood refractory. The result was a city which may not have been a nice place, but was certainly an exciting one. 'Have I not enough without your mountains?' wrote the impassioned Londoner Charles Lamb to those inveterate rural sentimentalists Dorothy and William Wordsworth in 1801.

> The lighted Shops of the Strand and Fleet Street, the innumerable trades, tradesmen and customers, coaches, waggons, playhouses, all the bustle and wickedness round about Covent Garden, the very women of the town, the Watchmen, drunken scenes, rattles – life awake, if you awake, at all hours of the night, the impossibility of being dull in Fleet Street, the crowds, the very dirt & mud, the Sun shining upon houses and pavements, the print shops, the old book stalls, parsons cheap'ning books, coffee houses, streams of soup from kitchens, the pantomimes. London itself a pantomime and a masquerade, – all these things work themselves into my mind and feed me . . . and I often shed tears in the motley Strand from fullness of joy at so much in life.

This vitality was also artistic and intellectual. London was never hidebound by the same network of royally sponsored academies and events (like the Salon) that dominated Parisian culture. Genius invaded from outside the Establishment and the most admired figures broke the rules rather than honoured them. Nor did Genius win official prizes: instead, it brusquely elbowed its way to the public's attention in a headline-hitting and sensational fashion. Lord Byron, mad, bad and dangerous to know; Edmund Kean, all flash and fire as Macbeth, Iago, Richard III – such were the heroes of the age.

In the visual arts there was far more experiment and variety than there was in Paris. Among the London cognoscenti, Joseph Turner's shimmering landscapes and John Constable's pure and subtle renderings of nature were increasingly admired. A broader public was thrilled and astounded by John Martin's vast, brash fantasies of apocalyptic scenes from the Old Testament – *Joshua commanding the Sun to Stand Still*, *The Fall of Babylon*, *The Destruction of Sodom and Gomorrah* – while lesser talents such as David Wilkie composed sentimental scenes in the manner of the Dutch school and Keats's friend Benjamin Haydon essayed the grand historical style.

The creative dynamism and ingenuity which pervaded British society in this era – Faraday's experiments with electricity, Stephenson's prototype locomotives, Dalton's chemical discoveries are all contemporary – also generated some remarkable technological innovation which gave London the edge in the commercial art market. English artists like John Cozens and Thomas Girtin pioneered the use of a full palette of watercolours, which younger men like Turner and Constable went on to exploit. Lithography, another medium more flexible than oil on canvas or ink on paper, may have been invented in Bavaria but it was only in London that its potential was first realised.

How much of all this Géricault appreciated when he made his decision to visit England we do not know – in the aftermath of the Napoleonic Wars, the culture of Paris in many respects lagged behind that of its rival metropolis and there is nothing in his letters to suggest a prior interest. It may well be that he simply wanted a change of scene and grabbed at the promise of money as a possible way out of his depression; it may be that he sensed that the high streets of London would provide a more receptive audience than had the Louvre Salon. But his readiness to take the risk on Bullock's offer certainly proved that when he shruggingly told his friend Cogniet that *The Raft of the 'Medusa'* '*ne vaut pas la peine d'être regardé*', he hadn't quite meant it.

And so, on 10 April 1820, accompanied by his friends Brunet and Charlet, Géricault set sail for England from Calais in the steam-packet *Iris*.* The entire journey from Paris to London would have

---

*There is mysterious and inconclusive evidence to suggest that Géricault might have previously visited England very briefly in 1819, apparently taking a short holiday from his labours on *The Raft of the 'Medusa'*. Passport records at Calais report his arrival at the port on 29 March (but oddly not his departure); the London magazine *Annals of the Fine Arts* simultaneously mentions that Géricault's friend Horace Vernet 'and a party of French artists, were hunting in Normandy, and on a freak they started for England, and gave a call on the different artists here'. See Christopher Sells, 'New Light on Géricault, his Travels and his Friends, 1816–23', *Apollo*, June 1986.

taken him about three days: one wonders if he spoke any English, or whether either Brunet or Charlet acted as his interpreters; one wonders, too, if he would have agreed with the Marquis de Vermont, who made the same journey around the same time and was delighted by 'the rapidity of the posting' on the Dover highway, 'the beauty of the horses and the civility of the drivers – the excellence of the roads – the rich variety of the landscapes – the ornamented grounds and villas of the gentry – the white cottages and neat gardens of the peasantry – the picturesque villages – the appearance of comfort so generally displayed in the dresses and dwellings of all orders of the people'; or whether he likewise deplored the overpriced accommodation and dreadful food ('the only real choice was between a tough mutton-chop and a hard beef steak, between an ill-cooked veal cutlet and a half-roasted leg of mutton, and between stale pastry and insipid jelly').

The Raft of the 'Medusa' followed a few weeks later – its surface has never recovered from the cracking caused by the necessity of rolling the canvas for the journey – after the final contract for the exhibition had been signed and Géricault had settled in a hotel. As he looked about, he felt encouraged by the absence of native artists painting proficiently in the grandly dramatic modern style he himself espoused. 'The English school distinguishes itself only by such subjects as landscape, seascape and genre,' he wrote to a friend in Paris. What led him to such an opinion? Most probably *Christ's Triumphal Entry into Jerusalem*, which had been put on display at the Egyptian Hall a couple of weeks before Géricault's arrival. This, the pretentious creation of Benjamin Haydon, had won popular acclaim and much coverage in the press: the high-minded, elderly doyenne of actresses, Mrs Siddons, gave it further kudos when she proclaimed that the figure of Jesus was 'completely successful'. It was big, it told a story, it looked to the Old Masters – yet Géricault could only have disdained its blatantly flat and inert composition, as well as its embarrassing technical crudity. The merits of British 'landscape, seascape and genre' – painting more modestly scaled and less obviously charged with emotion and narrative, the work of artists such as the young Landseer and Constable, and the watercolourists – he would find increasingly impressive and influential the longer he stayed in London.

To the wider public, all such aesthetic discriminations were of scant interest. Géricault appeared in London less as a great living artist, *confrère* to the masters of the British grand style like Reynolds or Lawrence, than as the author of a sensational image of a terrible yet picturesque calamity – and it was with an eye to its appeal to the prurient that *The Raft of the 'Medusa'* was unashamedly marketed. People came to the Egyptian Hall in the hope of experiencing a frisson of horror, not aesthetic exaltation: they wanted a theatrical spectacle, not a masterpiece of composition. Bullock, more a Barnum than a Diaghilev, was ready to oblige. Originally a Liverpudlian jeweller, his career as a showman started with an exhibition of curiosities taken from Captain Cook's antipodean voyages. In 1809 he came south and established the Liverpool Museum at 22 Piccadilly, at the heart of the flashiest and most glamorous part of London. This proved so popular – in 1811 even the hard-to-impress Jane Austen wrote to her sister Cassandra that she had drawn 'some amusement' from one of its exhibitions of exotic animals, a boa constrictor and a giraffe among them – that in 1812 Bullock moved to grander premises opposite the turning into Bond Street. Here he continued to flourish: the Egyptian Hall immediately became one of London's prime attractions, combining displays of stuffed fauna and dried flora (set amid representations of their natural habitats such as an Indian rain forest or Fingal's Cave) with historical relics (Napoleon's carriage, camp-bed and personal paraphernalia were reported to have drawn over 10,000 visitors a day in 1816).

It may be difficult for us to imagine the wide-eyed wonder such displays provoked, but we should remember that this was a culture still lacking the variety of visual possibilities which photography opened up, and that any depiction of an event or phenomenon otherwise experienced only through hearsay or the written word could provoke intense and naïve excitement. Peep-shows like those to be seen at the elegant Cosmorama in St James's, panoramic representations of the Alps or Himalayas (often unfurling on a spool to the accompaniment of atmospheric music or crude wind-and-rain sound effects), demonstrations of crackling electrical activity, and three-dimensional models of erupting volcanoes and famous shipwrecks garnished with small sulphurous explosions and puppet strings, seem to have exerted much the same effect on audiences that outlandish Hollywood epics do today.*

Like all good showmen, Bullock understood the value of constant novelty and surprise. In 1816 he sold off some of his natural history collection, turned the space over to something more like an antiques emporium (purveying 'Pictures, Marbles, Drawings, Books and Engravings, Cameos, Subjects of Natural History and Antiquity, rare works in Ivory, Japan &c. &c. China, Cabinet Work, and furniture of every description' for sale) and opened a 'Roman Gallery', devoted to classical statuary and examples of modern narrative or historical painting. One of the first exhibits here was *Brutus Condemning his Sons*, by the father of Géricault's friend Guillaume Lethière, who may well have provided the original channel of introduction to Bullock.

Bullock probably went to see *The Raft of the 'Medusa'* at the Salon (passport records certainly indicate that he visited France in September 1819, when it was still on display at the Louvre) and may have opened negotiations with Géricault in person. The terms eventually concluded in London sound fair enough: Bullock was to defray all expenses and receive two-thirds of the takings from tickets and catalogues. Such commercial deals were a newish phenomenon in the art world, increasingly used as an alternative to civic or aristocratic patronage, and allowing an artist more freedom and dignity at the expense of longer-term financial security. Géricault did rather better than others out of Bullock's sharp-nosed deals. For *Christ's Triumphal Entry into Jerusalem*, for example, Haydon ended up with a much less attractive arrangement: he simply paid Bullock £300 to rent a room 'upstairs on the right' of the Egyptian Hall (Géricault's foreign import occupied

---

*Forest Lawn Memorial Park in Los Angeles (better known as Whispering Glades, the cemetery satirised in Evelyn Waugh's novella *The Loved One*) displays *The Crucifixion*, a mediocre canvas by one Jan Styka. Advertised as 'the world's largest painting', 195 feet long by 45 feet high ('if it stood on end it would be as high as a twenty-storey building'), it is kept behind closed curtains on the stage of a sepulchral auditorium. Once an hour a congregation files in. After it has been seated, the lights darken, sacred music is heard and the curtains are slowly pulled. A spotlight and the solemn voice of an invisible narrator then pick out various features and personages represented, before the entire composition is revealed for a few minutes in all its upturned twenty-storey glory. This is very much the sort of spectacle that the public of Regency London would have appreciated, presented in a style that Bullock would have endorsed. The academic or aesthetic status of the painting is irrelevant; the scale on which it operates and the detailed 'realism' with which it pictures a mythical scene are the qualities which give it value.

prime wall space in the Roman Gallery) and while he grossed a total of £1,760 from the exhibition, after paying his dues to Bullock on top of all his managerial and promotional expenses, the net remainder hardly rewarded him handsomely for six years' work on the painting.

Bullock did not sell Géricault short. He flooded the newspapers with a series of advertisements composed in breathless fashion

> The Private Exhibition of Monsieur JERRICAULT's GREAT PICTURE from the Louvre, 24 feet by 18, representing the surviving crew of the Medusa French Frigate, after remaining thirteen days on a raft without provision, at the moment they discover the vessel that saves them, will take place in the Egyptian Hall, Piccadilly, on Saturday, and will be opened to the public on Monday next.

and charged 1s admission – the equivalent of something in the region of £10 today. The 'descriptive brochure', with a summary account of Corréard's and Savigny's story, cost 6d, and came with a crudely outlined, postcard-sized lithograph souvenir of the painting, probably executed by Charlet. A tellingly inappropriate quotation from Robert Southey

> 'Tis pleasant by the cheerful hearth to hear
> Of tempests and the dangers of the deep

was printed as an epigraph.

'Nothing is to be done in this town without great names,' complained the Marquis de Vermont about London. So to the private view on 19 June came dignitaries such as 'the Marquis of Stafford, the Bishops of Ely and Carlisle, Sir T. Baring Bart. and a number of the most eminent patrons of the Fine Arts together with several members of the Royal Academy. Several ladies of distinction also graced the throng.' Géricault wrote several of the invitations by hand.

The painting's general reception seems to have been friendly and admiring. Despite incidental criticism of the 'cold' colours and elements of 'pedantic' formalism, the reviews that followed were enthusiastic – more enthusiastic than they had been in reactionary Paris. 'In this tremendous picture of human sufferings, the bold hand of the artist has laid bare the details of horrid facts, with the severity of Michel Angelo and the gloom of Caravaggio,' announced the *London Literary Gazette*. 'The expression is energetic, true and full of pathos,' echoed *The Times*. 'There is more of nature, of the grand simplicity of art, and of true expression than is usual with the highest of modern French painters; and Mr Jerricault has displayed the deepest tragic powers,' concluded the *Morning Post*.

All we know biographically of this period is contained in one alarming incident, dubiously reported thirty years later in a memoir of Nicolas-Toussaint Charlet, who had accompanied Géricault from Paris. A painter and lithographer specialising in military subjects, this amiable heavy drinker stood out in Géricault's otherwise rather dandyish circle for his rough manners, and his brisk, bantering attitude countered Géricault's tendency to melancholy and depression. Returning to their hotel late one night, Charlet discovered from worried staff that Géricault had not been out of his room all day and the silence from within was causing alarm. His knocking unanswered, Charlet broke down the door and found Géricault lying unconscious on the bed. Charlet shook him back to life, banished the gapers and sat down with a serious air to talk sense. 'You have already tried to kill yourself several times,' Charlet reasoned. 'If you've made up your mind to do so, we can't stop you. In future you can do as you wish, but at least let me give you some advice. I know how religious you are' – sarcasm, that – 'and you know that once you're dead you'll have to appear before God to give an account of yourself. What will you tell him, you wretch, when he starts the questioning? You haven't even had your dinner yet!' At which Géricault burst out laughing and solemnly promised that this suicide attempt would be his last.

The story doesn't sound altogether plausible, not least in its feeble denouement. Charlet's memorialist suggests that London's climate was to blame (it 'affected Géricault's sickly constitution'), but it seems more likely that the desperate mess Géricault had made of his love life had overwhelmed him again. Whatever the truth of the matter, he cannot have had much time to mope: most of his time in London would have been consumed with the nitty-gritty of the mounting and launch of the exhibition.

More oblique evidence of Géricault's doings in these nine weeks comes from a little sketch, in pencil and wash, of a public execution in front of Newgate prison. Géricault was clearly fascinated by such events and the glimpse they gave into human extremity: in Rome some four years previously, he had made some lightning jottings of a man being led to the block, but they lack the haunting intensity that radiates from the London drawing. It represents, scholars agree, the demise of the Cato Street conspirators on the morning of 1 May. Five political radicals were hanged and – because they had been convicted of treason – decapitated. Their crime was participation in a pie-in-the-sky plot to assassinate members of Lord Liverpool's Tory cabinet and proclaim a provisional government. Through the dubious agency of an agent provocateur, the machinations of the conspiracy were exposed at an early stage, but no mitigation was accepted, no mercy shown. The harsh summary justice meted out was symptomatic of the anxiously reactionary mood of the times and the government proceeded to make hay with the propaganda opportunities.

But Géricault's interest would not have been primarily political. Public hanging was the most viscerally exciting form of street theatre, and victims often made the most of the histrionic opportunities the occasion allowed. Some were openly defiant and mocking, uninhibitedly exploiting their traditional prerogative to scream any manner of sedition, abuse or obscenity without being silenced by the authorities. Some bowed to the onlookers with eerie self-composure. Some dressed flamboyantly and relished their brief, bitter moment of stardom. Some staggered to the scaffold in a drunken stupor, some were paralytically convulsed. The crowds never knew what form the performance would take, and one can hardly blame them for turning out with such regularity and enthusiasm for what must have been an enthrallingly gruesome spectacle. Which is what it was for Géricault too.

Over 100,000 people were reported to have gathered outside the prison on the morning of 1 May, all edgily anticipating a roaring bloody drama and kept thirty yards at bay by a tight ring of soldiery. To accommodate the hanging and surgical decapitation of five men, a larger than usual wooden scaffold had been erected during the night. Extra security measures were enforced. Because an attempt at rescue or an insurrectionary riot was feared, there was a heavy presence of constables, as well as platoons of infantry and light cavalry, with six pieces of field artillery kept in reserve. To minimise the element of sensationalism, the usual practice of splaying traitors on wooden frames and dragging them from their cells to the place of execution was suspended. But the audience wasn't just a mob of bloodthirsty louts and *tricoteuses*: the fashionable fencing master Henry Angelo and intellectuals such as William Cobbett and Byron's friend John Cam Hobhouse were also among the witnesses. For a spot in the windows overlooking the scaffold, such quality folk were ready to pay as much as three guineas, and we can assume from his drawing that Géricault must have bought himself such a prime vantage point.

In G. T. Wilkinson's *An Authentic History of the Cato Street Conspiracy,* a book rushed out within weeks of the event, the climax of the hanging is graphically described. At 7.45 a.m. the five doomed conspirators mounted the scaffold. The most cantankerous of them was James Ings, dressed in the rough pepper-and-salt worsted jacket of his profession of butcher. He whooped three rousing cheers and sang 'O give me death or liberty!' as his manacles were removed ('his conduct was definitely bravado,' *The Times* condescendingly commented). Richard Tidd calmed him – 'There is no use in all this noise. We can die without making a noise' – and begged the executioner to do his job well and pull the knot tight. John Brunt took a pinch of snuff, while the leader of the conspiracy, Arthur Thistlewood, 'a gentleman', sucked on an orange. He is described by *The Times* as having a 'countenance somewhat flushed and disordered . . . on the cap being placed on his head, he desired that it might not be put over his eyes.'

The conspirators proclaimed themselves deists and therefore had no use for the ministrations of Newgate's Anglican chaplain, Revd Cotton. Only William Davidson, the half-caste son of the Attorney-General of Jamaica, gave in at last and asked for comfort. According to Wilkinson, he 'seemed inattentive to every thing but the journey he was about to take, and his lips moved in prayer until he was no longer able to speak. He made no request to have his eyes uncovered, but he was evidently preparing himself for bidding an eternal adieu to a world of which he had ceased to be an inhabitant.' The account in *The Times* confirms this: Davidson 'seemed engaged in prayer and was immediately joined by the Revd Mr Cotton, whose attentions were altogether rejected by the others'.

Perhaps their deepest terror was that death might not be instantaneous. Before the institution of the 'long drop', the end could take up to fifteen minutes, during which the half-throttled man would choke and quiver in unthinkable agony – in Edinburgh, a couple of years previously there had been a hanging so botched that it was necessary to haul the victim back up and take him out of the noose, kicking and screeching, only to hang him again as the crowd pelted the incompetent executioner.

At Newgate they were more expert, and at 8.06 a.m. the trap opened and the Cato Street conspirators fell into eternity. They were left to swing for half an hour. The one noose which failed was Brunt's: his knot slipped and for a few minutes he was dangling in the air choking, before the executioner could run underneath the platform and pull at his legs to finish him off. The threat of insurrection did not materialise; the fatal moment was met with a white-hot pin-drop silence and it was only when the surgeon began his somewhat inefficient decapitation that the mood briefly threatened to sour. There was violent hissing and booing when the severed heads were held up (with the prescribed proclamation of 'This is the head of X, the traitor!') and panicky shrieking when Brunt's was accidentally dropped, spraying a gush of blood. But this was the stuff of Grand Guignol rather than revolution and the Lord Mayor was able to report back to the Home Secretary, Lord Sidmouth, that 'there has seldom been a more tranquil Execution witnessed'.

It was, I believe, William Davidson, with the Revd Cotton to the left, on whom Géricault focused in this unique work of art.* No camera could ever capture with such vividness the appalling terror of staring into one's own imminent extinction, but the image does radiate a photographic immediacy: Géricault's aim is not to exalt the scene or bring it into conformity with classical models – instead, he produces something conceived, in the words of Lorenz Eitner, as 'sternest documentary sobriety, without embellishments or histrionics', registered on paper in what cannot have been more than one desperate ultimate minute. It is the first in a series of snapshots which Géricault made in England and, like all of them, it owes nothing to clichés of patriotism or the picturesque. The visitor perceives with clarity what the native's eye

---

*The names of Ings and Thistlewood have also been proposed, but the man's attitude suggests prayer, which would preclude them. What about Brunt? The *Morning Chronicle* of 2 May describes how 'the eyes of the man sent forth from their deep recesses glances of distressing keenness' and gave 'a degree of ghostly prominence to a forehead, cheek bones and chin, naturally very much protruded'. Maybe the figure is a composite, painted up from memory, on the basis of very rough sketches made at the execution. See Lorenz Eitner, *Géricault: His Life and Work* (London, 1983), pp. 223–4 and *Géricault*, Galeries Nationales du Grand Palais (Paris, 1991), p. 388.

is clouded against and inured to: Géricault's honest visual record amounts to some of the most powerful and telling evidence which remains of the harder realities of Britain in the post-Napoleonic era.

Shortly after the launch of the exhibition of *The Raft of the 'Medusa'*, Géricault returned to France for some months. But after travelling to Brussels to pay homage to the great master of neoclassicism, Jacques David (then living in political exile from Restoration France), he was back in London by the end of the year and would remain in England for virtually the whole of 1821, lodging for a spell with the family of Adams (or Adam) Elmore, a successful horse dealer with good connections who owned a stable near Hyde Park and lived near the Strand (Géricault bought three horses from him, on credit terms that he never paid off).

In February 1821, he wrote his friend Pierre Dedreux-Dorcy the most intriguing letter that survives of his English year.

> Since you are naturally given to pleasure, you will perhaps suppose , dear friend, that I have much of that here. Nothing could be further from the truth. I am scarcely amused at all; my life is just as it is in Paris. I work a lot in my room and then, for relaxation, wander the streets which are so full of constant movement and variety that you would never leave them, I am sure. But the reasons that would keep you there are the same ones that chase me away. I feel that prudence is increasingly becoming my lot . . .
>
> I have been extremely ill, but am better now. Don't mention this to my father, for it would only worry him. I am simply telling him that I had a cold. You might do the same, and this confirmation will keep him from suspecting anything more serious. Good friends have been taking care of me and keeping me from getting bored. It has always been my luck to meet people who are better than I am, and who make me wonder what I have done to earn their friendship. And I have also managed a little conquest, my dear Dorcy . . . A woman, not in the first flush of youth but still beautiful and surrounded with all the prestige of a great fortune, has got it into her head to fall madly in love with with me . . . She calls me the God of Painting and worships me accordingly. What upsets me is that her husband has nothing but good will towards me – but all these husbands are the very devil. Can you believe it – he wants me to go and live in their house and work there? Keep absolute silence about my passion, I beg you, because she is probably known in Paris.

Further evidence as to the nature of the illness or the identity of the infatuated woman (her age and marital situation reminiscent of the sad Alexandrine's) is lacking. Could the former be related to the attempted suicide that Charlet thwarted? Or the attack of sciatica and high fever, mentioned elswhere as the result of a damp walk along the Thames Embankment and perhaps a prelude to his final illness? Or do we credit Vernet's memory that Géricault had suffered infection after allowing a veterinary surgeon 'to treat a malady of which some indiscretion had been the original cause'? Could the latter be the hard-faced woman who appears side-saddle in the painting known as *Amazon* and could she even be Elmore's wife?

The solitude did not last. Géricault seems to have acquired friends and become sociable with other Frenchmen. In town, for instance, was a fascinating man he knew from his days in Rome, the dandyish Jules Auguste – who, according to some of his contemporaries, could have been a finer equestrian painter than Géricault himself had he not been so exquisitely fastidious and dilettante – and Simon Rochard, a miniaturist with a flourishing studio on New Bond Street. Through them he came to meet talented Englishmen of the younger generation such as the archaeologist and architect Charles Cockerell and the anecdotal painter David Wilkie. Eventually, Géricault seems to have penetrated the highest circles: he was mixing, as he put it in a lettter, with '*des gens meilleurs que moi*' ('people better than I am'). On 5 May, at the invitation of the Royal Academy's President Sir Thomas Lawrence, he attended the grand annual banquet which celebrated the traditional summer exhibition of new English work – London's closest equivalent to the Louvre Salon – where as 'Monsieur Jerricault' he would have rubbed shoulders with the Duke of Wellington.

Initially, in his concern for the reception of *The Raft of the 'Medusa'*, he had been nervously dismissive of English art. After its success, he could relax and look at it more disinterestedly. Much of what he saw, at the Royal Academy and presumably elsewhere, excited him. The grandiose pseudo-classical affairs produced by the numerous imitators of Sir Joshua Reynolds he could pass by unmoved, but in Lawrence's warm and fluent family portraits, in the freshness and freedom of works such as Constable's *The Hay Wain* (which, according to Delacroix writing in 1858, he was 'stunned' by), in the brilliant and virile sporting painting, he found a way forward for himself. 'The Exhibition just opened has again confirmed me in the belief that colour and effect are understood and felt only here,' he wrote to Horace Vernet back in smug Paris.

You cannot imagine the beauty of this year's portraits, and of many of the landscapes and genres, and of the animals painted by [James] Ward and by [Edwin] Landseer, aged eighteen – the Old Masters themselves have not done better in this line . . . I see that the painters here complain that their drawing is inferior, and envy the French School as the more accomplished. Why don't we, too, complain about our faults? What foolish pride closes our eyes to them? Can we bring honour to our country by refusing to see the good wherever we find it, and by foolishly insisting that we are best? . . . How I wish that I could show, even to some of our ablest artists, these portraits that so much resemble nature, whose easy poses leave nothing to be desired, and of which one could truly say that they only lack speech! . . . I am not afraid that you will accuse me of Anglomania; you know as well as I what is good in us, and what we lack.

Géricault's own work opened up and relaxed in this climate. His search for imposing melodramatic tableaux which could match those of the Italian Old Masters ceased and he began to play on a more intimate scale. There was commercial sense in this – the nouveaux riches of the Regency era wanted original works for the walls of their town-house drawing-rooms and watercolours, Dutch genre scenes and prints were in high demand – and in applying himself to one particular new trend, lithography, Géricault was at least partly motivated by a desire to reap more of the material rewards which the London market offered. To a friend in Paris he wrote:

At least I work and turn out lithographs with energy. I find myself here devoted for some time to this art which, being a novelty, is in astonishing fashion. With a little more tenacity than I possess, I am sure one could make a considerable fortune. I flatter myself that this will merely serve as my advertisement and that as soon as the real connoisseurs have come to know me I will be used for work worthier of myself. You will call it ambition, but, by God, it is just a matter of striking while the iron is hot.

But it wasn't a matter of mere avarice: whatever he pretends here, Géricault's involvement in lithography was not purely cynical. Its potential clearly engaged his creative imagination and nothing about the prints he published looks compromised: they are indeed among the most original of his works, entirely free of the mannerisms and stiffness which can taint his assumption of the Old Master manner and as rich in a sense of the tragic realities of the modern world as anything to come from the hands of Manet, Baudelaire, Dickens or Dostoevsky.

Lithography was a technological novelty, which developed quickly in an industrial Britain on the qui vive. How it worked is explained most simply by the historian of printmaking, Richard T. Godfrey: 'The marks made upon limestone with greasy chalk will accept printing ink, while the rest of the surface which has first been washed with nitric acid and then with gum arabic, will repel it.' For artists and printers, the method offered the advantages of speed and versatility: images could be drawn directly on to the stone without the labour of incising into a block of wood or etching on to a copperplate; wash-like effects could be rendered far more subtly than they could by the sort of mechanical cross-hatching which marked standard engravings; and what had previously taken a week or more to complete could now be achieved within the day.

Yet artists were initially uncertain how to use lithography's peculiar properties, mistrusting its mysterious chemical process (William Blake, for instance, the most inspired printmaker of the era, clearly didn't take to it: he only ever made one lithograph, in 1807, entitled *Job in Prosperity*). Géricault assayed it from several angles. When he first experimented with the technique in 1817–18, he produced several vignettes of the defeated Napoleonic forces. A blinded soldier on a dying horse trudges through the snow on the retreat from Russia; a wagon packed with wounded soldiers is led downhill by a peasant; a veteran with a wooden leg angrily displays his medals to a Swiss Guard who upholds some petty regulation which debars him from entering the courtyard of the Louvre (this illustrates an incident reported in the newspapers a few weeks previous to the publication of the print). Other of his lithographed images are more like a reportage photographer's snapshots of curious images of contemporary life: a black-skinned pugilist boxing a white-skinned opponent; two horses biting each other in the stable as a groom beats them apart with a broom.

None of these was very successful in Paris, their atmosphere being perhaps too sullen and aggressive to appeal, and Géricault reverted to the primitive art of oil painting instead. In London, however, his interest revived: the inventor of lithography had been awarded the prestigious Gold Medal of the Society in 1819 and suddenly, as Géricault's letter remarks, the process and its products shot into 'astonishing fashion'. What specifically stimulated him was his contact with Charles Hullmandel, a lithographer and printer based in Soho who had also trained as a painter in Paris. He must first have met

Géricault in 1820 when he was commissioned to print the postcard-sized souvenir lithograph of *The Raft of the 'Medusa'* (sadly, rather a crude job, probably executed in a tearing last-minute hurry by Géricault's friend Charlet, who was also a keen lithographer), at a time when he was engaged on a series of coloured lithographs of quaint scenes and characters of Rome.

Although these are conventionally picturesque and of little intrinsic merit, they must have been one inspiration for a collection of twelve lithographs, which Hullmandel printed the following year under the title *Various Scenes Drawn from Life and on Stone*. All of them are beautiful, but three of them stand out as startling, shocking, haunting masterpieces, unprecedented not only in Géricault's own work but in the history of Western art. They depict the poor – starkly and hopelessly, without a trace of sentimentality or didacticism. No element of the composition or subject matter is fixed in order to make a moral or political point, as Hogarth might have done; they owe nothing to the neat and dainty cut-out figures of street traders known as the *Cries of London*; there are no toothy, cheeky grins, pretty ankles and flirtatious glances, no mollifying chinks of comedy or redemption round the corner. Through Hullmandel's understanding of the refinements of the technique, lithography was no longer limited to reproducing the linear marks made by pen or chalk on the stone and had become capable of rendering the most delicate shadings and tints, which Géricault uses to give each scene a smoky, almost nightmarish atmosphere. But his images are not dreams, visions or revelations – 'the spiritual fourfold London eternal' of William Blake. Their power lies, in a sense, even deeper than that: all three lithographs are sternly truthful documentary works of art, which see things as they are, not as we see them.

The Piper depicts a ragged bulk of a blind man in a hard, grey urban landscape. He plays his music to nobody except a small, deadbeat dog who stands despairing beside him. Clément noted the way this lithograph conveyed 'the pallid light of London, the damp atmosphere which chills to the marrow, this profound and intense melancholy, the overall sense of distress which characterises "Merry England"', but it is the figure of the piper himself which dominates and the purpose of his music which mystifies – what ghosts does his piping summon or allay?

In *A Paraleytic* [*sic*] *Woman*, the eponymous subject lies (asleep or comatose?) straitjacketed in her crude wheelchair, against which the porter (her husband? her son?) leans exhaustedly for a moment. A straggling young girl (in social class a cut above the cripple?) scowls contemptuously at her: the neatly dressed infant whose hand she holds stands innocently waiting, her tiny wooden rocking horse a joking reference to Géricault's equestrian obsession. Behind them a hearse passes by; on the wall a tattered poster advertises some useless quack panacea, as if such abject misery could be cured by a potion.

Bleakest of the three is entitled *Pity the Sorrows of a Poor Old Man/Whose Trembling Limbs have Borne Him to Your Door* – a quotation from an obscure poem by Henry Moss, published in 1769 (how did Géricault come across it?). This lithograph shows a man destitute outside a baker's shop, too weak even to hold up his begging hand and knock at the window. His whimpering dog is plainly starving too. In the distance, where a pall of smog hangs over Blackfriars Bridge and St Paul's Cathedral, the city goes about its business obliviously.

Géricault's impressions weren't all so gloomy. Two earlier lithographs depict a dozing fishmonger about to have his wares filched and three ragged boys gaily tormenting a donkey; some quick pencil sketches of folk he spotted on his perambulations – fat-faced prelates, insouciant top-hatted young blades, exotic Dockland orientals – are salty Pickwickian caricatures reflecting the 'constant movement and variety' of London streets which he mentioned to Dedreux-Dorcy.

But the remaining prints in Hullmandel's volume of lithographs are further variations on one of Géricault's abiding themes – the horse. Their precise settings and subject matter are a puzzling jumble, how-ever: it's not clear what point, if any, the artist is trying to make by combining them. In *A Party of Life Guards*, we see members of the royal cavalry chatting before or after a parade or exercise. *An Arabian Horse* shows a fine representative of a breed much favoured by English owners, but its imaginary background of palm trees and desert stands in odd contrast to the grimy northern locations specified in the other images.

A more coherent succession of three lithographs shows the principal stages of shoeing a horse, as enacted in the forges of a Flemish, French and English farrier. Three more concentrate on drays, beasts of burden:

slowly they clomp out of the sunlight into the black hole of a vaulted tunnel at the entrance to the Adelphi Wharf; wearily they drag a coal wagon downhill against a grey sky; heroically they plod up a hill on their way to a horse fair. There is no pastoral prettiness in the air: the landscapes are bleak and hostile, and the men who drive the big-rumped horses are anonymous proletarian figures, unaware that they are being observed and turned into art. All they know is that they have work to do.

In terms of style, content and mood, these lithographs seem to be drawn in a world of their own – despite all Géricault's enthusiastic admiration for contemporary English art, there is no sign of its influence here, except inasmuch as the aesthetic mood of the time allowed more freedom of subject matter and put less value on grandiosity than was the case in stickier France. Depicting the back streets of London or the stoically struggling drays, he is out there alone, with the individuality of his genius to guide him. Only in the tenth of the Hullmandel set, *Horses Exercising*, with its two sleek galloping thoroughbreds, does Géricault pay homage to the uniquely English tradition of sporting painting.

But the dark and grainy nature of the lithograph did not suit conventional racing subjects. It was through the more fluid and impressionistic media of watercolour and pencil that Géricault interpreted the elegant world of equestrianism, with its fashionable canters along Rotten Row and its side-saddled ladies, nervous fillies and spry jockeys. Yet even here he deviates from the clichés of the run-of-the-mill practitioners. For all his technical interest in equine anatomy and physiology – he copied plates from Henry Alken's famous volume, *The Beauties and Defects in the Figure of the Horse Comparatively Delineated*, published in 1816 – his passion for these creatures had an almost erotic dimension, which precluded scientific detachment. The English painted their horses calmly and clinically, often showing them controlled by their grooms or clearly indicated as somebody's property. Géricault, on the other hand, was in love with their rearing, roaring, thunderous energy, their soulfulness, their variety of character. To capture those qualities in art was his aim. The English painters saw horses as trophies; Géricault saw them as beings.

The most brilliant example of this aspect of Géricault's work in England is an oil painting, now in the Louvre, of the Epsom Derby of

1821,* apparently a commission from – or a present to – the horse dealer Adam(s) Elmore, Géricault's landlord. At one level the canvas follows the standard format, popularised by Alken, of depicting the race in broad profile. At another it is strikingly original. Instead of facing the crowds and the tents, and the gay paraphernalia of the course, it turns the composition in the other direction and isolates the horses against a brooding sky, charged with the purple clouds of a summer storm as magnificent as anything in Constable's Suffolk. The horses are in flying gallop above the richly green turf, but pinned in absolute clarity against the haze of the landscape, as though photographed at a very high exposure – the effect, in the words of Lorenz Eitner, is to make it seem that 'the setting . . . rather than the horses are in motion'. Behind the picture, he continues, is 'an unmistakable note of melancholy . . . far removed from the festive conventionalities of normal sporting genre'. The painting is thus both a tribute to English painting and a transcendent criticism of it.

Perhaps that note of melancholy is one reason why Géricault doesn't seem to have caught on as a sporting painter in England: the atmosphere his art evokes, the resonances with which it echoes, must have been too complex and subtle to appeal to the hearty ridin' and huntin' class of the Regency era. The painters who prospered under such patrons understood market values and had no nonsense about them: John Ferneley, for instance, who lived in Melton Mowbray and charged ten guineas for a horse portrait and seven for a cow's; or James Ward, a masterly delineator of pigs and sheep, much admired by Géricault himself at the Royal Academy exhibition of 1821 – they provided unambiguous visual records of private property, not poetic evocations of disturbingly sensitive creatures.

Yet despite his failure to hit a winning streak, it's hard to doubt that Géricault enjoyed his year in England. The fecundity and variety of his output suggest that the high pitch and hustle of London life both stimulated and relaxed him; the painstaking long-term planning which preceded the execution of his great canvases in France vanished;

---

*The 1821 Derby was also notable for two other factors – the winner, for the first and only time until 1912, was a grey, Gustavus (possibly the horse second from the right of Géricault's painting); and a mob of drunken spectators, who became over-excited and surged on to the course, threatening to ruin the race. See Roger Mortimer, *History of the Derby Stakes* (London, 1962), p. 75.

instead, he began to feel free to improvise, to play – the sly humour which brightens some of his sketches struck a new note in his work. Effects of light and shade were more gentle; figures less obviously composed and more passingly 'natural', even humanely and affectionately rendered. One might conclude that Géricault found England and the English a haven, but that after a year the call of home, old friends and native habits had to be answered.

Aside from the reviews of *The Raft of the 'Medusa'*, it is difficult to gauge what impression Géricault had made on his hosts: we know nothing about his command of the language and his few letters reveal only the barest record of his doings. But we do have one tiny glimpse of the man to tantalise us. The archaeologist and architect Charles Cockerell kept an engagingly ill-spelt and erratically punctuated journal, in which an entry for 16 December describes his reflections on bidding farewell to his singular French friend. To posterity, the personality of Géricault is bafflingly opaque; but here, for a moment, he comes alive:

> . . . great admiration for his talent. his modesty so unusual & remarkable in a Frenchman his deep feeling of pity, the pathetique. at same time vigour fire & animation of his works . . . profound and melancholy sensible. singular life – like that of the savages we read of in America. lying torpid days & weeks then rising to violent exertions. riding tearing driving exposing himself to heat cold violence of all sorts – came to England chiefly to abstract himself from the idleness & no. of persons. company – fear he is in a bad way. – often said that England was the best place for study he had seen the air contributed & the habits of the people. – Géricault has not yet produced 10 works before the publick. yet his reputation is great everywhere –

And so he left for France. After a rough crossing from Dover to Calais – a light-hearted letter to Jules Auguste written some days later described the stomach-churning effect of *'une jolie tempête'* – Géricault was back in Paris for the Christmas of 1821. He was not 'covered with gold', as he had hoped – the lithographs hadn't sold well – but his year in England had been as pleasant and equable an epoch in his life as he would ever experience. His two remaining years were deeply unhappy.

Back home, he became extravagant and reckless, sinking money into foolish stock-market speculations and behaving with almost suicidal bravado – a bad riding accident caused an abscess on his spine, which he later tried to lance with a larding needle. To make some quick money he churned out lithographs on fashionable Byronic subjects, but these are bland and inferior works, which can have given him no satisfaction. His last great achievement was a series of portraits of lunatics in the grip of peculiar obsessions – child theft, compulsive gambling – probably commissioned for demonstration during the lectures of the celebrated psychiatrist Etienne Georget. Their faces evince a fiercely intense yet chillingly blank expressiveness, which recalls the condemned Cato Street conspirator staring into oblivion on the scaffold at Newgate. Consumed by his own demons, perhaps Géricault saw himself in the void too.

He died in January 1824, at the age of thirty-two, in unimaginable pain from a tumour on the spine, which had developed from the infected abscess. His estate, much encumbered by debt until a sale of all his works was held, passed to Georges, his son by Alexandrine. One obituary called him 'a young Romantic' – the first time that anybody had applied that loaded epithet to him. 'Romantic' was at that time a word used to suggest someone difficult, dangerous and antagonised, who disregarded the decorum of the classical rule book and wilfully concentrated on personal emotions and violent sensations, and no, it doesn't characterise Géricault's art – for all its remarkable originality and power – altogether fairly. But the label stuck and thenceforth posterity deemed him to belong to the Romantic tendency in culture, precursor to a generation of artists which included the wilder, more flamboyant genius of Delacroix and Hugo and Berlioz.

What of *The Raft of the 'Medusa'*?

Bullock's exhibition at the Egyptian Hall ran in London for over six months, finally closing on 30 December 1820. It is estimated that over 40,000 people paid their shilling to see it, netting Géricault something not far off £800 – equivalent to the annual income of a prosperous professional gentleman, but not the killing he had hoped for.* Bullock

---

*A senior civil servant like John Stuart Mill's father earned £800 per annum in the early 1820s. A starting salary, like that of J. S. Mill himself, was £30 per annum. Sir Walter Scott earned £10,000 in 1818. I would like to thank Drs Fram Dinshaw and José Harris of St Catherine's College, Oxford, for these figures.

then moved the painting across the water to Ireland, where it was overshadowed by another blockbuster.

> Messrs Marshall respectfully beg leave again to solicit the kind patronage of the nobility, gentry and the public of Dublin, and its vicinity, for their lately finished, entirely novel Marine Peristrephic panorama of the Wreck of the Medusa French Frigate and the Fatal Raft. Also the ceremony of crossing the line. Accompanied by a full and appropriate band of music. The picture is painted on nearly 10,000 sq. feet of canvas, under the direction of one of the survivors, in a superior style of brilliancy and effect – the figures on the Raft and on the boat being the size of life, and the Picture being of the Peristrephic form, give every appearance of reality . . . Admission front seats 1/8 – back seats 10d. – Children in the front seats at half price. The pavilion is always rendered perfectly comfortable by patent stoves.

Géricault's static version of the tragedy had no hope of pulling the public when pitted against this vulgar rolling attraction and Bullock was obliged to fight back with with an old commercial strategy – a price cut which poses as an altruistic gesture. After a month of poor attendances, another advertisement was placed, announcing that 'in order that all ranks may have an opportunity of viewing this stupendous production of the pencil [sic], the price of admission during the short time it remains in this city will be reduced to ten pence'. But the offer doesn't seem to have had the desired effect and the exhibition closed on 31 March 1821, pleading 'arrangements made in Edinburgh'. Whatever these arrangements were, they never materialised: the 'peristrephic panorama' had been exhibited in the Scottish capital only a few months previously and the hard-nosed Bullock would not have wanted to risk a repetition of the Dublin disappointment. Somebody's vague recollection that Géricault toured the Highlands (recorded in passing in Clément's biography) may relate to these plans, but there is no evidence to confirm that he did so.

The Raft of the 'Medusa' was returned to Paris, where it lay rolled up in a corner of the house of Géricault's friend Cogniet until it was sold at an auction some months after the painter's death. An English collector was said to have offered 23,000 Francs for the epic canvas, but through the good offices of his executor Dedreux-Dorcy, it was finally bought by the state for a quarter of that sum and entered the national collection in the Louvre. There it still hangs, its power and grandeur a match for the work of the great Italian masters, as Géricault had always hoped.

CHAPTER 2

Richard Wagner, Composer

Any account of Géricault's visit to London must be marked by a series of blanks and question marks, but what we can piece together from the exiguous surviving evidence suggests a theme fundamental to this book. Géricault was not motivated to cross the Channel by any sense of England as a place of artistic inspiration or even visual grandeur, and the castles, monuments and ruins then being made fashionable through the writings of Walter Scott seem to have held no charm for him. What he found to paint and draw is grey rather than green, modern rather than medieval, and empty of moonlight, poetry and sentiment. He didn't visit in order to sightsee – for ruins, he had already been to Rome – or to meet other artists – there were plenty of those in Paris.

No, he made for London as an actor today might make for Hollywood, drawn primarily by the lure of material gain. For the painter, England offered not revered teachers, splendid galleries, noble traditions or a discriminating élite, but a free market, a large audience, and lots and lots of money. Géricault came to England not to be garlanded as an academician, let alone a genius, but to sell his work and join the long queue of hopefuls waiting to cash in on the most prosperous and industrious nation on earth. What he found, of course, was something more complicated than that: a country pockmarked with appalling poverty and a culture in which art flourished more variously on hardy commercial soil than it did in the well-watered beds of aristocratic or ecclesiastical patronage. The mix was heady. Taste and craftsmanship may have been more exquisite in Paris, but London boasted an appetite for novelty and a liberality of spirit which made it a happier place for a young artist travelling his own journey.

Géricault's English experience stands in fascinating contrast to that of another egregious visitor – Richard Wagner, a composer whose art reached the highest watermark of Romanticism and a figure whose personality, behaviour and attitudes made him almost as controversial throughout Europe as Napoleon or Byron had been at the beginning of the century. Géricault was never remotely famous in his lifetime; but Wagner was hugely so and his three visits to London, in 1843, 1855 and 1877, are consequently documented in detail.

The England Wagner came to know had undergone convulsive revolution since Géricault's day, but not of the violent and volatile king-toppling kind epidemic on the Continent. The middle classes had consolidated their position through a prudent marriage of evangelical Christianity with Utilitarian economics; the rest of society had been stabilised by the extension of the franchise embodied in the Reform Acts of 1832 and 1867, as well as by government's new administrative efficiency and the boom that the building of the railways generated. The Empire spread, fortunes burgeoned, conditions improved and, until the great depression of the 1870s, anyone with stocks and shares, a profession or a job could be reasonably certain of continuing prosperity.

Britain in 1820 radiated the confidence of a nation which had triumphed in a long, hard and crucial war, then turned victory to its advantage. By the middle of the century it had developed another sort of confidence, a sense of inner moral righteousness which stiffened the nation's backbone to the point of inflexibility. The ethic of the Evangelist–Utilitarian nexus was simple: work to make money and attend church on Sundays. For your statistically average bourgeois Victorian, there were no commandments greater than these. In 1867 Matthew Arnold reviewed this phenomenon in a series of influential magazine articles entitled *Culture and Anarchy*. There he deplored the narrowness of the British spirit, its lack of 'sweetness and light', and made a celebrated call for society to leaven its devotion to Hebraism, or 'strictness of conscience', with Hellenism, 'spontaneity of consciousness'; to the middle-class obsession with the material and commonplace he stuck the durable label of 'philistine'. Two years earlier, in *Our Mutual Friend*, Dickens had harped on a similar theme: the prudish and purblind Mr Podsnap considered anything not British 'a mistake' and stopped short of anything calculated 'to call a blush to the cheek of a young person'.

But this has only the accuracy of caricature and the fact that such satire found a ready audience proves that there were also large sections of the middle classes with more open minds. Ultimately, of course, there were no statistically average bourgeois Victorians, only millions of men and women with their individual lives, thoughts and feelings. As much as there may have been 'strictness of conscience' among them, there was doubt, there was joy, there was nonconformity – one has only to think of the tonal richness, psychological variety and emotional warmth of the fiction of the period in order to feel the force of this.

There was nothing, however, which challenged the mid-Victorian middle-class psyche more strenuously than Wagner, whose art and personal behaviour fell way, way outside all the Hebraic norms and boundaries. Mr Podsnap's idea of music was 'a respectable per-formance (without variations) on stringed and wind instruments, sedately expressive of getting up at eight, shaving close at a quarter past, breakfasting at nine, going to the City at ten, coming home at half-past five and dining at seven'. Whatever Wagner was about, it wasn't that.

The first time his music had momentarily impinged on the British public was in 1833 when a musical journal entitled *The Harmonicon* mentioned in the course of a report from Leipzig that 'a symphony of Richard Wagner, scarcely twenty years of age' had been 'much and deservedly applauded'. After this, no more was heard of him until, six years later, he spent a week in London with his first wife Minna. The visit was brief and inconsequential. He was en route to Paris, having fled from Riga, where he had been resident conductor at the opera house and (typically) fallen prey to pressing creditors. The journey on a tiny Prussian ship across the Baltic and North Seas to London had been hellish – Wagner would paint in music the raging majesty of their tempests when he came to write *Der Fliegende Holländer* in 1843. After three weeks they reached the Thames estuary in a state of nervous exhaustion, and poor Minna became as terrified by the river's sinister warning lights and fog bells as she had been by the ocean's spray and swell. With their dog, Robber, and a large amount of luggage, they eventually disembarked at London Bridge and walked off their sea legs, before settling at the King's Arms on Old Compton Street in Soho, too fagged to brave the Channel crossing without a few days to recover.

Neither of them spoke any English and such communication as they managed with the natives was conducted in French. Wagner nevertheless resolved to make the most of his visit. Unfortunately, he failed in his quest to track down Sir George Smart, chief conductor of the

Philharmonic Society and a great friend to German music,* to whom he had once hopefully sent the score of an overture based on 'Rule, Britannia'. He then tried, equally in vain, to find the novelist Edward Bulwer-Lytton to discuss with him the possibility of turning his epic of medieval Rome, *Rienzi*, into an opera. Bulwer-Lytton balanced his literary career with a seat in the House of Commons and Wagner went to look for him there: after a lot of shaking of heads, frenzied sign language and no sign of his quarry, he ended up in the Strangers' Gallery of the House of Lords, listening to the ageing Duke of Wellington pontificating in a debate on an Anti-Slavery Bill.

Ignoring the dubious attractions of a summer season of Italian opera at Her Majesty's Theatre, Wagner and Minna then resorted to some more conventional sightseeing. In the company of the English-speaking captain of the ship in which they had travelled from Riga, they wandered round Westminster Abbey and took a train ride from London Bridge to Gravesend Park – the first time they had so much as seen a railway. A further trip to the splendours of Greenwich proved nearly fatal – as Wagner climbed the pilot's ladder on to the old *Dreadnought*, a treasured snuffbox given to him by his idol, the soprano Wilhelmine Schröder-Devrient, dropped from his pocket. Leaning into the Thames in a futile attempt to salvage it, he came close to losing his grip and drowning. That incident was the climax of his first London adventure: after enduring the shuttered-up dreariness of what he described as a 'ghastly London Sunday', Wagner, Minna and Robber took the coach to Folkestone (the rail link with London Bridge did not open until 1843) and reached Paris by Tuesday night.

*

---

*The composer Weber had been accommodated in Smart's house during his visit to London and died there in 1826 – the same year that Smart led the first British performance of Beethoven's Ninth Symphony. In his biography of Wagner, Ernest Newman amusingly footnotes Weber's disgust at the cost of living in London: dining alone in a restaurant one evening on soup, beef, vegetables, macaroni and wine, he was obliged to pay three thaler, or over 7s – which was indeed extremely expensive if one considers that a hundred years later a nutritious luncheon or dinner could be had in J. Lyons and Co. for less than half that price.

About the only thing Weber found cheaper in London than at home, Newman continues, was a haircut – 'this operation cost him 8 groschen (a shilling), which was apparently below the Dresden price – an illuminating economic detail that perhaps accounts for the traditional long hair of the German musician of that and a later period.' See *The Life of Richard Wagner* (London, 1933–47), vol. 1, p. 153; and below, p. 58.

Fifteen years later, following the production of four operas – *Rienzi*, *Der Fliegende Holländer*, *Tannhäuser* and *Lohengrin* – progressively more original and subversive of convention, Wagner was famous but far from prosperous and ever further from happiness. Exiled from Dresden in 1849 for his part in an aborted revolution, he had based himself in Zurich where his childless marriage to poor simple Minna began to break up in a morass of bad debts and worse temper. For four years or so Wagner wrote virtually no music, concentrating instead on writing the text for his great tetralogy *Der Ring des Nibelungen* and the development of his theory of a radical form of music drama more suited to the austere theatre of the Ancient Greeks than to the lavish opera houses of London and Paris. 'The artwork of the future', as he called it, would also be a return to the past: it would harmonise dance, music and poetry; it would be the product of a brotherhood of artists; it would be performed in democratic arenas; and it would be liberated from the profit motive, empty vocal display and vulgar spectacle which poisoned the work of Meyerbeer and other highly successful composers of the day. Meyerbeer was a Jew and it was on the Jews – a race of usurers, businessmen and bankers, without roots of their own, without vision or creativity: or so he thought – that Wagner obsessively laid the blame for all the trouble.

The rather dismally obvious irony behind Wagner's loathing of a culture based on money is that he himself required an enormous amount of the stuff, not least in order to buy the time to compose artworks of the future in present conditions of luxurious comfort. 'I cannot bed in straw or satisfy my soul with gin,' he wrote once, 'mine is a highly susceptible, intense, voracious, yet uncommonly sensitive and fastidious sensuality'. He needed, in other words, patrons – patrons who would give without counting the cost or expecting much in the way of return. A surprising number of these rare beasts materialised, and Wagner proceeded to treat them with a mixture of desperation, ruthlessness, arrogance and contempt. One victim of his Swiss years was the retired silk merchant Otto von Wesendonck, who sponged up most of Wagner's ocean of debt and provided him with generous living allowances and travel grants on the pitifully misguided premise that one day the sum would be paid back with gratitude. Wesendonck may have been besotted by Wagner, but by 1854 even he had had enough – he did not yet know that Wagner was also beginning to fall in love with his wife Mathilde – and not for the first time the composer was left in an embarrassing personal situation with a pressing need for income.

The possibilities of meeting this in Zurich were limited, and some distance from the increasingly hysterical Minna had become highly desirable. It was on these counts that Wagner decided to accept an offer – delivered by an emissary in an impressive fur coat – to come to London for a fee of £200 and conduct the orchestra of the Philharmonic Society in a series of subscription concerts. It was not a prospect he greeted with any positive enthusiasm: he had just been overwhelmed by his first reading of the grand but gloomy philosophy of Schopenhauer; his mind was burgeoning with the *Ring* project; and the irritating nitty-gritty of dealing with foreigners and mediocrities was the last thing he needed. 'They are not paying me much,' he grumbled in a letter, 'and as I have no accompanying speculation in view, I'm strictly going as nothing but a tourist, just to see what sort of things the people do there. If I have any ulterior motive at all, it would be that of assembling a choice German company in London some time in the future to present my operas.' In his autobiography, written a decade later, Wagner recalled his feelings somewhat differently: 'One thing only struck me as favourable and that was the prospect of again handling a large and excellent orchestra, after having been denied one for so long [i.e. in Zurich]; while the fact that I had attracted the attention to that remote world of music fascinated me exceedingly.'

But what exactly did that 'remote world' of London know of Wagner? Almost nothing. His notorious polemic of 1850, *Das Judentum in der Musik* ('Judaism in Music'), had not yet been translated into English. Among musical cognoscenti his name was vaguely associated with that of Hector Berlioz as a freak, an 'original', an 'ultra-red republican', writing incomprehensible stuff that nobody could make head or tail of. A pianoforte arrangement of the March for *Tannhäuser* had been published in 1855 (one wonders for whom it was considered suitable*), but only that opera's overture had ever been heard in concert. 'Such queer stuff that criticism would be thrown away upon it . . . so much fuss about nothing, such a pompous and empty commonplace has seldom been heard,' was the verdict of J. W. Davison,

---

*See p. 67–8.

correspondent for *The Times*. Such antagonism was to be expected. Davison's speciality was excoriation of anything modern – Chopin he called 'a morbidly sensitive flea' and Verdi 'the greatest impostor that ever took pen in hand to write rubbish'. Only one contemporary escaped his bile: the agreeable and melodious Jew, Felix Mendelssohn, dead since 1847 but still London's musical lodestar.

The Philharmonic Society was, therefore, acting on a hunch. Founded in 1813, it was London's most revered musical institution (granted a Royal Charter in 1912, it has continued to function as a charity). Its board of directors had commissioned Beethoven to write the Ninth Symphony, but a rival organisation had sprung up to threaten its status and, like the big orchestras of today, it needed to borrow the éclat of a glamorous foreign name as a means of attracting the smartest subscribers. For the 1855 season Wagner was not the board's first choice: top of the list was Berlioz, whose visits in 1848 and 1852 had enjoyed considerable success in aesthetically advanced quarters. But he was unavailable and, after a subsequent rebuff from Louis Spohr, Wagner's name was arrived at *faute de mieux*, on the strength of recommendations and rumours of the Continental success of *Tannhäuser* and *Lohengrin*.

Being German helped. In London in the 1850s the label had a special cachet, for this was the heyday of Prince Albert's influence on British culture, and all things Teutonic were imbued with an aura of high and earnest seriousness. Yet in other quarters there was a certain resistant spirit of 'British is best', and the prospect of Wagner inflamed it. 'The appointment of Herr Wagner can be regarded as nothing short of a wholesale offence to the native and foreign conductors resident in England,' spluttered Henry Chorley in *The Athenaeum*. 'We trust the Philharmonic Society's board will not be tempted into the Wagnerian waters,' thundered Davison in *The Musical World*, 'for if ever there was a veritable man-mermaid it is Richard, who looks fair enough above stream, but whose end is shrouded in a muddy quagmire of impenetrable sophistry.'

Too late: this bizarre hybrid arrived in England in March 1855, via the boat train service from Paris (the crossing from Calais took two hours, Wagner reported, but there was then an infuriating two-and-a-half-hour wait for a train up from Dover).

Once arrived in daunting London – 'a dreadfully large city, Paris is simply a village in comparison'* – Wagner put himself under the wing of some musical expatriate Germans who could alleviate his virtually non-existent command of the English language. Through the offices of the busy, talentless composer and pianist Ferdinand Praeger, characterised by Wagner as 'an unusually good-natured fellow, though of an excitability insufficiently balanced by his standard of culture', he was installed in rooms in a house in Portland Terrace, near Regent's Park, at £2 a week.

Initially he was optimistic, enchanted by a blue sky and the beauty of his sylvan surroundings. But the weather soon turned damp and dull. 'Though I spent four months in London, it seemed to me that spring never came, the foggy climate so overclouded all the impressions I received,' he remembered in his autobiography, and he was left with a stinking cold and the necessity of spending 'a shilling a day on coal alone' in order to keep himself warm in his poorly insulated rooms. Within weeks his expectations of 'a pleasant stay' had been totally flattened and by May he was writing to Liszt in a frenzy of despair. 'I live here like a damned soul in hell,' he complained. 'I see that it was simply a sin and a crime on my part to accept this London invitation.'

Things had gone badly wrong on a number of fronts. The fundamental problem was that the British musical scene was run on commercial lines entirely antithetical to Wagner's idealism. As Berlioz had noted in an essay on the subject, 'There is no town in the world where so much music is consumed as London,' but that vast appetite did not guarantee quality of performance, let alone discriminating audiences. There were no front-rank British composers, singers or instrumentalists, partly because standards of training for musicians were so low. Oratorio was a national obsession, with Handel's *Messiah* and Mendelssohn's *Elijah* repeated everywhere at regular intervals, like forms of religious service. The opera was focused on imported stars (the city had still not recovered from the Jenny Lind craze) and the most revered modern opera composer was the Jew Meyerbeer. In the Surrey Gardens, the bandmaster-showman Louis Jullien's Promenade

---

*A frequent reaction of visitors. Compare the gasp of the Parisian savant Hippolyte Taine, who discovered in 1861 that London 'adds up to twelve cities the size of Marseilles, ten as big as Lyons, two the size of Paris, in a single mass' and realised that 'you have to spend several days in succession in a cab, driving out north, south, east and west, for a whole morning' to encompass its boundaries. *Notes sur l'Angleterre* (Paris, 1872).

Concerts drew the masses with his 'monster' arrangements of classic favourites, played at deafening decibel levels, and punctuated with pyrotechnic effects, and a similar series had been inaugurated at the Crystal Palace. Foreign virtuosi might be received with curiosity and enthusiasm, but Lady Blessington's judgement of Liszt – that it seemed 'a pity to put such a handsome man at a piano' – was all too typical. The verdict of another great pianist of the modern school, Clara Schumann, on the London public was that 'they are dreadfully behind the times, or rather they can see only one thing at once. They will not hear of any of the newer composers except Mendelssohn who is their God.' Small wonder that the anti-Semitic Wagner was miserable.

He had more specific problems as well. Before signing his contract he had been given to understand that a deputy would be employed to conduct some of the less substantial works on a mutually agreed programme and that adequate rehearsal would be scheduled. This was not the case: there simply was no deputy and Wagner's idea of adequate rehearsal was not the Philharmonic Society's. In the matter of programming he gained one point only to lose another, and ended up lumbered with an omnium gatherum of overtures, concertos, symphonies and arias, a lot of them frankly mediocre. Worse, seven of the eight concerts contained items by Mendelssohn or Meyerbeer.

The orchestra itself, largely English in personnel, he found not bad. What it suffered from was a reluctance to depart from habit and a tendency to play everything with a jogtrot briskness which preferred manly *forte* to the subtleties of *piano*. (Ernest Newman suggests that the latter relates 'to the belief of Victorian England that any display of unusual sensitiveness was bad form', although this hardly squares with the equally strong Victorian penchant for the maudlin parlour ballad and the death of Little Nell). But these were irritations that Wagner could take in his professional stride and the players, with whom he communicated via their German-speaking, French-born leader Prosper Sainton, grew to like and respect him: 'You are the famous Philharmonic orchestra. Raise yourself, gentlemen, be *artists*,' he was heard to exhort in rehearsal, to some effect. 'Many of them assured me everything I conducted had been utterly *new*,' he told his wife Minna. 'They said they had never previously understood the works, in spite of the fact that they knew nearly all of them by heart.'

It was when he left the podium and floundered into the murky waters of polite society – not an area he inhabited happily at the best of times – that he fell out of his depth. Some of his gaffes were farcical: so befuddled did he become over English *bon ton* that he arrived at Sainton's house one day in full evening tails – at 9 a.m. Praeger told him that a top hat was necessary for all business and formal calls, but even the celebrated hatters of Regent Street had difficulty in finding a model to fit Wagner's enormous head. It was all very trying. 'I have stepped right into a morass of etiquette and custom and am in it up to my ears,' he wrote to Liszt. ' "Sir, we are not used to that sort of thing here" – that is all I ever hear, perpetually echoed back at me.'

On one point of politesse he refused to yield. Unfortunately, it was crucial. London's music critics were sensitive creatures, jealous of their influence and regularly in receipt of tokens of favour in return for 'puffs preliminary' and 'puffs direct'. Above all, they appreciated a courtesy call from visiting performers: it didn't involve much, but it made them feel important. Over some light refreshment in the drawing-room, Herr X or Monsieur Y could nod politely and scatter flattering compliments about the justice of Mr A's trenchant views of Signor Z's talents; a small gift, a souvenir, would not go amiss. It was all very comfortable and civilised, and favourable notices in the newspapers would surely follow. Berlioz and Meyerbeer had got the hang of the game, but Wagner was having none of it. 'I don't need the recommendation of blackguards,' he spluttered, contemptuous of well-wishers' arguments that this was how the system worked and that, in defying it, he would only be cutting off his nose to spite his face. One can but admire Wagner's integrity in this matter, but given the prejudices current against him and the half-baked misconceptions about his views (Davison, for instance, repeatedly told his readers that 'Wagner has little respect for any music but his own'), he was hardly justified in complaining of the treatment he subsequently received.

The eight concerts were held in the concert room in Hanover Square. It held around 800 and the fashionable audience of subscribers paid heavily for their seats. On 12 March the hall was 'well attended, though by no means crowded', as Wagner inaugurated the series with an early symphony by Haydn, the overture to *Die Zauberflöte*, a violin concerto by Spohr, Beethoven's *Eroica* and Mendelssohn's *Hebrides* Overture, interspersed with three operatic extracts; on 26 March came the overture to *Der Freischütz*, an aria by Cherubini, Mendelssohn's violin concerto, Beethoven's Ninth and, most significantly, some choral and orchestral highlights from *Lohengrin*.

There was some admiration for Wagner's conducting of the classics. 'Many portions of the great symphonies', admitted the *Morning Post*, 'have never, in our recollection, been so well played in this country . . . we can assert, without fear of contradiction, that they [i.e. Wagner's interpretations] were invariably intellectual, and frequently beautiful no less than new.' The key words here are 'intellectual' and 'new', for they are indicative of Wagner's disorientating refusal to follow the traditional tempi sanctified by Mendelssohn and emulated by other popular maestri of the day: in contrast, his beat seemed vague and 'poetic', his *andante lento*, his *presto prestissimo*. Other words often used in critiques include 'exaggerated' and 'fidgety'.

But the luminous grandeur of *Lohengrin* remained beyond comprehension. 'A great deal of this music is excessive and needlessly luxurious in mere loudness and meretriciousness of sound, [even if it] has very great merit in respect of instrumentation, and is also highly dramatic in character,' wrote W. H. Glover in the *Morning Post*. Chorley and Davison were even less generous: 'No melody, no form,' wrote Chorley; 'No definable phrase or rhythm, little else in short, but a sort of dull continuity,' added Davison. And so it went on: when the *Tannhäuser* overture was played in concerts in May and June, Davison became apoplectic: 'Wild, senseless dabbling . . . not music at all . . . a more inflated display of extravagance and noise has rarely been submitted to an audience.' Glover gave up on his effort to hear the good side and followed in Davison's corrosive wake, claiming the music to be 'destitute of melody, extremely bad in harmony, utterly incoherent in form and inexpressive of any intelligible ideas whatever . . . none but a terribly tormented soul could send forth such shocking sounds'.

Wagner's poor command of English might have prevented him reading such judgements in detail but he was aware of the general level of hostility and irately contemplated returning to Switzerland. 'I prefer not to dirty my hands by so much as touching a newspaper' he snarled. 'Anyone who understands anything and has a really independent opinion does not mix with this Jewish rabble' – a reference to Davison's fondness for Mendelssohn and a paranoid suspicion that the rest of them had been bought off by Meyerbeer. Still, he decided he had to stick it out, and to Liszt he wrote of his attempt to rise above the hostility. 'I don't quite know what I am here for. The only thing to interest me is the band, which has taken a great fancy to me, and is enthusiastic in my cause . . . All the rest, the public, press etc., is a matter of supreme indifference.'

The damp weather didn't let up and his cold got no better,* despite his adoption of what he describes as 'a heavy English diet'. At Portland Terrace he attempted to make himself comfortable, requiring an eiderdown quilt from his landlady, Mrs Henry, and renting a grand piano. A carpenter built him an easel, at which he slowly continued work on the scoring of *Die Walküre*, difficult though it was to concentrate on nobler things. In spare moments he read for the first time Dante's *Inferno* – all too appropriate, he thought, to his situation.

He battled to keep up his spirits and, however bad his cold or gloomy his lucubrations, he was clearly determined to make the most of his freedom from Minna and enjoy what London had to offer. His most regular companion was Praeger, who fetched and carried and generally attended to his needs (and later wrote a memoir of the visit, inflating his role in it all). Through him, Wagner became friendly with the orchestra's leader Sainton and his partner Charles Luders, a German exile with a passion for Wagner's theoretical writings. This latter were a pair of inseparable bachelors, 'living together in a pretty house like a married couple', as Wagner quaintly put it, 'each tenderly concerned for his friend's welfare'.

Another more consequential new friend was a young pupil of Liszt's called Karl Klindworth. Heroically handsome, impassioned and highly intelligent, Klindworth would become one of his most fervent acolytes. If only he had been a tenor, Wagner sighed, he would have carried him off and turned him into the perfect Siegfried.† One day Klindworth played him Liszt's new piano sonata, which he had not previously heard. His reaction was immediate. 'Beautiful beyond belief: great,

---

*Seven months later he was still complaining of it. 'Today I have just risen from my sickbed, to which – with a few days' exception – I have been confined for the last two months.' I think it was the same malady which afflicted me in London, gone into hiding but finally struck again . . . a collection of rheums and catarrhs which have only now finally left their cage.' (From a letter to Prosper Sainton, 19 December 1855).

†He also arranged the vocal scores of the *Ring*, *Die Meistersinger* and *Tristan und Isolde*. Klindworth's adoptive daughter, Winifred Williams, later married Wagner's son Siegfried. As his widow, she became a close friend of Hitler and controlled the Bayreuth Festival throughout the Nazi era.

lovable, deep and noble,' he wrote to the composer. 'I was most profoundly moved by it, and all my troubles here in London have suddenly been forgotten.'

There were other moments when the clouds lifted. He took daily constitutional walks with Praeger and his dog Gipsy in Regent's Park, where they fed the ducks on the pond and had a little joke about a swan who must have been Lohengrin's brother. He also toured the shops, buying silk for his own shirts and lace for Minna. In the evenings there was back-slapping conviviality and horseplay with Praeger, Sainton and Luders, some of it out on the town – according to Ashton Ellis, Wagner and his cronies went 'to almost every place of amusement then open, even those of a third-rate order'. This category embraced some Shakespeare (including a rotten performance of *Romeo and Juliet* in which Romeo was played by the American actress Charlotte Cushman), pantomime at the Adelphi and the big hit of the season, the burlesque melodrama *The Yellow Dwarf*, in which the title role was taken by the electrifying Frederick Robson (whose comic but macabre acting must have set Wagner thinking of his Mime in *Siegfried*). He also visited many of the standard tourist attractions and treated , Praeger et al. to a slap-up meal at the Ship Inn at Greenwich, home of the famous whitebait 'ministerial dinner', the centrepiece of which was a plate piled high with locally caught baby herrings, fried, devilled and otherwise, accompanied by bread and butter, and washed down with iced champagne or punch.

Of the music on offer, he took a dim view. One concert he attended 'was conducted in slip-slop fashion . . . and the next day all the papers said that this was the finest concert of the whole season . . . those same reporters who had written favourably about me accorded this other concert the very same praise they had given mine'. He was intrigued by a visit to the mecca of oratorio, Exeter Hall, where he felt he had come 'to understand the true spirit of English musical culture, which is bound up with the spirit of English Protestantism' and was amused at the sight of members of the audience 'holding their copies of the score in the same way as one holds a prayer-book in church'. At Covent Garden he saw a 'rather grotesque' performance of *Fidelio*, sung by 'dirty Germans and voiceless Italians', but avoided the chance to hear Meyerbeer's latest excrescence, *L'Etoile du Nord*, at Drury Lane. By ghastly mischance this supreme object of his loathing was in London too, and Wagner ran into him in person when calling at the house of the Philharmonic Society's secretary George Hogarth (Dickens' father-in-law). 'We greeted each other coldly without speaking,' Meyerbeer noted in his diary.

Nothing about England or the English particularly impressed Wagner. To hell with them – they were smug and narrow-minded and couldn't see the point of his music: 'I find it impossible to imagine anything more repugnant than the real genuine Englishman,' he wrote in a letter to Otto Wesendonck, as he launched into the sort of invective he normally reserved for the Jews (and the French, and the Italians). 'Without exception they are all like sheep, and the Englishman's practical intelligence is about as reliable as a sheep's instinct for finding its food in the open fields; of course, it finds its food, but the whole of the beautiful fields and the blue sky above might as well not exist, such are its organs of perception.'

But he felt a soft spot for a quaint little old composer, Cipriani Potter, who clung to him 'with almost distressing humility' while he rehearsed Potter's symphony for one of the Philharmonic Society's concerts; and he genuinely liked the sophisticated musical dilettante John Lodge Ellerton, not least because he was an ardent Wagnerian with no time for Mendelssohn. Less happy was Wagner's introduction to the Benecke family, friends of Wesendonck, of German extraction, who lived in a suburb that Wagner registered as 'Campervall' – actually Camberwell. A visit here involved the embarrassing discovery that 'I had dropped into the very family whose house Mendelssohn had made his home when in London. The good people did not know what to do with me, apart from congratulating me on the excellence of my Mendelssohn performances and rewarding me with descriptions of the generous character of the deceased.'

The concerts became progressively more exasperating. During the fourth, on 30 April, some idiot tenor made a false entry in an aria from Meyerbeer's *Les Huguenots* and indicated to the audience that his error had been the conductor's fault. Music of absolutely no merit whatsoever was as indiscriminately applauded and encored as Beethoven's *Eroica*. As Ernest Newman sympathised, 'To stand up like a performing dog and do his tricks for an audience that could demand a repetition of a second-rate work . . . must have been gall and wormwood to him.' Meanwhile the critics continued to be, at best, baffled and grudging. Wagner 'is capricious and erratic and wanders in the realms of fancy, when he should be humbly endeavouring to express the meaning and purposes of much greater men than himself', boomed the *Morning Post* in headmasterly tones.

To the seventh concert on 11 June came Queen Victoria and Prince Albert. Wagner was susceptible to such gracious royal attention, as radical socialists tend to be. 'She is not fat, but very small and not at all pretty with, I am sorry to say, a rather red nose,' he wrote to his wife Minna breathlessly, 'but there is something uncommonly friendly and confiding about her – and although she is by no means imposing, she is nevertheless a delightful and kind person.' They talked about Wagner's operas, in 'a conversation in which Prince Albert – a very handsome man! – joined with the most gratifying interest'. When the Queen ventured the view that 'my things could perhaps be translated into Italian in order to be given here at the Italian opera, the Prince retorted, very sensibly, that my libretti were unsuited to this, and, in particular Italian singers would have absolutely no idea how to sing them'.

The exchange sounds altogether fatuous, but Wagner was delighted. 'I do not think they understood me entirely,' he continued, 'but they expressed a concerned interest in what I was saying, and added that they were quite enchanted by the Overture [to *Tannhäuser*].'* The encounter gave Wagner a warm glow and left him feeling that he could leave London 'somewhat more reconciled' than he could before.

Another pleasant event cheered his final weeks in London – the arrival from Paris of Hector Berlioz, to conduct concerts for the Philharmonic Society's rival body, the New Philharmonic. Despite their profound differences, both as men and composers – Berlioz's Romanticism was subjective and unintellectual, Wagner's transcendental and meta-physical – they got on surprisingly well. 'Of a sudden, we found that we indeed were fellow-sufferers,' Wagner sighed, acknowledging in a rare fit of altruism that Berlioz's position was even worse than his own ('his whole being expressed weariness and despair . . . I could deem myself perfectly happy and almost floating on air, by contrast'). Berlioz felt, more guardedly, that 'even if we both

---

*In the same letter to Minna, Wagner also mentions the Queen's admiration for his satin trousers: 'I'm having to send them to the palace for her, so that she can have a pair made for Prince Albert.' One assumes this was a little joke, but you never know.

have our asperities, at any rate they dovetail' and the result was some lively and convivial evenings of conversation, conducted in French. What little each of them knew of the other's music they regarded somewhat sceptically, but their isolation in London united them in a shared sense of being persecuted radicals and misunderstood idealists, racked by contempt for the cynical commer-cialism of the modern world – more specifically for Meyerbeer who, according to Berlioz, was in the habit of inviting the Parisian critics to irresistibly elegant private dinners he held on the evenings before the premières of his operas. Wagner chortled grimly on hearing that.

As the time came for his departure at the end of June, the critics struck their most militantly John Bullish stance. 'Herr Wagner is a necessary evil,' decided Glover in the *Morning Post*. 'We believe him to be quite in earnest and perfectly conscientious . . . Germany, however, and not England, is the proper arena for his exploits. There he is at home, and natural – one of the last links in a chain which will soon end where it began, in artistic nothingness; the necessary expression of something which if he did not, somebody else must express; but here he is out of his element. England – young and fresh and full of musical feeling . . . cannot possibly relish corruption.' In *The Times*, Davison curtly concluded, 'Herr Wagner, it must be confessed, has cut but a sorry figure in this country, where plain common sense goes for something and a man is rather judged by his deeds than his professions . . . another such set of eight concerts would go far to annihilate the [Philharmonic] Society.'

The Society may have taken these words to heart. On its behalf, George Hogarth bade Wagner farewell in a perfunctory speech, which carefully avoided any implication that further invitations might be forthcoming. 'I am desired by the Directors of the Philharmonic Society to convey to you, before your departure, their most cordial thanks for the great attention, zeal and ability which, as conductor of the concerts this season, you have shown in carrying out their views; and also to add the expression of their best wishes for your welfare and happiness.' Wagner, fortunately, would have understood scarcely a word of this mouldy peroration, but he was moved by the massive applause, from both audience and orchestra, which greeted his final concert on 26 June – a programme consisting of a symphony by Spohr, a piano concerto by Hummel, overtures by Mendelssohn and Weber,

Beethoven's Fourth and arias by Weber, Haydn and Meyerbeer. Berlioz was in the audience: himself a conductor of Toscanini-like precision, according to David Cairns, he found Wagner 'unclear in his beat and self-indulgent in his changes of tempo'.

Afterwards Praeger, along with Berlioz, Klindworth and the cosy couple Sainton and Luders, drove Wagner back to his lodgings in Regent's Park, where they partied over champagne punch until 3 a.m., leaving Wagner to wake the next morning with 'the very devil of a headache'.

He left London a day later, without regrets. Despite the pleasant but superficial eleventh-hour acclaim, he summed up his visit as an utter waste of time and effort, at a point when he was desperate to be ploughing on with the *Ring*. Nor had the trip been as financially profitable as he had hoped: the horrendous expense of four months of London life ('places are so dreadfully far apart that I simply have to take a cab everywhere,' he complained to Minna, and 'half a bottle of Bordeaux in the worst restaurant costs three shillings') left him with even less than he had anticipated: a net profit, in fact, of a measly 1000 Francs, or £40. 'This is the hardest money I have ever earned,' he told a friend. 'I have had to pay for every one of these francs with a feeling of bitterness which I hope it will never fall to me to experience again.'

Within days of his departure, as if pursuing his fleeing enemy with a valedictory poison dart, Davison wrote a long and bilious invective against 'Herr Richard Wagner and his followers' in *The Musical World*. Less music criticism than hellfire-and-brimstone sermon in the style of Thomas Carlyle, it is almost comic in the excess of its foot-stamping and fist-shaking ambition to have the last word and rid England of the Wagnerian contagion.

> Shall music be condemned to the stake and burnt, to satisfy the insatiate craving for destruction of this priest of Dagon? Shall the nurse have no lullaby, to sing the child to sleep – no pretty tune, to rock it up and down – no snatch of melody to make its little eyes glisten through tears . . . Composition indeed! – *de*composition is the proper word for such hateful fungi, which choke up and poison the fertile plains of harmony, threatening the world with drowth . . . What he may think of musical London we are unable to guess; but if there be any truth in physiognomy the 'small man with the intellectual forehead' . . . must regard us as a community of idiots. Be it so. 'Where ignorance is bliss, 'tis folly to be wise'.

Poor Wagner! Posterity may now commemorate him as a despicable racist and egomaniac, but his second visit to England shows him in a more sympathetic, even pitiable light – not only a great creating artist but a thorough professional, staunchly determined to do the best possible job in a difficult situation; the provincial German outclassed by metropolitan London; the victim of prejudice and bigotry who wisely resisted the temptation to rise to a slanging match with his persecutors. Genius would finally triumph – who remembers J. W. Davison now? – but not quickly or easily. Twenty-two years later, in 1877, Wagner crossed the Channel again, still on the hunt for cash. He would make many of the same mistakes, with similarly unhappy results.

The circumstances, however, were rather different. For one thing, London had become somewhat more familiar with Wagner's theatrical work, and a cadre of supporters had consolidated. In 1870 Drury Lane staged *Der Fliegende Holländer* – Italianised, as custom dictated, as *L'Olandese Dannato*, with the famous Victorian baritone Charles Santley in the title role. Some reviewers continued to respond with knee-jerk hostility; others, like the anonymous man from *The Musical Times*, admitted that the music did exert a profound effect, even if they were not quite sure what it was or whence it came. '. . . that every one of the audience felt under the influence of a man who had struck out an original path for himself, and had power enough to make others accompany him, was apparent by the deep interest with which every note was listened to, and the enthusiastic applause with which the various pieces were received . . .'

'Pieces' is the significant word there – the writer recognises that the usual terminology of aria, duet and ensemble applicable to the operas of Verdi or Meyerbeer no longer quite serves, and by the time that *Lohengrin* and *Tannhäuser* reached Covent Garden in 1875 and 1876 respectively (albeit in severely cut versions, sung in Italian), some critics were beginning to understand the principles underlying Wagner's music. Journals like the *Fortnightly* and *Westminster Review* published serious and substantial articles on the Wagner question. Instead of berating him for meandering without obvious melodic direction, they gingerly acknowledged that his aim was to elevate opera from the level of a floor show to something approaching the nobility of the classic

Greek drama. In this rarefied aesthetic environment there were no encores, no bowing and curtsying by the stars, explained *The Musical Times* after witnessing *Tannhäuser* – 'no pretty song for the soprano, no high C "from the chest" of the tenor, no sensational passage "a due" patched in to evoke a storm of applause . . . from the first to the last one beautiful tone-picture is before us, the effect of which is not shown by audible marks of approbation at certain details, but by the burst of applause when the fall of the curtain, at the end of each act, gives time for reflection upon what has been passing before us.' From pieces, in other words, they began to perceive wholes.

What further lifted the Wagnerian cause in London was the presence of a sizeable German émigré intelligentsia, which took its music seriously and methodically as it took its socialist politics. As performers, both amateur and professional, and as members of the audience, its members formed an effective lobby and, in 1873, one of its number, the pianist and pedagogue Edward Dannreuther, went on to establish a British branch of the Wagner Society. This small but active organisation gave salon renderings of extracts from *der Meister*'s work and linked into an international network of such bodies, all designed not only to promote a deeper understanding of the operas, but also to raise cash for their composer's grander schemes and general well-being. Even if one refused to accept the view that his was 'the music of the future', the upshot was that Wagner could no longer justifiably be written off as a fraud or a charlatan, an arrant self-publicist or a priest of Dagon.

Yet although Wagner's music might have gained in respectability over the twenty-two years since his previous visit to London, his personal reputation had simultaneously blackened. 'We are sometimes told that Wagner has been a persecuted man,' wrote the *Daily Telegraph* on 9 May, in severe tones.

> Assuming the truth of this, we wholly decline to look upon him as an object of pity, since he has nobody but himself to blame. It was open to him, if necessity compelled the writing of pamphlets as well as music dramas, to set forth his principles with judicial calmness and moderation, instead of which he was content with nothing less than running a-muck like a mad Malay . . . That which is written remains, and we cannot forget – Herr Wagner does not permit us to forget – who turned upon the operatic composers of his own time with a fury which even now men wonder at; who ransacked the capacious German language for its strongest terms of contempt and scorn, who, in his boundless self-

consciousness, charged a whole race [viz. the Jews] with conspiring to ruin him; and who, heedless of the law against kicking a man when he is down, wrote a farce lampooning Paris in her distress and suffering [after the city had surrendered to the Germans at the end of the Franco-Prussian War], presumably because in her prosperity, she had rejected him [the first performance of *Tannhäuser* at the Paris Opera in 1861 had been a fiasco]. It is idle to talk of persecution when a man invites reprisals in this way. . . . Why do we write all this? That, in the midst of whatever honours are paid to Herr Wagner – and the deserts of his genius are great – there should be no false sentiment about the master's personality.

Below this, however, another level of disapproval was insinuated. Gossip whispered that Herr Wagner coveted other men's wives and, although the details never reached the newspapers, the accusation stuck – with some justification. Minna had died of a weak heart in 1866; for the previous ten years they had scarcely lived as man and wife. Wagner never totally abandoned her, but throughout that decade of estrangement he had certainly taken the unconventional view of marriage and, after the abrupt end of his affair with Mathilde Wesendonck, he indulged in several other infidelities. In 1863, however, he met his match: Liszt's daughter Cosima, then married to the conductor Hans von Bülow and the mother to two of his daughters. Mesmerised by a genius she never ceased to revere, Cosima left her husband (who magnanimously continued to champion Wagner's music) and, by the time she was able to remarry in 1870, Wagner and Cosima had become parents to three further children. But Wagner was never totally domesticated or comfortable with Cosima's adoration, and in 1876 he had begun some sort of clandestine relationship with another married woman, the French writer and intellectual Judith Gautier, daughter of Théophile.

The world didn't know the half of it: what it had gathered was that Wagner loathed Jews (or at least the Jewish race: his anti-Semitism, according to a starry-eyed Francis Hueffer, 'did not extend to individuals'), held revolutionary political views and had won the extravagant patronage of the young King Ludwig II of Bavaria. As for his music, it seemed to become ever more ambitious and unorthodox. Just as the opera public was beginning to come round to *Lohengrin* and *Tannhäuser*, up he came with three massive new challenges: *Tristan und Isolde*, a glorification of adulterous love 'scarcely to be tolerated on the boards of an English theatre', as *The Times* bristled on 12 May; the thoroughly Germanic comedy of *Die Meistersinger von Nürnberg*; and the four-part *Der Ring des Nibelungen*, given its first perfomance in 1876 when it inaugurated a new opera house in the Bavarian town of Bayreuth.

This was the most controversial and sensational of Wagner's artistic projects: a building, financed by a mixture of public appeal and state subsidy, which eliminated the hierarchical tiers of the standard auditorium and adopted a 'democratic' Greek-style amphitheatre instead. The orchestra was invisible beneath a hood; lights were dimmed to ensure silence during the performance; and the acoustics were of a heavenly clarity and sonority. It was to be a temple of art, Wagner insisted, where Mammon should have no place: artists would work for nothing but love, audiences would not pay for their seats. Stuff and nonsense, his opponents scoffed: the whole place was *folie de grandeur*, the expensive whim of a megalomaniac who had been over-indulged and deserved only the horsewhip.

Yet royalty and celebrity flocked to the opening season – the new theatre was considered a wonder of the modern world, or at least an irresistible curiosity. Among the musicians who made the pilgrimage were Liszt, Grieg, Tchaikovsky, Mahler, Bruckner and Saint-Saëns: like everybody else, including the sixty music critics in attendance, they responded to the *Ring* with a mixture of boredom and bafflement, admiration and excitement, and didn't know quite what to make of it. But many of the younger generation came away deeply moved and spirtually altered – among them the twenty-eight-year-old English composer Hubert Parry. One of his mentors was the crusty George Macfarren, whose overture *Chevy Chase*, Wagner had wearily con-ducted in 1855. Presumably the experience had been an unhappy one, for Macfarren wrote to his pupil sternly:

> I am sorry to hear you are going to Bayreuth, for every presence there gives countenance to monstrous self-inflation. The principle of the thing is bad, the means for its realisation preposterous. An earthquake would be good that would swallow up the spot and everybody on it, so I wish you were away.
> Yours, with kindest regards,
>   G. A. Macfarren*

The Bayreuth venture had left debts of over 100,000 Marks, for which Wagner himself was partially liable. Once again he was

---

*Quoted by Percy Scholes in *The Mirror of Music* (London, 1947), vol. 1, p. 254. This book gives many useful references to the early coverage of Wagner in the English music press.

desperate. Even though the tactic had scarcely worked for him in 1855, he returned to the idea of conducting some concerts in London as a quick way of reducing the ghastly sum. Quite how or where the scheme originated we do not know, but an enthusiastic firm of agents, Messrs Hodge & Essex of Argyll Street, had been in communication with August Wilhelmj, the London-based violinist who had led the orchestra for the Bayreuth *Ring*, and with Dannreuther of the London branch of the Wagner Society. The plan that emerged was for Hodge & Essex to present a series of twenty concerts at the Royal Albert Hall, then a new and relatively untried musical venue – it had opened in 1871 – but one large enough – it could accommodate 8000 – to offer the possibility of considerable profit to anyone who could fill the house.

Hodge & Essex opened their negotiations with tempting talk of a profit-share of £500 for Wagner on every concert, but by the time arithmetic had been done and signatures put to contracts, the figures had been whittled down to six concerts, to be given over a fortnight in May, for a total fee of £1,500 – providing, of course, the box-office takings reached a certain level. Colleagues who had yielded to such deals before and come away with burnt fingers sounded Cassandra-like warnings about the terms, but Wagner had no option. He engaged many of his Bayreuth singers for the ordeal and, on 1 May, a week before the first concert, arrived in London with Cosima via the boat train from Dover. 'Almost the entire orchestra is gathered on the platform at Charing Cross,' reported Cosima in her diary. After a drive to the Albert Hall – 'which we like very much,' Cosima commented, 'in spite of its enormous dimensions' – they made their way half a mile or so across Kensington Gardens to 12 Orme Square in Bayswater. Here Dannreuther and his wife Chariclea (*née* Ionides, a clan involved with the Aesthetes and Pre-Raphaelites) accommodated them for the duration in their newly built terraced house (now demolished), decorated in the style of William Morris: it was a pleasant place to stay and an economical one.

Unfortunately, it soon became clear that the visit had been planned on shaky foundations and even before the first concert, there were ominous rumblings of disaster. On 3 May Cosima noted that 'H. and Essex seems to be very good people, but they are very inexperienced and the whole of Israel is once more working against us'. (What provoked this latter remark is unknown – perhaps it was nothing more than quotidian Wagnerian persecution mania.) Still, the first rehearsals went quite well. 'He is very cheered by the sound of the orchestra,' wrote Cosima on 4 May, an impression confirmed by the other diarist of these weeks, Hubert Parry – a pupil of Dannreuther who shyly attended every concert and rehearsal, and was an awestruck guest at Orme Square. 'The hero was there and in good humour, and pleased with the band,' he wrote after the morning session at the Albert Hall, adding after another session on 7 May that 'Wagner's conducting is quite marvellous; he seems to transform all he touches, he knows precisely what he wants and does it to a certainty. The Kaiser Marsch became quite new under his baton and supremely magnificent. I was so wild with excitement that I did not recover all the afternoon.'

A massive 169 players were involved – about a third more than any modern performance would use. With Wilhelmj as Leader, they divided into forty-eight violins, fifteen violas, twenty cellos, twenty-two double-basses, twenty-eight woodwind, eight horns, five trumpets, five trombones, five tubas, seven harps and six percussion: united at *fortissimo*, they must have lifted the roof off the Albert Hall (and God knows how they ricocheted round its notorious echo). Dannreuther had taken some preliminary rehearsal, but it was Wagner's trusty deputy Hans Richter, conductor of the first Bayreuth *Ring*, who was the linchpin of the operation. Wagner himself, almost sixty-four, was not in sufficiently good health to undertake the entire assignment unaided and remained unable to speak coherent English, so Richter did most of the donkey work. During performances it was often unclear to what extent Wagner himself was in direct control: he presided at all times, but for many items sat to one side while Richter took over the baton and attempted to fulfil the composer's barked instructions. The press took a dim view of this arrangement and on 15 May the *London Figaro* brutally talked of Wagner's 'total and absolute failure as a conductor . . . performing a little in dumb show early in the evening and resigning the baton to Herr Richter when his own arm begins to tire'. And what he did manage himself was 'fidgety and fussy . . . he loses his head at the slightest provocation, his tempi are invariably slow, and he cannot even beat the measure with regularity'. This from a critic who professed great admiration for Wagner's music.

Back at Orme Square, the social carousel began to whirl. There was a dinner with Wagner's old friends from 1855, Sainton and Luders, there were visits to the Zoo in Regent's Park and meetings with Browning and

George Eliot – to whom Cosima had been introduced via a letter from her father Liszt – as well as many others less celebrated. On 5 May the Dannreuthers invited a crowd to an 'At Home', where the great man and his wife were guests of honour. 'A goodly company of artist folk to meet Wagner, who was in great fettle and talked to an open-mouthed group,' wrote Parry. 'He talks so fast that I could catch but very little of what he said.' 'R. annoyed at the visitors,' was Cosima's terse view of the event.

But he could not complain of being ignored. The concert programmes were to be exclusively devoted to Wagner's own music, in what amounted to a retrospective of his oeuvre. The press was full of it and on 7 May *Punch,* the principal organ of middle-class British philistinism and no friend to highfalutin art of any kind, had characteristic fun at its expense:

> The following regulations have been issued by the Police for the maintenance of order and the satisfaction of the Great Composer on the occasion of the Wagner performances at the Albert Hall. The public will be admitted to the Albert Hall on presentation of vouchers signed by HERR WAGNER or HERR DANNREUTHER, and on production of a certificate from any two Professors of Aesthetics in any University at home or abroad. No person who has ever been heard to scoff at the Music of the Future, or is known to prefer MOZART's, BEETHOVEN's or MENDELSSOHN's works to the recitatives in *Lohengrin* and the *Ring des Nibelungen*, or who has ever confessed to having derived pleasure from the Operas of AUBER or ROSSINI, BELLINI or DONIZETTI, or who has at any time degraded himself so far as to listen to the garbage of OFFENBACH, HERVE, LECOCQ, or STRAUSS, will on any account be admitted to the honour of assisting in this audition.
>
> Any one of the audience assembled who shall blow any one's trumpet but that of RICHARD WAGNER (always excepting the ninety-nine trombones in the orchestra), or who shall sneeze, cough or blow his own nose, or any one else's, during the ceremony, or who shall show any sign of disapproval or weariness, either by audible words, gesture, exclamation or whisper shall on detection, be removed by the police agents at the first pause in the programme.
>
> Only specified admirers will be permitted to bring up to the dais on which the august WAGNER will be enthroned crowns, wreaths or bouquets for his acceptance. . . .
>
> The Police have special orders to prevent the audience in their enthusiasm carrying HERR WAGNER round the galleries, or crowding to kiss his hand, so as to impede his respiration, or otherwise interfere with his personal comfort.

A powerful limelight will throw a halo round the head of the Professor during the performance. Three of the most noted aurists of Savile Row will be in attendance at the Hall for the reparation of defective [ear] drums.

Sal volatile and chloric aether, for the use of persons of exceptionally fine strung nerves, may be had in the basement of the Hall, on application to the Chemist of the Medicines of the Future, who will have his laboratory on the premises, with every description of restorative appliance and apparatus.

Special trains will run from the Kensington High Street station to Colney Hatch, Hanwell and Earlswood [sites of noted lunatic asylums] after each concert.

This was excellent publicity – probably more effective than the sort of advertising with which Hodge & Essex had saturated the newspapers: on 7 May, for example, the central column of the front page of the *Daily Telegraph* was dominated by a tedious scroll of names, which must have been enough to put anyone off:

WAGNER FESTIVAL
ROYAL ALBERT HALL
FIRST GRAND CONCERT
THIS EVENING AT EIGHT O'CLOCK
Kaisermarsch
Rienzi
Tannhauser
Ring des Nibelungen – Das Rheingold
Wagner, conductor
Wilhelmj, leader of the orchestra
Vocalists:
Frau Materna (Vienna)
Frau von Sadler-Grun (Coburg)
Fräulein Waibel (Munich)
Fräulein Exter (Munich)
Herr Hill (Schwerin)
Herr Unger (Bayreuth)
Herr Schlosser (Munich)
Herr Chandon (Vienna)
Orchestra of 200 instrumentalists
Private Boxes, from Five Guineas
Amphitheatre Stalls, One Guinea
Arena Stalls, 15s
Balcony (first three rows), 15s
Balcony (back rows), Half a Guinea

Orchestra and Organ Gallery, 5s
Gallery, Half a Crown
etc.

Did it live up to expectations? Cosima, for one, thought not: 'I sit with
the two Leweses [George Eliot and her common-law husband G. H.
Lewes] in the grand tier and am horrified by the sound, a double echo,
no impression possible! On top of that, our singers very feeble.' The
reviews were mixed. The extracts from *Rienzi* and *Tannhäuser* – by
now becoming staple concert fare – were generally appreciated; the
orchestra was magnificent. In *The Times*, the ever-implacable J. W.
Davison found the evening's novelty, a potted version of *Das
Rheingold* 'simply dreary . . . the audience listened for a time, and then
treated the entire affair like a too elaborate conundrum, and simply
"gave it up" and quitted the Hall by ones and twos and finally by
scores'. But for all his strictures, even he had to admit that 'the audience
was large and the applause almost overwhelming'. The *Daily
Telegraph* managed more enthusiasm for *Rheingold*, praising 'the
wonderful beauty of the scoring' and the performers, but bemoaning
the absence of 'scenic effects' without which the action could make
little sense.

It could have been worse, and the next evening the Wagners went off
in what Cosima describes as 'cheerful spirits' to enjoy a performance of
Rip van Winkle. On 9 May the concert featured the first act of *Die
Walküre*. In *The Times*, Davison's review was excoriating – 'the shrieks
of railway whistles, the lowing of cattle, the grinding of machinery, are
all more endurable than the music of *Die Walküre*', he blustered. It was
indeed 'a severe test on the public, without the assistance of the scenery
and dramatic action and many went out,' admitted Parry, 'but the
applause at the end was great nonetheless.'

If only there survived some indication as to who attended these
concerts! Even if the Albert Hall was half empty and a lot of people
came to several concerts, something in the region of 20,000 individuals
must have bought tickets. The figure is impressively large and speaks
highly of Victorian London's musical sophistication, or at least its
curiosity: one would be hard pushed today to draw such a number to a
series of concerts of a 'difficult' contemporary composer. But who
made up this audience, from what classes or professions or addresses
did it emanate? The Wagner Society cannot account for more than a

few hundred. The intelligentsia may have provided a thousand or so more, the hard core of cultured German immigrants perhaps a couple of thousand at most.* Where did the remainder come from? How had they heard about Wagner's music and what did they think of it all? Were they part of the new middle-class, suburban audience for theatre and concerts, the sort who over the next twenty years would flock to the works of Gilbert and Sullivan and Oscar Wilde? Were they God-fearing people who sang in the great choral societies of the day? Or the sort of folk who papered their houses with the patterns of William Morris and risked reading Flaubert and Baudelaire?

We just don't know. Our only reasonable general inference is that Wagner appealed to the fashionable young. In *The Times* of 13 May, Davison had written:

> 'Bad form not to be well up in Wagnerism, don't you think?' said a swell in our hearing. There it is. Society must have materials for small talk, and for the time being Richard Wagner is served up as a topic of conversation in the clubs and drawing-rooms of Belgravia and Tyburnia. 'Heard Wagner's latest operas?' say the young dandies to the pretty girls they admire, and the pretty girls make reply 'oh yes, I don't know what they mean, but they're awfully sublime, I understand'.

This is a sneer, but one based on authentic observation, as we can see from the charming way that Hubert Parry proselytised on behalf of his idol.

> Eddie [Hamilton, his cousin] came to luncheon [on 12 May] and I gave him a good preparation in Walküre, so that he might know the story and the chief subjects; and we went to the concert together. It was a triumphant success. The great last act of Walküre was overwhelming! and very few went out before the end, and the cheering and clapping was prolonged and enthusiastic. Eddie went to sleep once or twice, especially in the scene between Siegmund and Brünnhilde, but I think on the whole he appreciated it.

On 14 May Parry dragged his adored fiancée Maudie to a rehearsal,

---

*There was a large German immigration to Britain in the nineteenth century. 'Whereas the other foreign colonies in London are more or less limited to certain quarters, the Germans are distributed over all the districts of the colossal city. According to some, their number is 35,000, others make it 70,000, a third estimate even doubles this last calculation; but throughout England there can hardly be fewer than a quarter of a milllion . . .' Leopold Katscher, 'German Life in London', *Nineteenth Century* (May 1887), p. 726 and Ian Buruma, *Voltaire's Coconuts* (London, 1999), Chapter 9.

'very anxious to know if she would like it or not'. Maudie, possibly more out of loyalty than genuine ardour, 'entered into it thoroughly and was delighted'. Four days later she was taken back, to hear parts of *Tristan und Isolde*. 'I enjoyed them fully,' Parry continued, 'and so did Maudie, who is keener about Wagner's music than I ever saw her about anything except the Rights of Women.' He had less joy of his stepsisters Linda and Beatrice, who 'came to luncheon with us and I quarrelled with the latter for saying that the poems of the Nibelungen were "horrid stories" ', but fell gratefully on one Susie Stephenson, who is 'as fervent a Wagnerite as I am; saying even that it moved her so much that she could hardly talk about it'.

Did Parry ever encounter Jeannette Marshall, one of Dannreuther's piano pupils? She was the twenty-two-year-old daughter of a Savile Row surgeon, with a pert and brusque personality characteristic of 'the Girl of the Period'.* She shopped at Liberty, favoured Aesthetic fabrics and jewellery, and had advanced literary and artistic tastes. On 14 May, with Dannreuther's encouragement, she attended Wagner's fourth concert at the Albert Hall and tartly recorded her impressions in her diary. 'He is certainly clever looking and there is something dashing in his face. He looks a genius and as if he knew it.' But the extracts from *Lohengrin* and the *Ring* broke through her defences, and the effect on her of the 'Ride of the Valkyries' was 'indescribable':

> The scrapes of the violins wh. begin it and accompany the first giving out of the theme by the trumpets has an uncanny and wild effect past all description. Then the drums roll like the clatter of horses' hoofs, louder and louder, and nearer and nearer, while the violins sigh like the wind and then comes the theme agn. The finale works up to a *ff* and then breaks off suddenly. Most marvellous, and enough to convert anyone . . . I feel to want [*sic*] very much to hear some more of Wagner's music, I shd soon be a disciple.

Which in due course she was – in 1882 she went to the first British performance of the *Ring* at Covent Garden and in 1889 made a

---

*A much-used journalistic phrase in the 1870s and 1880s, originating in 1868 and the title of a polemical essay written by Mrs Eliza Lynn Linton in the *Sunday Review*. Mrs Linton contrasted 'the simple and genuine girl of the past . . . with her tender little ways and pretty bashful modesties' to the 'loud and rampant modernisation, with her false red hair and painted skin, talking slang as glibly as a man . . . whose sole idea is plenty of fun and luxury'. Gwendolen Harleth in George Eliot's *Daniel Deronda* is a deeply perceptive portrait of the type. See also p. 191.

pilgrimage to Bayreuth, where she heard *Parsifal* and *Die Meistersinger*. But were there many more like her?

In any case, the enthusiasm of such as Parry and Jeannette Marshall was grist to the scoffer's mill. In the pages of *Punch*, Wagnerism was interpreted as a ludicrous pretension, a magnet for what the Victorians called 'humbug' – and we would call 'pseudery'. On 19 May, for example, it published a spoof report by 'THE HOOKY WALKYRIE':

> Having been a considerable time accustomed to play the trilogy [i.e. the Ring] with one finger on the accordion, I was naturally anxious to hear the same work of art performed by a band of two hundred, at the Albert Hall. HERR RICHARD WAGNER wrote to me in his best low Bavarian: *'Ich bin gleich nach London gekommen mit den Trompeten und Drummen, der Brassen, der Winden und der Fiddelstückeren. Du bist ein Musik Kritiker. Wie viel? Leben sie wohl. R.W.'*

After more nonsense in this vein of prep-school humour, 'THE HOOKY WALKYRIE' attends a concert at the Albert Hall in the company of a supposed true Wagnerite

> Suddenly, a burst of enthusiastic applause. I could not see whom they were applauding. I appealed to my Well-Informed Friend. 'Is it Wagner?' I asked.
>
> 'Well,' he replied slowly, 'I fancy it must be Wagner.'
>
> 'Is he there?' I asked, authoritatively, for you see I had treated this man, and treated him well, on the strength of his being Your Own Well-Informed Correspondent at Bayreuth.
>
> 'Well,' he began, 'I rather think he –' But before the egregious humbug could commit himself to an assertion, a mysterious whisper passed round – 'It is Wilhelmj [the orchestra's leader]!'
>
> 'Ah!' exclaimed my Well-Informed Friend, suddenly waking up. 'That's Wilhelmj!'
>
> I frowned; he cowered. So we sat, I frowning, he cowering, until an enthusiastic greeting announced the appearance of HERR WAGNER.
>
> A lady near me gave a great start.
>
> 'Is that WAGNER?' she exclaimed; and then added, in a tone of considerable disappointment, *'Why, he is quite a respectable-looking, quiet, elderly man!'*

Having recognised that the Wagnerite is a fraud ('Spare me! Oh spare me! I never was at Bayreuth!'), THE HOOKY WALKYRIE begins to listen to *Das Rheingold* and considers its 'leitmotifs' – those melodic themes which run through Wagner's music and which the critics and musicologists of the time were at great pains to elucidate and label.

The Music hall of the Future is evidently paved with good motives . . . Before it was a quarter over, didn't I feel an irrepressible 'drink motive'? Later on wasn't I powerfully moved by a 'more-drink-motive'? Then by a 'go-away-before-the-crowden-motive'? . . . Didn't the 'drink-motive' recur strongly again, and often times during the remainder of the evening, not to mention the 'supper motive' and the 'cigar motive', uniting together to form one irresistible 'stop-at-the-Club-till-three-in-the-morning-motive'?

This essay must have provoked great hilarity in the *Punch* office, because next week it was followed by *The Master and Missis' Ring*, a skit on *Rheingold* in which three Kitchenmaidens [the Rhinemaidens] clean the house in imitation of the Rhinemaidens' cry of 'Weia! Waga! Woge, du Welle!'

> Waggala! waggala!
> Waggala dusta
> Over the crockery
> Waggaladusta
> Waggala! Wiggala! Waya!

and guard a cold shoulder of mutton (representing the ring itself) from the lecherous Pleesmannex (Policeman, otherwise the dwarf Alberich), a 'Nibbeling' who adopts the thump of the *Ring*'s alliterative verse

> Atishoo! Atishoo! Atishoo!
> How the dashed dry dust
> Nebulous Nothing
> Nettled my Nasal
> Nostrils, you Noodles!
> Atishoo! Atishoo! Atishoo!

Neither Wagner nor Cosima makes any reference to such satires, or indeed to any of the newspaper coverage of their visit. Outside the routine of rehearsal and concert they continued to lead a busy, sociable existence. They visited the Tower of London and Hampton Court, two spectacular historical monuments 'recreated' by Victorian architects, and on 17 May went by train to Windsor, where Wagner was briefly received by Queen Victoria. (Cosima, being a stigmatised divorcee, must have waited outside, but she does not remark on this.) On 25 May, Wagner rather touchingly took Cosima on the same jaunt that he had enjoyed with Praeger in 1855, down to the Ship Inn at Greenwich for a whitebait dinner. They returned by steamer, according to Cosima, in mild, grey weather. 'The industrial landscape made a tremendous impression,' she continued, recording a passing remark of Wagner's, which endorses the view that he envisaged *Das Rheingold* as an allegory of modern capitalist society. 'R. says, "This is Alberich's dream come true – Nibelheim, world dominion, activity, work, everywhere the oppressive feeling of steam and fog."'*

While Wagner was engaged with rehearsal, Cosima went out on her own and had a fine old time. She visited the flower show at Crystal Palace and went to Westminster Abbey to hear the preaching of the celebrated proponent of the 'Broad Church', Dean Stanley, but it was the art world which claimed most of her attention. Her interest was not focused on the Old Masters: she enjoyed the National Gallery and the collection of drawings at the British Museum, but made a greater point of acquainting herself with the new movements in painting. One evening she graced a soirée at the sumptuous Grosvenor Gallery, founded by Sir Coutts Lindsay, a cousin of Lord Lindsay, patron of the Wagner Society, and opened only that very month. With its air-conditioning and basement *salle à manger*, it was the last word in Victorian chic, positively scandalous, according to the *London Figaro* of 5 May, in its 'combination of luxury and taste which, together with the most complete disregard of economy, prevails throughout the building'. (Later in the year its walls would display *Nocturne in Black and Gold* by Whistler, a painter often described as 'Wagnerian' inasmuch as his canvases lacked obvious subjects and classical form: Ruskin, who also loathed Wagner's music, described *Nocturne* as

---

*In the same year Henry James described the same journey more evocatively but to the same end. 'A damp-looking, dirty blackness is the universal tone. The river is almost black, and is covered with black barges; above the black housetops, from among the far-stretching docks and basins, rises a dusky wilderness of masts . . . like so many aspects of English civilisation that are untouched by elegance or grace, it has the merit of expressing something very serious. Viewed in this intellectual light, the polluted river, the sprawling barges, the dead-faced warehouses, the frowsy people, the atmospheric impurities become richly suggestive. It sounds rather absurd, but all this smudgy detail may remind you of nothing less than the wealth and power of the British Empire at large; so that a kind of metaphysical magnificence hovers over the scene.'

The Greenwich fish dinner he calls 'the most amusing of all dinners. It begins with fish and it continues with fish: what it ends with – except songs and speeches and affectionate partings – I hesitate to affirm. It is a kind of mermaid reversed; for I do know, in a vague way, that the tail of the creature is elaborately and interminably fleshy.' See 'London at Midsummer', *Lippincott's*, November 1877; reprinted in *English Hours*, ed. A. L. Lowe (London, 1960).

tantamount to 'flinging a pot of paint in the public's face', precipitating a notorious suit for libel.) She also met Millais, had dinner with William Morris, his hands stained blue from dyeing experiments (in 1876 he had published *Sigurd*, a verse adaptation of the Norse sagas, and he didn't like what he heard of Wagner's 'pantomime' version of the *Nibelungenlied*), called at the studio of G. F. Watts, and sat for both Burne-Jones and the young émigré Bavarian, Hubert von Herkomer.

George Eliot and G. H. Lewes provided her with the necessary introductions: the couple were her most regular companions during these weeks – although Cosima's English was very good, she may have been relieved that they both spoke fluent German, and they would have had many friends and interests in common, even though their private enthusiasm for Wagner's music was more tepid than they let on.* 'We are both in love with Madame Wagner,' wrote G. H. Lewes on 19 May to Barbara Bodichon. 'No such woman has appeared on our horizon for a long time.' 'A rare person, worthy to see the best things,' is how George Eliot more temperately described her to Burne-Jones in a letter of 8 May.

In his free hours Wagner went to Whiteley's, Bayswater's smart new department store, in company with Chariclea Dannreuther. She 'helped to choose frocks for his own girls and he bought a rocking horse for my boys which we called Grane' [after Brünnhilde's horse in the *Ring*]. He also dropped into a *Tannhäuser* at Covent Garden, sung in Italian and starring the genteel Canadian soprano Emma Albani as Elisabeth (according to Francis Hueffer, Wagner deemed the performance 'the worst he had ever seen for ensemble'). Dannreuther later recalled (in an interview with *The Musical Times* in October 1898) how, as the March in the second act struck up, Wagner whispered to him, 'Let us march too'. The two men excused themselves from their wives and 'trotted down Drury Lane to The Strand, where he had discovered a German restaurant. The opera seemed to be entirely forgotten; as if to make up for it, he poured out dozens of comic anecdotes. I had to remind him that the ladies were

---

*In *Half a Century of Music in England*, Francis Hueffer describes George Eliot's appreciation of Wagner's music as being of 'a very Platonic kind'. See also George Eliot's fine essay of 1854 'Liszt, Wagner and Weimar', republished in *Essays*, ed. T. Pinney (London, 1963). This is one of the most judicious early attempts in English to treat Wagner's music seriously. Her scepticism may have moderated by 1877, but it had not fundamentally altered.

waiting – and so we went back and listened to the end of Tannhäuser's pilgrimage.'

Dannreuther also recalled a less attractive aspect of Wagner's personality. After a rehearsal at the Albert Hall one day

> I took Wagner to the grill room at the South Kensington museum [viz. the Victoria and Albert]. There, over a chop and a pint of Bass's ale, he began to pour out story after story . . . about German Jews, told in their peculiar jargon. A young foreigner, a painter apparently, had taken his seat at a table opposite, and was quietly watching and listening. Soon, his face began to twitch – I could see that he was making efforts to look serene. But the twitches increased – and when one of the stories came to the final point, he snatched up his hat and vanished.

The German community claimed a piece of him as well and three hundred expatriates gathered on 22 May to celebrate his sixty-fourth birthday with a grand dinner at the Cannon Street Hotel. Wagner made a speech: 'He who had been so little accustomed to public festivals could rejoice in the sympathy shown him in England.' And there was another party organised by the Dannreuthers at Orme Square. 'Before the Wagners left us we decided on the spur of the moment to give our friends another opportunity of seeing him', recalled Chariclea Dannreuther.

> We invited one hundred people to an 'At Home' at two days' notice. Two hundred came! The crush was so great my husband nearly fainted, everyone had brought a friend. We had dined early to give Wagner time to have a nap before the guests arrived, but no sooner had he lain down than a barrel-organ began to play outside in the square. Wagner sent the man sixpence, but he still played on; so he sent down a shilling, which still encouraged the man; then he tried half a crown, but even then the man would not go!

This was probably the occasion which Parry records in his diary for 20 May. 'There was a great company to meet him. They love not his work, but they would be glad to get to hear him because he is big and they could tell their friends lightly that they had met him and then cast some more dirt, no doubt. Young [Lord] Stuart-Wortley was there, full of complacent criticism of an adverse kind and scornful chaff.'

More artistically elevated had been the intimate gathering at Dannreuther's on 17 May, during which Wagner recited the text of what would be his next and last opera, *Parsifal*. Parry, with his *nicht so gut* German 'only got a hazy notion of it, part from hearing & part from other people's explanation', but G. H. Lewes, with his *perfekt* German, thought that he read 'with great spirit and like a fine actor'. Chariclea Dannreuther recalled that 'he had a wonderful emotional voice which was most beautiful. His whole personality was most fascinating and dwarfed that of anyone else in the room with him. The reading lasted two hours.' Nobody seems to have ventured to express any view as to the content, but 'it's awfully sublime, I understand' would have served.

Was it on this occasion – at which all three parties were present – that George Eliot was overheard by the music critic Francis Hueffer remarking to Cosima, 'with that straightforwardness which was so conspicuous and so lovable in her character, "Your husband does not not like Jews; my husband is a Jew" '? George Eliot had another reason to dwell on this vexed point. Her great novel *Daniel Deronda* had been published the previous year: one of its major themes was the position of Jewry in modern European society and she was very sensitive as to the way it had been received.* The subject must have come up in one of their many conversations during these weeks: one wonders how Cosima dealt with it.

Despite all the lionising, Wagner was not happy. Egoist though he undoubtedly was, flattery and acclaim from ignorant quarters did not mollify or fool him. The concerts were fraught with problems, exacerbated by complaints from certain sections of the orchestra that they were being paid less than other sections and the mutinous indignation of the amateur chorus when their complimentary tickets were withdrawn. On 12 May, the presence of the Prince of Wales and members of the Royal Family ensured a good house, but the players lost Wagner's beat – never very precise – during an extract from *Tannhäuser* and they greeted Richter 'almost uproariously' when he took over for the next item. More royalty appeared on 14 May, but now it was the singers who started to play up: and to be fair to them, projecting into the cavernous Albert Hall over the full blast of the enormous orchestra must have put unnatural strain on their vocal

---

*In February 1877, G. H. Lewes had written to his friend Edward Dowden that George Eliot 'has been pained to find many dear friends and some of her most devoted readers, utterly dead to all the Jewish part [of the novel]. The phrase uttered to one lady which was reported to me, "I never did like the Jews and I never shall", expresses pretty much the general state of feeling.'

cords. Cosima: 'Herr Unger already shows signs of hoarseness in the *Lohengrin* duet, and he declares he will be unable to sing the Forging Song [from *Siegfried*]; it is decided to repeat 'Wotan's Farewell' [from *Die Walküre*], but Herr Hill has already gone home – persisting confusion, finally Mr Hodge tells the audience that the 'Ride of the Valkyries' will be played instead of the forging scene, but the concert ends, after all, with the Farewell scene between Siegfried and Brünnhilde, though indeed only Frau Materna can be heard.' The audience was totally baffled by all the chopping and changing and, according to the *Daily Telegraph,* 'the *Götterdämmerung,* or *Twilight of the Gods* became such Cimmerian darkness to the visitors that despairing of finding any light, they quitted the hall in crowds.'

With some rejigging to compensate for the continuing indisposition of Herren Unger and Hill, matters improved two days later. In Parry's view, indeed, the occasion was 'a perfect triumph'. The melancholy Prelude to Act Three of *Die Meistersinger* was encored, but best of all, he thought, was Siegfried's 'Funeral March' from *Götterdämmerung.* 'The greatest thing in the world,' he wrote, which left him 'quite cold with ecstasy. The applause was tremendous for nearly quarter of an hour after the concert, shouting and clapping renewed again and again.' On 18 May, however, there was another run-in with the orchestra. 'Wagner got into a charmingly unsophisticated rage at some of the band for beginning badly,' Parry attests, 'and threw down his baton and seized his coat and comforter and put them on (for no ostensible reason except the need of doing something) and walked up and down the platform in front of the orchestra till time and the appeals of those of the orchestra more in favour had calmed him down a bit.' Happily, as in 1855, the last scheduled concert turned out a triumph, and even J. W. Davison was drawn to admit to the readers of *The Times* that the duet from *Tristan und Isolde* contained 'music of supreme beauty'. 'Proceeds of £1600 and a very animated audience,' reported Cosima. 'Very un-English, we are told. R. crowned with a laurel wreath and unending cheers.'

Laurel wreaths paid no bills, however, and once again London failed to live up to its reputation as a cash cow. As early in the visit as 10 May, Cosima had exclaimed in her diary, 'Messrs H&E [Hodge & Essex] are on the verge of bankruptcy. The last concert brought in £600 – in such circumstances there is no question of even covering the costs. Great despondency.' It transpired that Hodge & Essex had acted in puppyish naivety and done their sums wrong: they had under-capitalised the concerts, apparently in ignorance of the fact that a third of the seats at the Albert Hall were privately owned and not available for public sale. The upshot was that they were unable to fulfil their contract with Wagner, who had part-paid several of the singers out of his own funds and scrabbled to pay the remainder of their fees. Once again he was pushed to the edge of the verge of total ruin. Hysterically, he and Cosima discussed selling up their home in Bayreuth and emigrating to America: only temporary loans and guarantees resulting from abject pleas to his long-suffering bank manager Friedrich Feustel in Bayreuth pulled him back.

In a last-ditch attempt to drum up money any how, two extra concerts were slotted in at bargain prices. On 26 May, buried at the bottom of the front page of the *Daily Telegraph* was an announcement somewhat less prolix and trumpety than the one it had carried three weeks previously:

WAGNER CONCERTS
ROYAL ALBERT HALL
MAY 28, at three, AFTERNOON
MAY 29, at eight, EVENING
REDUCED PRICES OF
ADMISSION – 1s, 2s 6d,
4s, 5s, 7s 6d,10s 6d, 15s

The first of these concerts passed without incident, but on 29 May the proceedings approached farce. The tenor was again 'indisposed' or truculent and everyone else in a foul mood. Cosima: 'Herr Unger produces not a single note, does not ask to be excused, but stands there utterly unperturbed, with poor Materna exerting herself in the awakening scene [from Act Three of *Siegfried*], Richter cursing, R. sending him looks to turn him to stone, not making the slightest effort. R. tells him afterwards that he was not hoarse, but had lain down tired after eating too much and clogged his palate.' Even the Pollyanna-ish Parry was forced to admit that it was 'dismally catastrophical', despite what Cosima felt was a 'very good-natured' audience. The net financial result, according to Ernest Newman, was that Wagner received a total of £700 for his pains – less than half the projected amount. This sum was immediately sent back to Feustel to relieve the most pressing debts hanging over Bayreuth. All the performers at the Albert Hall were paid their fees; only Wagner himself made not a penny for his efforts. Dannreuther subsequently persuaded patrons of the Wagner Society to raise a subscription and in August he went to Bayreuth to present the composer with a cheque for £561, 'as an expression of gratitude for the pleasure he had given the donors by the London concerts'. Wagner decently refused to accept the money for himself.

After a last weekend filled with final dinner parties and sight-seeing expeditions, the Wagners left London on 4 June. A party of well-wishers, Parry, Hueffer and even Davison among them, saw the pair off from Victoria station: Wagner ceremoniously shook hands with one and all, and kissed the cheeks of an intimate few. Davison told him in French that he looked forward to hearing *Parsifal* and his cheeks were kissed too. As the train drew away, Wagner is said to have called from a window, 'All is lost except honour' – a joke, one hopes because, viewed in the longer term, his third visit to London had been a great success – exhibiting his music to a vast new audience, which had responded with everything except indifference. In 1855 Wagner's music had been freakish, marginal; by 1877 it assumed a central position in the vanguard of Victorian culture. The Priest of Dagon had been received at Windsor Castle, crowned with laurel, and – at a service on 23 May, attended by Cosima – had his music (an arrangement of Elisabeth's '*Allmächt'ge Jungfrau*' from *Tannhäuser*) played as an exit voluntary in Westminster Abbey. There may have been a feeling that the Albert Hall had not shown the music to its best advantage – the *London Figaro* of 22 May only wished that 'a set of four performances of the [*Ring*] trilogy had been given, with a band of 80 players, at St James' Hall' – but as *The Musical Standard* of 16 June insisted,

> not even the most adverse criticism can ignore the significance of the unprecedented occurrence of a living musician giving six concerts on an enormous scale, of his own compositions exclusively, in the largest concert hall in the world, with the élite of English aristocratic and musical society crowding [a pardonable exaggeration] to listen. The event was a singular triumph for the man who has boldly braved a generation of adverse criticism . . . it was astonishing to us that so much enthusiasm and real appreciation were elicited.

Astonishing, but incontrovertible. Over the next twenty years, fuelled by the first British performances of the *Ring* and *Tristan* in the 1880s and the passionate writings of the young George Bernard Shaw in the 1890s, the individual skirmishes against Wagner would continue – they still do. Nevertheless, one can look at his 1877 campaign in London and see that it had won him the war Within a generation, the 'Music of the Future' would become the music of the present, increasingly acknowledged as one of the supreme and defining cultural achievements of the century.

Appendix

So much of the criticism of Wagner published in London during his lifetime was either ill-informed, prejudiced or conditioned by extra-musical considerations that a short piece published in *The Musical World* on 12 May 1877 is all the more remarkable. Its title, 'Amateur Madman at Bayreuth', and signature 'Thersitis Grumpus Wizzell, Asylum opposite Theatre, August 1876', suggests that it is another *Punch*-type spoof. But it isn't: instead, it is a brief impressionistic account of a performance at Bayreuth of *Rheingold*, written on the spot by someone who was plainly extremely musical and intelligently attuned to what Wagner was trying to do – for sheer analytical sensitivity, nothing of its time can match it.

J. W. Davison was the editor of *The Musical World* and also attended the first *Rheingold* at Bayreuth, but Thersitis Grumpus Wizzrell's views scarcely seem to match those of *The Times*'s critic, who found the extracts from that opera as played at the Royal Albert Hall 'simply dreary'. What, one wonders, was the true identity of 'Thersitis Grumpus Wizzell', who could have been Wagner's great British lobbyist?

For some reason, it is addressed to 'Mortimer Collins, T. Hood, F. C. Burnand, Tom Taylor etc.', all prominent comic-sketch writers of the day.

> E flat Rhine bottom – fifths, ensuing – restless modulation, keys, everywhere and nowhere, *ff*, fifths, dim sevenths!!! – orchestra (under) wonderful effect – of more sensation of hearing music *somewhere* – now near now far – now loud now soft – now 'twixt the two. In to, and on Wagner's own – let no one attempt to follow or inspect it for fear of danger (kaleidoscopic) – *never* a true burst of *ff* without the aid of brass – strings restless and rambling about basses queerly used – combinations of wind often queer – anvils – too much. XXXXXXXX (Verdi) heard before – form none, proportion, completion (ending or beginning) none – more than rainbow colours – snatches of melody always

streaming about, reminding of *Tempest* and *Midsummer Night's Dream* – all a dream – in fact every melody belongs to somebody and comes in somehow or other unexpectedly whenever that somebody is alluded to – two or three notes sometimes constitute the remainder. This all through the four dramas to the end (cite the Rhine maids – Dwight by the way [sic] – compare *Götterdämmerung* with *Rheingold* for that. pity no continued music – no chorus. Gods ensemble *never* – giants *a due* NEVER- Niblungs, although all under same tyranny *never* in chorus – (good characteristic chance lost) – against Wagner's system (*Götterdämmerung*, retainers of Hagen, Gunther exception) – even no duets – each says what he has to say in his own manner – never mingles voices – only dialogue (few soliloquies) – orchestra mingles up themes (see *Götterdammerung*) ad lib – but no free bass – no counterpoint &c.

Aug. 1876 – Stage management unparalleled – all act, to the smallest Niblung, and with significant meaning – name the characters – Wagner stamps each indelibly with his melodic – beautiful or queebish [*sic* not listed in *Oxford English Dictionary*], unmistakable figures (return in snatches or fragments). The unexpected appearance of fixed melodies, or fragments of ditto, at time perplexes – all the parts well played – though voices! Machinery, painting, decorations (name authors) – Conductor Richter (Bülow's successor). When themes come together one above another, &c. – the tremolando shift occurs – this is in *oppressive excess,* and one gets tired, as of the XXXXXXXX [sic] &c. Orchestra superb – nevertheless should like to hear it for once above ground. Wilhelmj's solos ravishing – W. condescends occasionally to *that* means of effect happily. But all sounds wonderful! Are there no angels or something of the sort in Walhalla and thereabouts to welcome Wotan and train (followed by the discarded Loge) to the huge battlemented castle. Opportunity for grand chorus of invisibles lost. Duet in form, for Alberich and Mime would have been welcome – surely they may respect their sentiments. Wagner always goes on, spinning out, referring and re-referring to same figure for his gathering intensity – orchestra assisting at want. Nowhere independent bass for orchestra.

Aug. 1876. Ah! poor Mozart, poor Beethoven, who W. is said to have said never had such homage!

CHAPTER 3

Ralph Waldo Emerson, Philosopher

'Who has society? People to talk to? People who stimulate? Boston has 120,000 and I cannot now find one.' In the clean, sober town of Concord, Massachusetts, early in 1847, sat Ralph Waldo Emerson, unchallenged and frustrated. He was in his prime – forty-three years old, a conscientious husband and father, with property and a thriving career as America's most renowned lecturer, preacher, essayist and intellectual. Yet he felt underused, torpid – 'We must have society, provocation, a whip for the top,' he confessed to his journal. He needed to escape from the thin air of New England and, with members of his family to support and bail out of debt, he needed money too.

Some months previously he had written to his inspirational friend and advocate Thomas Carlyle in London that 'somebody or somebodies in Liverpool and Manchester have proposed once or twice, with more or less specification, that I should come to those cities to lecture. And who knows but I may come one day? Steam is strong & Liverpool is near . . .' From his house in Cheyne Walk, Carlyle replied warmly: 'A prophet's chamber is ready for you in Chelsea, and a brotherly and sisterly welcome, on whatever day at whatever hour you arrive.'

So Emerson decided to make the transatlantic journey and join a succession of visitors whose dreams of the 'old country' were intense with expectation, doomed to disappointment, and fraught with a heavy cargo of misunderstanding and recrimination.

For the first fifty years of American independence, the traffic had largely moved the other way. Britons visited the upstart 'democracy' and looked its rebel colonists up and down with a seigneurial sense of cultural superiority. Some of them pronounced without the bother of undertaking the trip – Sydney Smith, for example, the witty and Whiggish cleric, who in 1820 asked in the pages of the *Edinburgh Review*: 'In the four quarters of the globe, who reads an American book, or goes to an American play, or looks at an American picture or statue? What does the world yet owe to American physicians or surgeons? . . . finally, under which of the old tyrannical governments of Europe is every sixth man a slave, whom his fellow creatures may buy and sell and torture'?

These barbs hit hard and wounded because they could not be easily gainsaid – even Emerson himself, the most profoundly American of Americans, was obliged to admit that 'from 1790 to 1820 there was not a book, a speech or a conversation or a thought in Massachusetts' – but other attacks irritated by their gratuitous cattiness and assumption that the English way of doing things was by definition correct. Most widely disliked was Fanny Trollope's *Domestic Manners of the Americans*, published in 1832 and notable for its jibes *de haut en bas* against the Yankees' general 'want of refinement', including their ill-bred habits of slouching, 'remorseless spitting' and garnishing ham with apple sauce. The galled American press and its caricaturists made hay with the implications of Mrs Trollope's surname and accused her of being motivated by anger over the failure of her attempt to make money out of Americans by establishing a version of Bullock's Egyptian Hall in the boom town of Cincinnati. To which Mrs Trollope, restored to the elegant gentility of her residence in Harrow, made cool retort that 'one of the most remarkable traits of the national character of the Americans' was its 'exquisite sensitiveness and soreness respecting everything said or written concerning them'.

Yet for all such scratching, Americans of British ancestry felt deeply possessive and respectful of what a book of Nathaniel Hawthorne's would evocatively call 'Our Old Home'. Their notions of this *dulce domum* were, of course, sentimental and over-coloured: just as a later generation would envisage London as it appeared in the Sherlock Holmes stories, shrouded in gaslight and pea-soupers, so ordinary Americans of the 1820s and 1830s imagined England through the glaze of pastoral mezzotints and engravings, and the poetic prisms of Shakespeare, Milton, Thomson, Gray, Scott and the Romantics. Half-timbered Stratford-upon-Avon, mysterious Stonehenge, the ruins of Warwick and Kenilworth, the sublime landscape of the Lakes – these were what the American visitor expected and wanted, not the filthy, seething ports of Liverpool and Tilbury or the smoke-belching mill chimneys that in reality they were more liable to find. 'Our Old Home' was falling victim to the onslaught of industrialism and, to the dismay of pure-hearted, sensitive New England souls who came in search of a welcoming hearth, its walls were crumbling in rot and corruption.

Emerson himself had first visited his ancestral roots in 1833, as part of recuperation from a period of personal unhappiness and spiritual crisis which changed his life.

Born in 1803, the descendant of a long line of New England clerics, he studied at Harvard and became a Unitarian pastor in 1829. Although he set out ardently and ambitiously, the death of his first wife after only sixteen months of marriage and his discovery that Unitarianism was as 'cold as a cucumber' led him to resign from the ministry in 1832. Instead, he felt impelled to pursue another sort of Christian belief, free of sacraments, dogma and institution, but drawn on the individual's own experience of nature and the intuitions and emotions flowing from it. He wanted, it could be said, a religion which would allow him to think for himself.

Meanwhile, an abbreviated Grand Tour of Europe would provide him with an opportunity to clear and recharge his mind, as well as the dry, warm air and mental rest deemed beneficial to his widowered state and tubercular tendency. In February 1833 he arrived in Malta, passing on through Sicily to Naples and Rome. But Italy was not the place for him. Shy and quiet in manner, simple in his personal tastes and habits, and uncomfortable with the deeper possibilities of sensual or aesthetic pleasure, he could only allow himself a half-measure of admiration for Catholic architectural magnificence, the artistic treasures of the Renaissance and Baroque or the glamorous extravagance of the opera. Then he was impelled to become moral again: people and the state of their souls were what mattered, not ritual and flummery. 'One act of benevolence is better than a cathedral,' he wrote in his journal. 'Here's for the plain old Adam, the simple genuine self against the whole world.' To be unbeholden in foreign parts brought an odd sort of freedom, in which 'you feel always in prison, & solitary'.

He was lonely, in other words, and wanted not sights or monuments, but the company of 'men who are great or interesting'. In Florence he found the expatriate Walter Savage Landor, author of a series of 'Imaginary Conversations' between 'great or interesting' people of the past. Back in Massachusetts Emerson had relished these dialogues, but in person he found Landor a boisterous dilettante, full of scholarship and a rare connoisseur, but short of moral gravity. 'Men of talents want simplicity and sincerity as much as others', Emerson concluded in a letter home. 'They have the vulgar ambition of keeping fashionable company & are more afraid of intrusion than they are desirous of truth and sympathy.' In such a downcast state he moved on through picturesque towns and villages to Venice, which from a distance 'looked like nothing but New York' and which close up became 'a city for beavers', thence to Geneva, where he visited Voltaire's château at Ferney and Paris, which he thought a 'loud modern New York of a place', abounding in 'all the conveniences of an easy, fat, amused life'.

In July he arrived in England. Here lay three goals of his quest for beings 'great or interesting' to guide him along the new path he was uncertainly exploring. At the funeral in Westminster Abbey of the Evangelical reformer and campaigner against slavery William Wilberforce – itself a vastly impressive occasion – he found himself with a good view of the Duke of Wellington, probably at that time the most famous living personage in the Western world. Emerson, however, was in pursuit of men of wisdom, not action, and the personage who met his criteria of 'great or interesting' in London was not a politician or soldier, but the poet of 'The Rime of the Ancient Mariner' and the theologian of *Aids to Reflection*. Samuel Taylor Coleridge was now in his sixties, a frail and reclusive lodger in the house of a Dr Gilman in Highgate, where he still struggled against the demon of opium. Of that addiction Emerson would have known nothing: what would have attracted him were reports of Coleridge's wonderful conversation – or 'one-versation', as the poet himself quipped in acknowledgement of the monologic nature of his discourse. But 'the short thick old man' with 'a clear clean face' who appeared in response to Emerson's call on the Gilmans was 'anything but what I imagined'.

Taking copious quantities of snuff, 'which presently spoiled his cravat', Coleridge first asked whether Emerson knew of his old friend the American painter Washington Allston (whose portrait of the poet now hangs in the National Portrait Gallery). He then drifted into a diatribe against 'the folly & ignorance' of a noted American divine Dr William Ellery Channing and pooh-poohed the creed of Unitarianism. Emerson managed to slip in that he too was a Unitarian. ' "Yes," he said, "I supposed so", & continued as before.' Hearing that Emerson had been in Sicily, which he too had once visited, he remarked that the island 'was an excellent place to study political economy, for in any town there it was only necessary to ask what the government enacted & reverse that, to know what ought to be done . . . There were only three things, which the government brought on that garden of delights, namely, itch, pox and famine.' Emerson felt he had read this little spiel somewhere before and went away disappointed: Coleridge was 'old and preoccupied, and could not bend to a new companion and think with him'.

But there was another name on Emerson's list – Thomas Carlyle, a Scots intellectual whose writings he had admired in the *Edinburgh Review* and elsewhere. Beyond what he had read, Emerson knew nothing about Carlyle or his circumstances, yet he could sense someone who shared his impatience with sectarian nit-picking and his revulsion from life and religion without the dimension of awe or faith or wonder. One extraordinary essay, 'Signs of the Times', published in 1829, romantically bemoaned the way that throughout modern society a mechanical, standardised and administrative philosophy was replacing a sense of the wonder of the creative individual human soul. It was a hugely influential statement, which continues to mean something today, and in Emerson it struck a deeply resonant chord. He needed to talk to someone who thought like this, someone concerned to signpost a spiritual direction for a world being stripped of the comfort blanket of institutionalised religion and denied the image of God as either a figure of unquestionable authority or – in the evocative phrase of A. N. Wilson – 'a great love-object'.

Assuming that Carlyle must live in or near Edinburgh, Emerson duly made his way north, via Oxford and York, in the hope of meeting him. But the trail was longer than he had anticipated.

During his time in Rome he had encountered a young French savant who had recently met and corresponded with Carlyle. From him Emerson received a note of introduction, but no home address – for that information the Frenchman advised him to consult another of his friends, a Mr John Stuart Mill of the India Office. But Mill, whose reputation as a thinker in his own right was yet to be made, had little more to tell Emerson, except that Carlyle lived not in the city but somewhere unmapped called Craigenputtock. Mill nevertheless agreed to write to Carlyle to forewarn him of Emerson's intended visit: this was not quite the kindness it appeared, as the letter he sent expressed little enthusiasm for the earnest American ('I do not think him a very hopeful subject').

On arrival in Edinburgh, still redolent of its reputation as 'the Athens of the North' and a centre of enlightenment, Emerson was truly befriended for the first time since leaving America. A journalist with a radical turn of mind called Alexander Ireland not only showed him the sights but also arranged for him to speak in the Unitarian Chapel – which Emerson did with his usual lightness of oratorical touch and irresistible sincerity of manner.

Landor, Coleridge and Mill failed to penetrate beyond Emerson's demure politeness, but the more generous-spirited Ireland took a little trouble and was delighted with the wry, original person he uncovered. The two remained in lifelong correspondence and, after Emerson's death, Ireland would commemorate his pulpit voice as 'the sweetest, most winning and penetrating of any I ever heard'.

After a few pleasant days in the capital, Emerson finally tracked down Carlyle's precise whereabouts. Craigenputtock, it transpired, was nowhere near Edinburgh, but some sixty miles south of Glasgow, near Dumfries. Emerson, a tourist, after all, as well as a pilgrim, decided to take a long way round and view the splendour of the Highlands en route. The weather – in mid-August – was characteristically dour: cold, driving rain accompanied his steam-boat up the River Forth to Stirling and continued to drench him over the Trossachs. By the time he reached the sublime shores of Loch Katrine, the air was dry but the wind so strong that an attempt to row across its waters had to be abandoned, obliging the party to walk fourteen sodden miles to the hut, where oatcakes and whisky awaited it. Another steamboat, another coach and yet another steamboat took Emerson to Glasgow and thence, two days later, to Dumfries, the town in which Robert Burns had ended his days in 1796.

Like so many of his generation, Emerson held Burns's unique candour and manly charm in high esteem, and he was moved to walk past the tenement house in which the poet's widow Jean, now over eighty, still lived and to spot his son, standing on a doorstep and evincing 'some resemblance to the points of his father's head'. After dinner, he paid his respects to Burns's grave. 'On his tomb was no inscription but his name. I asked the sexton's boy who admitted me, who Burns was? "A ploughman." & what else? "A maker of poems." Did he ever hear any of his songs? "Ay." This was all I could get.'

Early next morning he hired a creaking gig and set out along a track through 'the wild and desolate heathery hills' to Craigenputtock. Set in a bleak valley amid desolate grazing land, the house was seven miles from another human habitation. Inherited from the father of Carlyle's wife Jane, it was a large and solid building, with a piano, a servant and a modicum of amenities. Carlyle and Jane had lived there for five years, during which his satirical-philosophical-fantastical novel *Sartor Resartus* had been written and his wider literary reputation flourished. But visitors of any sort were rare and foreign ones unheard of. When Emerson rolled up at midday, the Carlyles were eating Sunday dinner. Mill's letter had been so unspecific that they had no reason to expect him, and he was welcomed with a mixture of panic, delight and sheer astonishment (Jane called it 'the first journey since Noah's deluge undertaken to Craigenputtock for such a purpose'). After an exchange of initial courtesies, the gig was sent back to Dumfries with orders not to return until the next morning.

An immediate bond was established between the two men, both of them cut off from a community of like minds. All that summer's afternoon they roamed the hills together, talking hungrily through what Carlyle described as 'the whole encyclopaedia' of their mutual interests and enthusiasms. In manner, in personality, in experience, they were as different as they were alike, but they had covered much of the same territory and felt impelled to ask many of the same questions.

Carlyle, more voluble and excitable by nature and obviously flattered by the attention, seems to have taken the lead. He celebrated the greatness of Goethe, whose poised moral wholeness made other modern literary figures look hysterical and adolescent – Carlyle had translated several of his works into English, corresponded with him, and at that time he and Jane were downcast that shortage of funds had prevented them from travelling to Weimar to confront his genius in person. His heroes, as Emerson later analysed it in a letter to Alexander Ireland, were not supreme rationalists like Socrates or Gibbon, but men like Burns and Dr Johnson, and 'whoever has given himself with all his heart to a leading instinct & has not calculated too much'. He discussed other writers, past and present – Rousseau, Hazlitt, Scott, Gibbon, as well as Landor and Coleridge. Of his contemporaries, he spoke highly of the brilliant mind of his London acquaintance John Stuart Mill (a thinker who had bravely emancipated himself from the deathly Utilitarian philosophy which had enslaved his father James), but otherwise railed against the mediocrity and corruption of the literary scene. One publisher alone spent £10,000 on the 'puffery' that we now call hype, 'and hence it came to be that no newspaper is trusted & now no books are bought & the booksellers are on the eve of bankruptcy'.

Emerson was enthralled by Carlyle's bravado, charmed by his broad Scots locutions, exhilarated by his stock of witty stories; Carlyle – an angry, but never a cold man – delighted in Emerson's honesty, simplicity and clarity. But even in this first ecstatic flush of friendship they seem to have instinctively avoided digging into more intimately religious and ethical matters, conscious perhaps of the potentially alienating distance between their positions. Safer, the liberal-minded Emerson may have thought, to let Carlyle boom and rant against social and political reform. His line was unashamedly authoritarian, dismissive of cant, impatient of whingeing and vacillation. 'Government should direct poor men what to do,' he asserted, giving as an example the wandering Irish immigrants, daily begging from his wife at the back door of Craigenputtock, who could more usefully be put to forcible work cultivating the moors. What he liked best about the United States of America, as he understood it, was its simple principle that 'a man can have meat for his labor'. Emerson would have put it more gently and seen other aspects of the question, but he had primarily come to Europe to listen, not to argue.

That evening Jane prepared the men the best supper that her modest housekeeping could muster and joined in the talk. Herself a highly intelligent and articulate woman, she was as delighted by the American visitor as her husband was and in his honour proudly wore a gold chain that Goethe had sent her as consolation for the aborted trip to Weimar. Now they spoke of Carlyle's plans to write a grand account of the turning point of modern history, the French Revolution, and to move down to London, where at least he would have access to the books and facilities denied him in the wilderness. 'The baker's boy brings muffins to the window at a fixed hour every day,' he added, 'and that is all the Londoner knows or wishes to know on the subject.' Contradicting the views expressed in 'Signs of the Times', he admitted that there was something rather appealing about such workings of the 'huge machine'.

Back in Dumfries the following evening, Emerson wrote lyrically in his journal that his meeting with Carlyle amounted to 'a white day in my years. I found the youth [in fact, Carlyle was thirty-eight and looked older] I sought in Scotland & good & wise & pleasant he seems to me.' For his part, Carlyle was left in a rare fit of cheerfulness. He reported the episode to Mill, concluding that 'above all, what I loved [about Emerson] was his health, his unity with himself; all people and all things seemed to find their quite peaceable adjustment with him'. But to Jane the warm glow cast by Emerson's brief sojourn also became a poignant reminder of how cold the rest of her life at Craigenputtock was: 'It was like the visit of an angel,' she told another American visitor, Henry Wadsworth Longfellow two years later, 'and though he staid with us hardly twenty-four hours, yet when he left us I cried.'

Emerson now moved south to the Lake District in pursuit of his last trophy – an interview with William Wordsworth. This proved quite dull. The poet he found at home in Rydal Mount was 'a plain looking elderly man' of sixty-three, wearing green goggles to protect his inflamed eyes, whose romantic and creative spirit had long withered. Decent and honourable he may have been, but Emerson concluded that his mind was 'narrow and very English . . . off his own beat, his opinions had no value'. Something joyless and unimaginative underpinned his deep-dyed Tory view that the idea of social 'progress' was a delusion, and that morality – hard, simple, no-nonsense Biblical truths – and 'circumstances' – the school of hard knocks – should be the basis of all education, not scientific rationality. 'Society is being Enlightened out of all proportion to its being restrained by moral culture,' he told Emerson. 'Sin, sin is what he fears.' America, he felt, prophetically, 'needed a civil war . . . to teach the necessity of knitting the social ties stronger'. As things stood, he suspected that Americans were 'too much given to making of money, & secondly to politics.' Emerson appears to have listened to all this with equanimity, but then became embroiled in a disagreement over Carlyle, whom Wordsworth thought 'insane sometimes'. This view seems to have been provoked by his flamboyant translation of Goethe's rambling and eccentric *Wilhelm Meister*, a novel Wordsworth had found replete with 'all manner of fornication' and then thrown across the room in disgust.

Perhaps to ease a certain tension in the air, the poet at this point led Emerson into his garden and showed him the gravel walk, which he paced as he composed. Suddenly he announced that he had recently returned from a trip to Fingal's Cave and would it please Emerson to hear three sonnets which it had inspired? Emerson was acquiescent, but startled: 'This recitation was so unlooked for and surprising – he, the old Wordsworth standing apart, and reciting to me in a garden walk, like a schoolboy declaiming – that I at first was near to laugh; but recollecting myself, that I had come thus far to see a poet, and he was chanting poems to me, I saw that he was right and I was wrong and gladly gave myself up to hear.'

After touching on further miscellaneous subjects, Wordsworth 'walked near a mile with me talking and ever & anon stopping short to impress the word or the verse & finally parted from me with great kindness & returned across the fields'. Emerson then made his way to Manchester, where for the first time in his life he boarded a railway train. The journey on Stephenson's pioneering line to Liverpool, some thirty miles along one of the world's first lines, took an hour and a half, about a third of what it would have taken in a stagecoach on a hard macadamised road. At a minimum fare of 5s, however, such speed did not come cheap and Emerson does not seem to have much enjoyed the ride. 'Strange it was to meet the return cars; to see a load of timber, six or seven masts dart by you like a trout,' he wrote in his journal. 'Strange proof how men become accustomed to the oddest things: the laborers did not lift their umbrellas to look as we flew by them on their return at the side of the track.' Surprisingly, the dirt, noise, danger and intense suspensionless discomfort, the sheer intrusiveness of this novel mode of transport elicited no comment from him.*

At Liverpool, ill wind and bad weather kept him waiting ten days for a transatlantic crossing home. The city he disliked ('the least agreeable . . . to the traveller in all England'), but he attempted to improve the shining hour in the company of his compatriot inventor Jacob Perkins, who escorted him round the railway depots and initiated him further into the mysteries of steam and locomotion. In his solitary hours he reflected on what spiritual nourishment the visit to Europe had brought him. Only in Carlyle did he feel he had found a true personal friend –

---

*Asked what he thought of the innovation of railway trains, the Duke of Wellington, a guest of honour at the opening of the Liverpool–Manchester line in 1830, made the laconic, immortally disapproving response: 'They encourage the lower classes to travel about.' See Frank Ferneyhough, *The Liverpool and Manchester Railway* (London, 1980).

'Carlyle is so amiable that I love him' – but otherwise the chief value of the seven months abroad had been to strengthen his sense of his own worth. Without arrogance, he recognised that 'great or interesting' personages had nothing to teach him about his beliefs. If anything, his spirituality went deeper than theirs:

> I thank the great God who has led me through this European scene . . . he has shown me the men I wished to see – Landor, Coleridge, Carlyle, Wordsworth – he has thereby comforted and confirmed me in my convictions. Many things I owe to the sight of these men. I shall judge more justly less timidly, of wise men forevermore. To be sure not one of these is a mind of the very first class, but what the intercourse with each of these suggests is true of intercourse with better men, that they never fill the ear – fill the mind – no, it is an *idealised* portrait which always we draw of them. Upon an intelligent man, wholly a stranger to their names, they would make in conversation no deep impression – none of a world-filling fame – they would be remembered as sensible well read earnest men – not more. Especially as they are all deficient all these four – in different degrees but all deficient – in insight into religious truth. They have no idea of that species of moral truth which I call the first philosophy.

This last point may be arguable – no Coleridge scholar today would describe him as deficient in 'insight into religious truth' – but Emerson needed to uphold it, in order to clear the necessary patch of mental space. He had already decided that he did not need to subscribe to Unitarianism; now he could feel that there was nothing about the wisdom of the Old World which need intimidate him either. He set sail, elated by the certainty that he had graduated from his 'last schoolroom' and now had something more, something different, something *of his own* to say. 'This is my charge plain & clear – to act faithfully upon my own faith, to live by it myself, & see what a hearty obedience to it will do . . . Glad I bid adieu to England, the old, the rich, the strong nation, full of arts & men & memories; nor can I feel any regret in the presence of the best of its sons that I was not born here. I am thankful that I am an American as I am thankful that I am a man.'

Emerson's surge of confidence reflects the spirit of greater assertiveness which was starting to motivate his compatriots. Enraged by the sneers and strictures of Mrs Trollope and her sort, the Americans went on the offensive. The Irish question was raised: even a genteel New England travel book like Mrs Fanny Hall's *Rambles in Europe*, published in 1834, could sarcastically inquire 'in what respect the condition of the Irish peasant is superior to that of our African slaves for whom the English profess so much sympathy'. The point was well made and over the next twenty-five years it would frequently be reiterated, for the want of a good answer. That deafening silence emboldened scribbling Americans to mention other forms of British slavery, as manifested in pauperism and prostitution, mines and manufactories, prisons and lunatic asylums.

The next visitor from the Old World to reopen the wound was Charles Dickens. He visited America in 1842 and, although he found much to praise in New England's schools, work-places and philosophies of can-do and self-help, he caused tremendous offence by publicly demanding that the republic acknowledge Britain's new copyright laws and allow authors to collect royalties abroad. Dickens may have had right on his side – he hadn't received a cent from any of his American editions – but his attitude was interpreted as an aggressive breach of the code of hospitality, thinly concealing self-serving greed. Further offence was subsequently caused by an episode of *Martin Chuzzlewit* (1843–4), in which the eponymous hero emigrates hopefully to America, only to be battered and bamboozled by the relentless fire of Yankee verbosity, pomposity, chicanery and chauvinism.

Its satire is a good deal more heavy-handed than anything in Fanny Trollope's *Domestic Manners of the Americans*, but the odd potshot hits a fair target. One such bull's-eye in this part of the novel is the momentary but impressive appearance of Miss Toppit, a literary lady in a brown wig. 'Mind and matter glide swift into the vortex of immensity,' she booms portentously. 'Howls the sublime and softly sleeps the calm ideal, in the whispering chambers of imagination. To hear it, sweet it is. But then outlaughs the stern philosopher, and saith to the Grotesque, "What ho! arrest for me that Agency. Go, bring it here!" And so the vision fadeth.'

This tosh is a parody of the philosophy of Transcendentalism, newly fashionable and popular among the American educated classes.* As the bewigged lady's vatic utterances suggest, it is not a lucid, pragmatic or logical philosophy. Its profound appeal to a young republic, thin in history and culture, and populated by pioneers, settlers and loners, was

---

*In *American Notes* Dickens had been more cordial. 'Among much that is dreamy and fanciful,' he wrote of Emerson's essays, 'there is much more that is true and manly, honest and bold . . . if I were a Bostonian, I think I would be a Transcendentalist.' But Dickens never had any patience with literary ladies.

its emphasis on the paramount importance of the individual self following its own path, according to its own inner light. From one perspective such a gospel seemed mystical and pantheistic – God, 'the universal soul' is apprehended through nature, as the majestic, uncharted 'New Eden' of America symbolised – but its doctrines could also justify the practices of capitalistic business and bolster the political agenda set out in the Monroe Doctrine of 1823, with its insistence that the USA dissociate itself from Europe ('we look too much abroad . . . let us become real and true Americans'). Democracy in the eighteenth century had primarily been conceived as a rational, legal contract between its citizens; in the nineteenth century, Transcendentalism made it into an article of Romantic faith.

The broad sweep of these ideas had been drawn from German Romantic philosophers like Schlegel and Novalis, first mediated into America through the divinity schools via scholarly Unitarian theologians like Dr William Ellery Channing (whom Coleridge so scorned). Among this first wave of Transcendentalists, Emerson, with his poetic turn of phrase and gifts as a charismatic public speaker, was the most imaginative and communicative. No longer a pastor, he made his living as a freelance preacher and lecturer, travelling the length and breadth of New England, and drawing huge crowds. Even those who couldn't follow his always meandering, often vaporous train of thought felt warmed by the glow of his moral radiance. 'I like to go and see him stand up there and look as though he thought everyone was as good as he was,' explained one of his most ardent fans, an elderly 'scrubbing-woman' who simultaneously admitted that she couldn't understand a word of what he was on about.

Many of his sermons were published as essays, which brought him an even wider audience. Two of the most celebrated of these, written in the mid 1830s, muse on thoughts resulting from his visit to Europe. 'Self-Reliance' reflects that 'travelling is a fool's paradise. At home I dream that at Naples, at Rome, I can be intoxicated with beauty and lose my sadness. I pack my trunk, embrace my friends, embark on the sea, and at last wake up in Naples, and there beside me is the stern fact, the sad self, unrelenting, identical, that I fled from.' What matters is not where you are, but who you are: 'Nothing is at last sacred but the integrity of your own mind . . . whoso would be a man must be a non-conformist.' 'The American Scholar', an address to the Phi Beta Kappa students of Harvard, makes what a sage of the next generation, Oliver Wendell Holmes, would call 'our intellectual declaration of independence' and looks westwards. 'We have listened too long to the courtly muses of Europe,' it concludes. 'We will walk on our own feet; we will work with our own hands; we will speak our own minds.' 'Insist on yourself; never imitate,' he reiterated in 'Self-Reliance'. Such injunctions are echoed to this day in every high-school valedictory and every heart-on-sleeve Hollywood movie: they are still at the heart of what it is to be American.

Yet although his message was heard with rapture and Transcendentalism became the rage among nervous theological students and ladies in brown wigs, Emerson remained listless and dissatisfied: prim he may have been, smug he was not. Superficially, his life was probably agreeable enough. His second wife Lidian was companionable, if sickly and religiose in disposition, his children were charming. He took pleasure in cultivating his garden, he read promiscuously. He had admirers, neighbours, friends; intellectuals like Bronson Alcott, Henry David Thoreau and Margaret Fuller thought as he did on many matters. But for all his cherished solitude and talk of self-reliance, he felt a great void in the 'Lilliput' of New England. His circle was 'without adventure, connexion, or wide information'. Where could he find a great inspiring man, 'a whip for the top'?

Thus in 1847 he resolved to return to Europe, with the more specific aim of visiting Carlyle, now resident in London and tremendously famous. Out of that memorable encounter in Craigenputtock a warm and copious transatlantic correspondence had developed. What chiefly sustained it, however, was business – Emerson showed an enthusiastic and disinterested readiness to act as Carlyle's unpaid American literary agent, thereby ensuring him a regular flow of dollar royalties and saving him from the copyright evasions and pirated editions that had so infuriated Dickens. For his part, Carlyle was more ready to reciprocate with his inimitable style of verbose compliment and extravagant praise of Emerson's work (after reading 'The American Scholar', he wrote to him that 'it was long decades of years that I had heard nothing but the infinite jangling and jabbering and inarticulate twittering and screeching, and my soul had sunk down sorrowful, and said there is no articulate speaking then any more, and thou art solitary among stranger creatures? – and lo, out of the west comes a clear utterance, clearly recognisable as a man's voice, and I *have* a kinsman and brother') than he was to undertake the nitty-gritty of negotiating contracts and pestering publishers.

Over-generous to relatives and those in need, Emerson needed his second visit to England to be financially as well as spiritually profitable and, with the help of his Edinburgh friend Alexander Ireland, now established as the editor of a radical newspaper in Manchester, he began to map himself out an extensive lecture tour. Ireland arranged the bookings, confident of his friend's drawing power – in 1833, Emerson had travelled as a nonentity, but fourteen years later, through the dissemination of his principal essays, he had a burgeoning reputation in more radical circles as the outstanding American writer and thinker of his age. Some more conventional commentators may have thought of him nervously as 'queer' – allusive, esoteric, elliptical in style, a disciple of the school of Carlyle and therefore disturbingly indifferent to organised religion – but he was universally recognised as a man 'in good earnest', a couple of cuts above the run of brash Yankee-Doodledom. Emerson himself was no longer daunted: in 1833 he had listened to England with reverence; in 1847 he would do more of the talking himself.

Despite all Emerson's sterling efforts on his behalf, Carlyle was anxious not to become too embroiled – since the angelic visitation to Craigenputtock, visiting Americans had become a bane of his life, presenting their cards at his house at 5 Cheyne Row, Chelsea* and invading his precious solitude with their banalities and compliments. One of the more welcome was the stammering Henry James, father of the novelist, then engaged on a critique of the Book of Genesis. Others got shorter shrift. 'These Yankees form a considerable item in the ennuis of our life,' complained Jane in November 1843, after 'a tall, lean, red-herring-looking man' had appeared 'to congratulate Dr Carlyle on his increasing reputation' and made a great nuisance of himself. 'I counted lately fourteen of them in one fortnight of whom Dr Russel [*sic*] was the only one that you did not feel tempted to take the

---

*Then a modest address, far from the hurly-burly – Carlyle described Chelsea in 1834 as 'a singular, heterogeneous kind of spot, very dirty and confused in some places, quite beautiful in others'; today, it has become much grander. Carlyle's house is now owned by the National Trust and open to the public. See also Thea Holme's delightful *The Carlyles at Home* (Oxford, 1979).

poker to.' Still, Emerson had been a true friend and hospitality must be offered, so Carlyle made a brave show of offering open house and claimed to be in keen anticipation of some stimulating conversation. 'A prophet's chamber is ready for you in Chelsea, and a brotherly and sisterly welcome, on whatever day at whatever hour you arrive . . . I do not know of another man in all the world to whom I can speak with clear hope of getting adequate response'.

Emerson eventually sailed from Boston on 5 October 1847 – one of an estimated 50,000 Americans who made an eastward crossing every year. Steam was still a novelty then – Brunel's celebrated screw-propelled ship *Great Britain* had been launched only two years previously – and whatever advantage it provided in terms of speed was considered to be offset by the noise and stench, as well as the increased danger of collision. Perhaps in deference to his nervous wife, Emerson entrusted himself to the more sedate power of sail and took a packet boat, the *Washington Irving*. Nobody need have worried: the passage was uneventful. Large meals were consumed, shoals of porpoises observed, novels by Dumas, Dickens and Captain Marryat circulated; Emerson also read the Transcendentally inclined second volume of *Modern Painters*, which despite its anonymous title-page he knew to have been written by 'a young man named Ruskin'. But no tempests or icebergs were encountered, and even the sublimely patient Emerson confessed in a letter to his family that he found the days tedious: 'It is forlorn to have the room in which you stand or sit always sloped at an angle of from 20 to 40 degrees, and besides what seems some one at every moment actually tipping it up.'

In addition to the eighty-six passengers (Emerson was accommodated in the 'first cabin', along with the captain, four ladies with nine children and four gentlemen, on a part of the ship sectioned off from the sixty-five in steerage) came a poignant stowaway. Every ship on the route seemed to have one, and Emerson was touched by 'the poor boy who hid in the bread closet that he might go to England, though he had no money to pay his passage & not even a coat over his shirt-sleeves'. His fate was not so bad: the captain treated him mercifully and found him employment. 'His name is Walters, and it seems he is English & came out to America, in the same way, in the "Ocean Monarch"; & not finding republics to mind, smuggles himself back. He says he likes the work of the ship "firstrate" &, if the captain will take him, means to go back again. The mate tells me, that this is the history of all sailors . . . nine out of ten are runaway boys.'

On 21 October the *Washington Irving* passed along the southern coast of Ireland. The country was being racked by one of the most terrible episodes in its generally tragic history: a famine, precipitated by the failure of the potato crop. Within four years, something like a million people had died of malnutrition or related diseases, and nearly half of the remaining population were being fed by charity and government handouts. A vast diaspora began, as tens and hundreds of thousands of angry, desperate people emigrated both to America and to the industrial north of England in search of the means of bare survival. The newspapers had woken to the full horror of the situation but Emerson the Transcendentalist, always reluctant to believe in evil or confront despair, glided past, seeing only 'a country as well cultivated & plentiful as Brookline & Brighton. I see towers & grain & turnip fields, & fishermen, but no curse.' Late the following evening, he reported to Lidian, 'We dropped anchor in the port of Liverpool, and in a little dangerous-looking dangerously dancing boat, first by oars & then by sail, four of us passengers with the captain have touched the land.' Arriving in London by train three days later, he headed straight for 5 Cheyne Row and the supposedly open house of Thomas and Jane Carlyle.

In a letter to Lidian he wrote how he and Carlyle had sat up that first evening talking until 1 a.m. and 'at breakfast next morning it begun again'. Towards midday they walked over to the Strand, 'Carlyle melting all Westminster and London down into his talk & laughter as we walked.' To a man accustomed to the quiet manners and modest clapperboard of Massachusetts, the city itself provided a backdrop of gloomy apocalyptic grandeur. 'The smoke of London, through which the sun rarely penetrates, gives a dusty magnificence to these immense piles of building in the West part of the City, which makes my walking rather dreamlike.' That evening Carlyle's brother John came to dinner and they had another late night. Over the next couple of days Emerson presented himself to the American ambassador, made arrangements at a bank, and visited Westminster Abbey and the National Gallery before setting off for Liverpool – via a train which covered '212 miles in 6 hours . . . nearly twice our railway speed' – and the start of his lecture tour.

But the worm had turned. With a reluctance born of painful disappointment, Emerson began to admit to himself that the intensity of that brief encounter at Craigenputtock had blinded him to aspects of Carlyle's character which put a gulf between them. 'I find my few hours' discourse with him in Scotland, long since, gave me not enough knowledge of him,' he explained to Lidian, 'and I have now at last been taken by surprise by him. He is not mainly a scholar, like most of my acquaintances, but a very practical Scotchman, such as you would find in any sadler's or iron dealer's shop.' There seems to have been one specifically sensitive topic: Emerson was unable to show sufficient partisan ardour for the hero of Carlyle's latest tome, Oliver Cromwell. But the deeper problem was the emergence of a dyspeptic, cynical side to Carlyle's personality which Emerson – essentially someone earnest, hopeful and benign – found inimical and perhaps a little frightening. 'All his qualities have a certain virulence. He talks like a very unhappy man, profoundly solitary, displeased & hindered by all men & things about him, & plainly biding his time, & meditating how to undermine & explode the whole world of nonsense which torments him.' With some relief he turned 'to the king of all friends & helpful agents', Alexander Ireland, busily and happily negotiating his engagements. 'I think there is a pool of honey about his heart which lubricates all parts of his system,' he wrote to Thoreau.

And the Carlyles? Well, it never took much to infuriate them and, setting aside the years of selfless literary agency Emerson had discharged on Carlyle's behalf, they regarded his visit as a cursed nuisance. From the start there had been problems. A letter sent from America announcing the details of his arrival had gone astray and created a flurry of confusion; Jane, a furiously energetic yet resentful housekeeper, had felt obliged to renovate the guest room, but could not find a seamstress to help her with 'the quantity of sewing that lies in a lined chintz bed'. So with her customary manic determination she had set to work with the needle herself, as Carlyle dashed off another fulsome letter to Liverpool: 'Know then, my friend, that in verity your Home while in England is *here*; and all other places whither work or amusement may call you, are but inns and temporary lodgings. I have returned hither a day or two ago, am free from any urgent calls or businesses of any kind; my wife has your room all ready – and here surely, if anywhere in the wide earth, there ought to be a brother's welcome and kind home waiting you. Yes, by Allah!'

In the event the invasion was even more of a strain than they had imagined. Not only did Emerson talk, he wanted Carlyle to talk too, and because he went to bed late and rose early, there was no escaping the constant passive demand for attention. Only a day after his arrival his mere presence was grating and Carlyle wrote to his mother: 'Emerson is now here with us; arrived just about an hour after my operations [an essay on Cromwell's letters] were completed – and there has been nothing but *talk* talk ever since. He is a fine pure gentle ingenious creature; and we think we shall both like him very well . . . No more of him at present.'

By the end of the week the pitch of irritation had risen and before Emerson had even left Cheyne Row, Jane's pen was scratching the paper. 'I do *not* like him the least bit,' she snarled in a letter to a friend.

> C says he is a 'most polite & gentle creature – a man really of a quite seraphic nature'; & all that may be true, at all rates C has good cause to say it; for Emerson with a tact as laudable as prudent avoids all occasions of dispute, & when dragged into it, by the hair of his head, so to speak he receives the most provoking contradictions with the softness of a feather-bed . . . But with his politeness and tolerance my approbation ends. The man has no '*natur*' about him, his geniality is of the head not the heart . . . you can get no hold of him – nor yet feel held by him . . . His very face is two or rather ½ a dozen faces that change into another like 'dissolving views.

Soon it was Carlyle's turn to let rip against Goody Two-Shoes. 'Emerson went on Friday night last,' he wrote to Lady Harriet Baring on 3 November.

> I was torn to pieces talking with him; for his sad Yankee rule seemed to be, That talk should go on incessantly, except when sleep interrupted it: a frightful rule. . . . A pure-minded elevated man; *elevated* but without *breadth*, as a willow is, as a reed is; no fruit at all to be gathered from him. A delicate, but thin pinched triangular face, no jaws nor lips, lean hook nose; face of a *cock* . . . a certain sensitive fastidious *stickishness* . . . No getting into any intimacy with him, talk as you will . . . I wish him honestly well, do as I am bound respect him honestly; but *Friends*, it is clear we can never in this world, to any real purpose, be.

Still, at least no doors had been slammed. The veneer of civility had been maintained, honour satisfied – and the Carlyles could further console themelves that, although he had portentously left his umbrella hanging in their hallway, the visitor planned to rent lodgings when he returned to London after the first leg of his lecture tour.

For the entire month of November Emerson alternated between two institutions of self-improvement: the Athenaeum in Manchester and the Mechanics' Institute in Liverpool. Here he addressed nonconformist, freethinking audiences – anti-Corn Law men, sharing many views of the anti-slavery lobby in New England – on a selection of 'Great Men' and the lessons offered by their self-realisation: 'Swedenborg the Mystic', 'Shakespeare the Poet', 'Montaigne the Sceptic', 'Goethe the Man of Letters' and 'Napoleon the Man of Action'. Such courses of celebrity lectures had become hugely popular in the early nineteenth century – Coleridge, Hazlitt, de Quincey, Thackeray, Dickens and Carlyle were only the more prominent among the many who took to the secular pulpit and attempted to satisfy a general appetite for undoctrinal moral and intellectual nutrition.

The appeal of what Emerson had to say was not obvious or overt. His style of delivery was gravely unemphatic: he read from a script, displaying no emotion and often appearing to be sunk in a low-level trance. Crop failures and a commercial slump were depressing the industrial north, but Emerson serenely ignored such temporal matters and looked to higher realms where 'the opaque self becomes transparent with the light of the First Cause'. He grew on his listeners. Although much of his import must have been hard to grasp – one man, according to the reporter from *Howitt's Journal*, was heard to ask his neighbour 'if he did not think he could understand it better if they stood on their heads' – he was also blessed with a gift for coining poetically memorable images ('a foolish consistency is the hobgoblin of little minds') which shone like sun through the clouds and kept his audiences if not gripped, at least intrigued.

According to the newspapers, Manchester and Liverpool received him with enthusiasm, and even if orthodox brows furrowed at his denial – or his evasion – of doctrines of Evil and Damnation, it was impossible to resist his aura of modest, selfless goodness. On 18 November he earned even broader Northern fame by virtue of his participation in the Athenaeum's glamorous annual soirée at the Free

Trade Hall, where he sat on the speakers' table alongside the Anti-Corn Law agitators Cobden and Bright, the comic illustrator George Cruikshank, the historical novelist Harrison Ainsworth, the publisher Robert Blackwood and the Dean of Manchester.* An astonishing total of 8000 guests attended, at the cost of 5s for a pair of tickets. But the event wasn't all high-toned talk. It had its less intellectual attractions too, including dancing motivated by a double quadrille band and lavish refreshment (sides of roast beef, ice-creams, punchbowls full of port and sherry negus, coffee brewed in a two-hundred gallon boiler).

The speeches must have seemed interminable, even to an audience hungry for self-improvement and self-congratulation. Formal proceedings opened at 7.15 p.m. when the Athenaeum's chairman launched into an elaborate encomium of the city of Manchester, coloured by that favourite Victorian piety – the way that successful commerce and industry nurtured domestic refinement and appreciation of the arts – and garlanded with quotations from Bacon, Johnson and Gibbon. He was followed by sturdy Richard Cobden, striking a harder-headed political and economic note, for the battle for Free Trade was not yet won. And then came Emerson, misty-eyed, rhapsodic and innocently racist. 'That which lures a solitary American in the woods with the wish to see England [is] the moral peculiarity of the Saxon race – its commanding sense of right & wrong – the love & devotion to that – which is the imperial trait, which arms them with the sceptre of the globe.' After praising 'the thoroughness & solidity of work' which characterised traders and mechanics and 'that fidelity of fellow-ship, that habit of friendship, the homage of man to man, running through all classes', he began to expatiate on his childhood vision of 'the British island . . . no paradise of serene sky, & roses, & music, & merriment, all the year round . . . but a cold, foggy, mournful country, where nothing grew well in the open air, but robust men & virtuous women, and these of a wonderful fibre & endurance'. Their nature was to be 'good lovers, good haters . . . and you could know little about them, till you had seen them long, & little good of them, till you had seen them in action: that in prosperity, they were moody & dumpish,

---

*Dickens was also expected, but withdrew at the eleventh hour: he was preoccupied with an overdue episode of *Dombey and Son*, and the inauguration of Urania Cottage, the refuge for prostitutes in which he was philanthropically involved. See *The Letters of Charles Dickens*, ed. G. Storey and K. J. Fielding, vol. 5 (Oxford, 1981), pp. 192–3

but in adversity, they were grand'. Experience had verified all this, and more: whatever temporary vicissitudes of material fortune Britain suffered, 'she has a secret vigour, & a pulse like a cannon. . . . Seeing that – I say, All hail! Mother of nations – Mother of heroes – with strength still equal to the time; still wise to entertain and swift to execute the policy which the mind & heart of mankind requires in the present hour, and thus only hospitable to the foreigner, & truly a home to the thoughtful & generous, who are born in the soil.'

To his journal, however, he privately expressed deeper anxieties and moral reservations about this triumphant alma mater and her brood. Superficial good breeding he found everywhere, but compared with New England 'by no means any superiority of understanding or culture'. To his wife he wrote that she 'should see the tragic spectacles which these streets show, these Manchester & those Liverpool streets, by day & by night, to know how much of safety and dignity & of opportunity belongs to us so easily that is ravished in England. Woman is cheap & vile in England – it is tragical to see – Childhood, too, I see oftenest in the state of absolute beggary'. In Liverpool, a port swarming with Irish migrants and a miscellaneous transient population, Emerson was seized with the sense of alienation which enveloped so many intellectuals confronted by the chaotic activity and filth of the nineteenth-century industrial city. He felt out of place and out of scale, unable to make ordinary human contact among people living without community. 'I am oppressed by the seeing of such multitudes,' he wrote to Lidian. 'There is a fierce strength here in all the streets, the men are bigger & solider far than our people, more stocky, both men & women, and with a certain fixedness & determination in each person's air . . . in America you catch the eye of everyone you meet; here you catch no eye almost . . . if they bow in the street, it is no trifle, but a duty performed. They rarely introduce persons to each other, & mean something when they do, & they are slow to offer the hand.'

Manchester felt less oppressive, partly because of Alexander Ireland's gentle presence. Emerson took lodgings in its tranquil suburb of Higher Broughton, renting a bedroom and parlour from the obliging Mrs Massey, who fed and watered him, '& discovers when my boot needs a stitch & carries it to the cobbler'. 'I breakfast at 8, dine at 2 and sup at 6 – all alone,' he wrote to Lidian. He appears to have been generally low in spirits, homesick even: the weather alone was depressing: 'It is a strange drizzling climate, raining, I should think, a little in every day since I was in England.' Correspondence took up much of his spare time – 'In this land of cheap postage, where letters arrive to you hourly from all parts of the kingdom for 1 penny' – as did visits from 'various young men whose expectations I am doomed to disappoint.' He wrote to Carlyle to thank him for the days in Cheyne Row, signing the letter 'ever your lover', but mused in his notebook, 'I wonder the young people are so eager to see Carlyle. It is like being hot to see the mathematical or the Greek professor, before you have got your lesson.'

In the first week of December he embarked on an arduous itinerary, which would take him to most of the major industrial towns of the North and Midlands. Most of the lectures were given at Mechanics' Institutes, to aspirational working-class men of proud independence of mind and, given Emerson's alluring platform manner and uplifting, if capaciously vague, moral message, they were invariably well received. Newspaper reports allow us to trace his precise schedule. Between 6 and 13 December he alternated between Nottingham and Derby (lecturing on 'Napoleon', 'Shakespeare', 'Domestic Life' and 'Reading'); on 15 December he was in Preston ('Domestic Life'); on 16 December, Birmingham ('Napoleon')'; 17 and 18 December, Huddersfield ('Napoleon' and 'Domestic Life'); 20 and 21 December, Leicester ('Shakespeare' and 'Domestic Life'); 22 December, Chesterfield ('Domestic Life'); 23 December, Birmingham ('Domestic Life'); and 29 and 30 December, Worcester ('Eloquence' and 'Domestic Life'). Such mobility, facilitated by the ever-expanding railway network, still seemed almost miraculous. 'I ride everywhere as on a cannonball (though cushioned & comforted in every manner) high & low over rivers & towns through mountains in tunnels of 3 miles & more at twice the speed & with half the motion of our cars & read quietly the Times newspaper,' he explained in a letter to Thoreau written just before Christmas. But at the same time the sense of churning it out was relentless and, inundated as he was with further demands from all quarters, he could hardly keep up with himself. 'The newspapers here report my lectures and London papers reprint so fully, that they are no longer repeatable, & I must dive deeper into the bag & bring up older ones, or cease to read.' So in January 1848 he added 'Uses of Great Men' and 'The Humanity of Science' to his repertory, and passed through Leeds, Halifax, Ripon, Sheffield, York, Beverley, Bridlington and Driffield. It was exhilarating, it was exhausting. 'There is great advantage to me in this journeying about in this fashion, I see houses, manufactories, halls, churches, landscape & men. There is also great vexation.'

'Droll passages' too. Emerson did not lack a quiet sense of humour – in fact, it became somewhat louder the longer he was in England – and he told Lidian how particularly amused he had been by the officious Mr Dunning, Secretary of the Yorkshire Union of Mechanics' Institutes, who followed him from Beverley to Bridlington to Driffield, greeting him at railway stations, opening the applause at his arrival at the lectern and encouraging the audience to rise to its feet in acclaim after he had finished. 'Mr D had obviously charged himself with making the whole thing succeed; & wished to convince the audience that they were a great crowd, & that they were filled with enthusiasm.' It transpired that there was an agenda behind Mr Dunning's persistent cheerleading, in the form of 'some quarrel between the Yorkshire Union of Institutes & the town of Hull, which refuses to come into the same; and it was designed to punish the contumacy of Hull by exhibiting this triumph of these little towns in sending across the ocean for a Lecturer & getting him; whilst great Hull cannot have him'.

On 22 January Emerson returned to his Manchester lodgings to recuperate. A week later he organised a sort of 'At Home' there, partly to thank those who had given him hospitality and partly to bring together some of the awkward, intense young men who had attached themselves along the road. They were a rum crew: one of their number, a sardonic journalist called Francis Espinasse, described them as 'a strange collection of mystics, poets, prose rhapsodists, editors, schoolmasters, ex-Unitarian ministers and cultivated manufacturers' – almost a mid-nineteenth-century equivalent of the brown-rice-and-sandals brigade. The loyal Alexander Ireland, of course; Joseph Neuberg, a German-born merchant based in Nottingham who had put Emerson up and who was later to become, on his recommendation, a long-suffering research assistant to Carlyle for his biography of Frederick the Great; Thomas Hornblower Gill from Birmingham, a writer of hymns, squeaky voiced, gesticulating and twitchy; the tall, thin, timorous Henry Sutton, a Shelleyan vegetarian horrified by all 'sensual propensity' ; and George Searle Phillips, a radical and writer-of-all-sorts so impoverished that he could not afford the train fare, who had trudged twenty-five miles from Huddersfield in order to be present. The young socialist and industrialist Friedrich Engels had left Manchester in 1845, having published his impassioned study of the city's proletariat, *The Condition of the Working Class in England*. Had he still been resident, one likes to think he would have been there too.

Those who did attend were nonconformist in every sense, not least that of their own mutual incompatibility, and one doesn't imagine that the party they made up offered much in the way of whoopee. At dinner, according to Phillips's account of the evening, Sutton sat apostolically on Emerson's left, Gill on his right. The latter was so short-sighted and excitable that he knocked his plate of food into his own lap and then dropped a glass of red wine over Phillips's shirt-front. The conversation lacked ease and flow, and Emerson himself, as was his wont in numerous company, contributed little. Remarks were made, anecdotes exchanged, but there was none of the high discourse for which the host must have hoped. After the meal, perhaps to freshen the general fug of social discomfort, Emerson read aloud his new essay on Plato. Then Phillips went outside to smoke a cigar. By the time he returned the company had drifted away, leaving only the irrepressible Gill and Sutton. In the small hours Emerson lit up and became eloquent, and the four of them sat talking gently and listening ruminatively until the wintry morning dawned.

On 7 February the tour resumed: Halifax, Barnard Castle, Newcastle, then on to Scotland, with a new lecture entitled 'Aristocracy' and another addition, 'The National Characteristics of the Six Northern States of America'. His purpose being not just to lecture but to observe, Emerson copiously recorded his passing impressions and deeper thoughts in his notebooks. The signs of the times were awesome indeed: 'I look at the immense wealth & the solid power concentrated, & am quite faint.' Like Carlyle, he admitted to a certain admiration for a strong nation in its prime, flexing, expanding, marching inexorably onwards – and to Thoreau, in early December, he wrote of that remarkable moment, profoundly symbolic of the age, at which the whole of Great Britain synchronised its watches in order to keep up with its own movements:

> Everything centralizes, in this magnificent machine which England is. Manufacturer for the world she is become or becoming one complete tool or engine in herself – Yesterday the time all over the kingdom was

reduced to Greenwich time. At Liverpool where I was the clocks were put forward 12 minutes. This had become quite necessary on account of the railroads which bind the whole country into swiftest connexion, and require so much accurate interlocking, intersection & simultaneous arrival, that the difference of time produced confusion . . . the proceeding effects of Electric telegraph will give a new importance to such arrangements.

Driving this vast complex engine was a national force of character, described by Emerson as 'pluck' – 'the merchants have it, the bishops have it, the women have it, the newspapers have it' – and an independence of mind which meant that 'each man walks, eats, drinks, shaves, dresses, gesticulates & in every manner is, acts, & suffers without the smallest reference to the bystanders & in his own fashion'. To illustrate which generalisation he offers the charming image of a clergyman he spotted in a first-class train carriage, shamelessly taking 'his stout shoes out of his carpet bag' and putting them on 'instead of thin ones' as he approached his station. An American in that position would never have casually ventured so close to impropriety.

All this was irresistible. Yet Emerson struggled not to be intimidated by England and the English. His tenor when dealing with them remains ambivalent, not least because he was conscious that brazen British confidence aimed to leave his own more callow American identity threatened and enfeebled. 'If I stay here long,' he fretted, 'I shall lose all my patriotism & think that England has absorbed all excellences.' He was determined to be alert to its shortcomings. The cancerous smugness of 'a nation where mediocrity is entrenched & consolidated, funded & decorated, in an adamantine manner'; a cumulating mass of wealth and power, which left 'little girls running barefoot thro' the rain with broom in hand to beg a half penny of the passenger at the crossing'; sheep in a field near Leeds black-coated from the grimy soot belched from the city's chimneys; the booming brag of the leading articles in *The Times*; 'the incuriosity and stony neglect of each other', which was the bleaker implication of the shoe-changing clergyman's disregard for convention; and worst, the 'unreligion' of a country in which 'I have never heard, I believe, but one man in England [who?] speak of "Our Saviour".'

Smaller things fascinated him too. He transcribed, for instance, oddities of idiom and pronunciation, as in

'He is poorly'   The common phrase for sickness
'Aye'   for   yes
'You know you know you know you know'
'Oh!'   for   'Indeed!'
'I beg your pardon'   for   'I did not hear you'
engine   ingin
interesting   interrr esting
Europe   Yer-up
More   is almost   mar
curious curate   kyerious &c

concluding, as many have, that 'it is certain that more people speak English correctly in the United States, than in Britain'. He also noted that

people eat the same dinner at every house in England. 1. soup, 2. fish; 3. beef, mutton or hare, 4 birds, 5 pudding & pastry & jellies. 6 cheese, 7. grapes, nuts & wine. During dinner hock & champagne are offered you by the servant, & sherry stands at the corner of the table. Healths are not much drunk in fashionable houses. After the cloth is removed, three bottles, namely, port, sherry, claret, invariably circulate. What rivers of wine are drunk in all England daily! One would say every guest drinks six glasses.

Underpinning these disparate insights is his romantic sense of the British as a heroic stock. This was something he felt you could actually see – several times he insists on what he first noticed at Liverpool, that people here possessed 'a fierce strength' and physical superiority, which the callow American breed could not match – but it was not just a matter of muscle and brawn.

One would say that the island has so long been the abode of a civil & free race, that the very dust is the remains of good & brave men, & the air retains the virtue their souls have shed into it, & they who inhale it, feel its quality . . . The first name for intellect in the human race is Shakspeare [sic] – the first for capacity in exact science is Newton; and where out of his country has Milton his superior in epic or in lyric song? What lawgiver in learning & reason has excelled Bacon? . . . These heroes of peace have been flanked by the heroes of action, by the Drakes, Blakes, Cavendishes, Cooks, Marlboros, Nelsons, Wellingtons . . .

What troubled Emerson – and it troubled Carlyle too – was the problem of reconciling this supremacy with the mercantile thrust of British society in the mid-nineteenth century and the weakening of the religious dimension of life. Both thinkers looked to outstanding individuals for inspiration, leadership and salvation, but Emerson could not quite bring himself to concur in Carlyle's belief, expressed in his lectures *On Heroes, Hero-Worship and the Heroic in History*, published in 1841 and later regrettably influential on Fascist ideology, that 'the history of the world is but the history of great men' and that 'every advance which humanity had made was due to specific individuals supremely gifted in mind and character, whom Providence sent among them at favoured epochs'. Emerson's own attitude was more subtle and democratic; instead of 'heroes', he talked of 'representative men' (the title of a collection of his lectures published in 1850), like Shakespeare or Napoleon, whose value lay in qualities 'representative' of the 'capacity' of all men. They weren't what we would call 'role models', however, for Emerson recognised no human being as entirely exemplary – 'we cloy of the honey of each peculiar greatness. Every hero becomes a bore at last' and we are all 'teachers and pupils in turn'.

Yet Emerson was still hungry for 'people to talk to, people who stimulate' – and the prospect of exciting, abrasive conversation with minds richer and deeper than those possessed by the good souls of his quiet New England kin was as strong a motivation of his second visit to Europe as it had been of his first. In 1833, he had earmarked and collared only four British sages: Landor, Coleridge, Wordsworth and Carlyle. By 1848 the number of worthies he was determined to encounter had greatly increased. Shortly before his return to America later that year, his notebook lists

Wordsworth	P. J. Bailey
Landor	J. S. Mill
Carlyle	Arthur H. Clough
Tennyson	W. Sewell
Wilkinson	James Moseley
Stephenson	Henry Taylor
Hallam	Edwin Chadwick
Faraday	Duke of Wellington
Owen	Robert Peel
Edw. Forbes	Richard Cobden
Samuel Brown	Robert Browning
De Quincey	Matthew Arnold
David Scott	John Bright

And he notes, with some satisfaction at the foot of the page, 'All these I have seen except Chadwick, Browning, Taylor & Sewell & Moseley.'

Emerson was himself the object of much curiosity. His weeks in

Scotland brought him accruing celebrity: in Glasgow, his lecture attracted '2 or 3000 people' to 'a vast lighted cavern called the City Hall' and in Edinburgh enlightened folk turned out in force to meet him – none more poignantly so than the frail septuagenarian figure of Thomas de Quincey, the once-great essayist and opium addict, with 'a face marked by great refinement,- a very gentle old man speaking with the utmost deliberation & softness', hopelessly impoverished but quite serene in his pitifully reduced circumstances, who braved driving wintry rain and walked ten miles from his cottage in Lasswade in order to attend a dinner (Emerson worried that their hostess was unable to lend him a dry pair of 'pantaloons'). His conversation, however, didn't match the expectations aroused by his splendiferous prose style. Emerson enjoyed de Quincey's chatter, but he had 'fancied some figure like the organ of York Minster would appear'. Another Scottish disappointment was Judge Francis Jeffrey, founder and former editor of the biting, cutting and profoundly influential *Edinburgh Review*, who materialised as a vain old windbag, 'every sentence interlarded with French phrases speaking a dialect of his own, neither English, not Scotch, marked with a certain petitesse, as one might well say, and an affected elegance . . . but here he is the chief man, has it all his own way, and is a mere Polonius'. Emerson's sweetness was not without a sharp tang.

At the end of February he moved south again via the Lake District. Here, in her comfortable house overlooking Lake Windermere, he stopped a few days with Harriet Martineau, the no-nonsense campaigning radical recently recovered from terminal illness through (or so she claimed) the influence of mesmerism and now the author of a blasphemous tract in comparative religion positing 'Egypt as the Cradle of the Four Faiths'. Together they paid a visit to Wordsworth, now nearly eighty and close to death. They discovered him asleep on a sofa, and 'a little short & surly as an old man [is] suddenly waked before the end of his nap'. Harriet Martineau found Wordsworth tiresome, and soon went off home, leaving Emerson to manage the encounter. It was even less of a success than their previous meeting. Wordsworth proceeded to spend the next hour and a half grumbling at news of the outbreak of republican revolution in France – the French 'were an idle people' – and harrumphing at Emerson's account of his time in Scotland. 'No Scotchman can write English,' he said, describing Carlyle as 'a pest to the English tongue'.

Although impressed by his hale and healthy appearance (marked by a huge 'corrugated' nose), Emerson concluded that Wordsworth was not much more than a 'bitter old Englishman' with altogether ordinary views. What had become of his poetic wisdom? 'His conversation is always simple and not usually distinguished by anything forcible,' Emerson wrote. 'His opinions of French, English, Irish & Scotch &c. seemed rashly formulized from little anecdotes of what had befallen himself & Mrs Wordsworth in a diligence or stagecoach . . . Occasionally, his face lights up & he says something good but I thought I could easily supply such table talk as this without the cost of journeys.' Afterwards, Harriet Martineau told him that the poet 'had no personal friend – he was not amiable and he was stingy . . . in his earliest housekeeping at the cottage [he] was accustomed to offer his friends bread & plainest fare. If they wanted something more, they must pay. I heard the story with admiration, as evincing English pluck, more than any anecdote I knew.'

Back in London by the beginning of March, Emerson tactfully evaded Carlyle's half-hearted invitation to lodge in Cheyne Row and installed himself instead in a modest suite of rooms owned by the publisher Edward Chapman at 142 the Strand. Here he had privacy (in the Carlyles' small house there can have been no physical escape) and found some space to think. Letters from home demanded his attention – Lidian reported that she had been bedridden with jaundice and their children had also been ill, that debtors were pressing, and that she felt isolated and unhappy. Perhaps he knew that she exaggerated, perhaps he resented the pressure exerted between the lines to cut short his visit and return home: but whatever his reaction to the news, this kindest and least egocentric of men certainly did not go out of his way to provide his wife with any sensitively pitched reassurance. 'A photometer cannot be a stove,' he told her, in a cursory attempt to mitigate his marital frigidity and uncommunicativeness. 'I truly acknowledge a poverty of nature, & have really no proud defence at all to set up . . .' But then, just like a man, he did try to defend himself. 'Besides am I not, o best Lidian, a most foolish affectionate goodman & papa, with a weak side towards apples & sugar & all domesticities, when I am once in Concord? Answer me that. Well, I will come again shortly and behave the best I can. Only I foresee plainly that the trick of solitariness never never can leave me.'

Reading his letters, Lidian could be excused for wondering wryly as to exactly what he meant by his 'trick of solitariness'. Free of lecturing engagements and unsure what next to do, Emerson allowed himself to be drawn into the giddying, glamorous whirl of the capital. It was all very interesting, often amazing too. 'One goes from show to show, dines out, & lives in extremes. Electric sparks 6 ft long, light is polarized, Grisi sings, Rothschild is your banker, Owen & Faraday lecture, Macaulay talks, Soyer cooks.' Everyone wanted a piece of the philosopher American and, as one smart dinner party followed another, he could tick another name on his wish list of worthies. 'At Mr Bancroft's I dined with Macaulay, Bunsen, Lord Morpeth, Milman, Milnes & others,' he wrote,

> Carlyle, Mr & Mrs Lyell, Mrs Butler & others came in the evening. At Mr Milman's I breakfasted with Macaulay, Hallam, Lord Morpeth, a certain brilliant Mr Charles Austin here who makes or 'has made £30,000 in one year by his profession' (of law) and Mr and Mrs Bancroft. Guizot was expected: unhappily for me he did not come . . . At Mrs Drummond's I found Mr Cobden and Lord Mounteagle, and saw but did not speak to the Archbishop of York & Mr Panizzi. Carlyle carried me next to Lady Harriet Baring, who is a very distinguished person and the next day to Lady Ashburton her mother. And I am to dine with them both. Then Mrs Bancroft procured me a card to Lady Morgan's soirée . . .

And so on, without satirical intent. Even Emerson's cool head was turned a little. He plainly relished, for instance, his honorary membership of the Athenaeum, the exclusive and lavishly appointed Pall Mall club where he could continue to enlarge his acquaintance with the cream of the British Establishment in style, and discuss great issues of the day like the revolution in France – by now it had sent King Louis Philippe into exile and inflamed the Chartist agitation for universal suffrage in England. Yet in the end he wasn't fooled: although his social diary at one level represented precisely the intellectual 'whip for the top' that he had so desperately craved when he was pining in Concord, a man of his discerning moral taste was never going to be satisfied by a parade of sophisticated urbanity and fast living.

Against all the endemic British energy and self-confidence – its industry and inventiveness, its 'indescribable material superiorities' – he continued to feel undercurrents pulling society in the wrong direction. Particularly repellent to him – his own sexual appetite being, on all the evidence, permanently dormant – was the prevalent attitude to prostitution. For all the reverent lip-service paid to the sacrament of marriage, ragged women stood on every street corner begging to have their bodies bought for next to nothing. Sexual incontinence was something his clubbable friends accepted as a fact of life – even if, like Dickens, they made courageous attempts to help individual women who fell victim to it. But Emerson could not take it for granted and, at an all-male dinner at Lincoln's Inn he talked

> with Forster, Dickens & Carlyle, on the prostitution in the great towns, & said, that, when I came to Liverpool, I inquired whether it was always as gross in that city as it then appeared to me? for it looked to me as if such manners betokened a fatal rottenness in the state, & especially no boy could grow up safe; but that I had been told, that it was not worse nor better than it had been for years. C & D replied, that chastity in the male sex was as good as gone in our times; and in England was so very rare that they could name all the exceptions. Carlyle evidently believed that the same thing was true in America. I assured them that it was not so with us: that for the most part, young men of good standing & good education with us go virgins to their nuptial bed, as truly as their brides. Dickens replied that incontinence is so much the rule with them that if his own son were particularly chaste, he should be alarmed on his account, as if he could not be in good health.

In the face of so much that was disappointing or disconcerting, what could Emerson hold on to? Who were the adequately 'representative men' of Victorian Britain? Perhaps surprisingly, he seems to have fastened on types who made up in solidity and amiability what they may have lacked in far-sight or spirituality. The thirty-nine-year-old Alfred Tennyson, for instance, who showed, in Emerson's words, 'a great deal of plain strength about him, and though cultivated, is quite unaffected . . . there is an air of general sanity & power in him that inspires confidence' (an image which the publication of *In Memoriam* two years later would destroy). Or Richard Cobden, framer of the Anti-Corn Laws and a reforming MP, 'the object of honor & belief to risen & rising England, a man of great discretion, who never overstates, nor states prematurely, nor has a particle of unnecessary genius or hope to mislead him, no wasted strength, but calm, sure of his fact, simple & nervous in stating it, as a boy in laying down the rules of the game of football which have been violated'. Or Richard Monckton Milnes, the

Liberal MP of a literary bent (he wrote a *Life and Letters of Keats*), 'the most good natured man in England . . . fat, easy, affable and obliging', who slipped Emerson into membership of the Athenaeum and opened doors for him into high society. 'He is on the best terms with all men from dukes and Archbishops down to Chartists,' Emerson wrote of him affectionately. 'When he breakfasted somewhere with the Abp. of Canterbury, his friend said "Now I beg you, Milnes, don't slap him on the back & call him Canterbury, before breakfast is over". . . He makes very bad speeches of exquisite infelicity, & joins in the laugh against himself. He is very liberal of his money, & sincerely kind & useful to young people of merit.' (What Emerson did not perceive was the other side of Monckton Milnes's bonhomie: a devotion to flagellation and sado-masochistic sexual practices.)

In May, Emerson left London for Paris. The trip had always been part of his itinerary and he refused to let the political situation (or Lidian's worries) deter him. Shortly after he arrived the revolution conveniently took an interesting turn, as a crowd of working-class radicals invaded the National Assembly and attempted to overthrow the newly established government of the Second Republic. Order was soon restored, but only with a huge show of force. Emerson saw it all, he told Lidian, 'The sudden & immense display of arms when the rappel was beaten . . . the streets full of bayonets, and the furious driving of the horses dragging cannon towards the National Assembly; the rapid succession of proclamations proceeding from the government, & pasted on the walls at the corners of all streets, eagerly read by crowds of people.' He rejoiced in what he called 'the Shopkeepers' victory', but found the proto-socialist radicals them-selves tremendously impressive. Although he himself was too much of an individualist to subscribe to any sort of collectivist ideology, he respected their integrity. 'The men are in terrible earnest,' he wrote after visiting one of their debating clubs. 'The deep sincerity of the speakers who are agitating social not political questions, and who are studying how to secure a fair share of bread to every man, and to get God's justice done through the land, is very good to hear.'

It was this level of commitment and idealism that British politics lacked, whatever the personal niceness and decency of a Cobden or Monckton Milnes. Shortly before Emerson left London for Paris, the climactic – or anticlimactic – Chartist rally had taken place on

Kennington Common. With a keen eye on the wave of insurrections then spreading throughout Europe, the British government had anticipated that the event would spark an outbreak of revolution and accordingly fortified the city with seven regiments. But last-minute bargaining behind the scenes, combined with that most effective of dampeners, a long, heavy rainstorm, quite literally washed out the threat of mass violencet, turning the rally into one of history's most intriguing might-have-beens. Emerson deplored the Chartists' feeble and prevaricating leadership, the intellectuals' failure of nerve (writers, for instance, who were 'bold and democratic' until matters came to a head) and the absence of 'the terrible earnest' that motivated the Parisian workers. The English were not just quietist and traditionalist, but fundamentally venal. 'There will be no revolution, none that deserves to be called so,' he stated, in a prescient analysis. 'There may be a scramble for money. But as all the people we see want the things we now have and not better things, it is very certain that they will, under whatever change of forms, keep the old system.' But in the longer term, he knew, the Chartist movement had right on its side and 'will have it at last'.

In Paris, he could not predict the future so confidently – 'For the matter of socialism, there are no oracles,' he wrote. 'The oracles are dumb.' Yet the sun shone and the city put Emerson into a rare holiday mood. Compared with London, with its hierarchies and snobberies, Paris seemed open and democratic, and infectiously gay. 'Knots of people converse everywhere in the street . . . Nothing like it could happen in England. They [the French] are the most joyous race and put the best face on everything.' Mostly he socialised with fellow expatriates, although he did pay a call on Alexis de Tocqueville, author of the celebrated critique of his homeland, *Democracy in America*. Otherwise he was content to drink in the enveloping exhilaration of a city high on the promise of new liberty. One night, there was a '*fête de la Concorde, de la Paix et du Travail*' and the city magically lived up to its sobriquet of *la ville lumière*. 'The illumination in the Champs Elysées was delicious,' he told Lidian. 'They understand all the capabilities of the place & of the whole city as well as you do your parlour and make a carcanet of jewels of it all . . . festal chandeliers . . . hung up & down a mile of avenue gave it all the appearance of an immense ballroom in which the countless crowds of men & women walked with ease and pleasure. It was easy to see that France is far nearer to Socialism than England.'

Shortly before Emerson left London for Paris, Carlyle, Dickens and other literary lions had petitioned him to give a course of lectures in London, making incidentally encouraging noises about the profit he could clear if he charged a subscription of one guinea. Reluctantly he agreed to do so and in Paris he jigged up some existing material under the catch-all title *The Mind and Manners of the Nineteenth Century*. The premises of the Metropolitan Early Closing Association in Marylebone were hired and, in early June, the 'Massachusetts Indian', as Emerson drily referred to himself in letters home, returned to give London the benefit of his wisdom. The price of the tickets meant that the tone of his audiences was fashionable and aristocratic, their numbers disappointingly small: Emerson felt heavy hearted about the entire enterprise, especially as a renewed round of dinners and soirées meant that he did not have time to polish the lectures as he had intended and polite compliments rather than real emotional engagement was the general response they provoked. Carlyle was in the audience. From the platform Emerson was amused to hear him making 'loud Scottish Covenanter gruntings of laudation, or, at least, of consideration, when anything strikes him, to the edifying of the attentive vicinity'. 'Very Emersonian,' was his verdict on one of the lectures – which, suggested Francis Espinasse, 'considering that Emerson had been the lecturer, was not striking or enthusiastic praise'.

Elsewhere, alongside the dozing duchesses and the loyal Monckton Milnes, sat the elderly Henry Crabb Robinson, a barrister and literary hanger-on whose diaries record encounters with most of the great writers of the first half of the nineteenth century, Goethe included. His befuddled comments probably indicate the general level of comprehension. 'Full of brilliant thoughts,' he wrote of Emerson's disquisition on 'Politics and Socialism'. 'But I was unable to connect them. He praised [Robert] Owen [the philanthropic mill owner] & called Fourier [whose ideas about communal living had been influential in New England] a great man; yet he seemed to speak of all their efforts as hitherto unsuccessful. Wilkinson whipered to me "All lies", but my attention was at the moment flagging.' On other occasions he grasped at stray ideas – 'the high dignity of *Instinct* . . . the influence of the

Individual' – and was relieved that his views on aristocracy 'contained nothing to offend the highborn', but it was Emerson's personal charm rather than the gospel of Transcendentalism which penetrated.

To compensate for the shortfall in the takings – and perhaps, too, to take away a bad taste left by addressing an élite congregation – Emerson also gave three lectures at Exeter Hall, bastion of oratorio, nonconformism and the respectable lower-middle classes.* At lower prices, these seem to have gone down better and Emerson enjoyed them more, smiling happily when his final appearance on the platform was greeted, according to *The Reasoner*, by an audience 'rising en masse, hearty cheering, and waving of hats &c'. The flat fee he received of thirty-five guineas paid for his steamship passage across the Atlantic, booked for 15 July.

The pace and glamour of his social life did not abate in these last weeks. He toured the picturesque charms of Eton, Windsor and Cambridge and wondered at the splendours of Chatsworth. He paid his respects to Gray's country churchyard at Stoke Poges and to the Shakespeare memorials at Stratford-upon-Avon, breaking his journey in nearby Coventry at the house of the freethinker Charles Bray. At breakfast he encountered Bray's lodger, a horse-faced young woman of evident intellectual genius called Mary Ann Evans, whose anonymous translation of a great work of German biblical criticism, Strauss's *Life of Jesus*, had been published two years previously. She had read and admired some of Emerson's essays and they talked in earnest of higher things. He asked her what had first awakened her to philosophical reflection. Rousseau's *Confessions*, she replied. Emerson was impressed: Carlyle had said the same. The future George Eliot was impressed too, remembering the tall, gaunt and soft-spoken American as 'the first *Man* I ever saw'.

Back in the Great Wen, he met Byron's widow and their daughter Ada (in private, a brilliant mathematician and pioneer of computing) and chatted to Shelley's friend, the dilettante essayist Leigh Hunt. He gloried in an exhibition of the landscapes of Turner – that most Transcendentalist of painters – but felt cloth-eared when confronted with the mysteriously beautiful art of another contemporary visitor, Fryderyk Chopin. 'And there is no end to London & the Londoners,' he sighed to Lidian.

---

*See also p. 54.

There remained the problem of Carlyle. No rift had been acknowledged between them and they could meet pleasantly with other people in attendance, but Emerson was now under no illusions about the man he had formerly supposed to be his soulmate. 'I seldom see Carlyle & I do not see him with much pleasure: he is always strong, but always pounding on the same strings, one endless vituperation of all people & things in the modern world . . . He breaks every sentence with a scoffing laugh, "windbag", "monkey", "donkey", "bladder" and let him describe whom he will, it is always "poor fellow". . . . I fancy, too, that he does not care to see anybody whom he cannot eat, & reproduce tomorrow, in his pamphlet or pillory.' At the parade of his views – 'a protectionist in political economy, aristocrat in politics, epicure in diet, goes for murder, money, punishment, slavery and all the pretty abominations' – Emerson was left speechless. But still he did not want to think ill of him.

Carlyle for his part emptied hot scorn on the 'poor *washy* set of people, chiefly friends of humanity &c' with which Emerson kept company and persisted in dismissing his thinking as 'moonshiny'. One anecdote – first reported by George Eliot in a letter of 1851 – neatly illustrates the gap between them, even if it is only apocryphal. 'Carlyle was very angry with [Emerson] for not believing in a devil, and to convert him took him amongst all the horrors of London – the gin shops etc. – and finally to the House of Commons, plying him at every turn with the question "Do you believe in a devil noo?" ' But with Emerson's departure safely fixed, Carlyle must have felt a twinge of conscience and began to take a more charitable view. 'There is really something of excellent in him,' he wrote to his mother. 'His present visit has not done much for me, nor could I in any way, do much for him: but he has and keeps up from old a very friendly feeling for me, and the very separations that lie between us add themselves to this probably final parting to make it sad and affectionate!'

At this point of delicately balanced goodwill they managed a rapprochement. One Sunday evening they had a long talk alone – 'to much more purpose than we commonly attain,' as Emerson told Lidian – which led to an agreement to take a little trip away from London (and, incidentally, away from the cantankerous Jane Carlyle, whose nagging psychosomatic ailments exacerbated her irritation with Emerson). As Carlyle explained to his mother, 'Emerson has asked me to make a little journey with him to see a strange old Antiquity, old almost as the hills, which bears the name *Stonehenge*, near Salisbury in Wiltshire . . . some 4 hrs by railway.' On the morning of 7 July they duly set off. In *English Traits*, the book about his visits which he subsequently worked up from his journals, Emerson published a sanitised version of what followed.* Carlyle's letter to his wife, written from their inn in Amesbury, adds some bilious addenda to his account.

They travelled by South-Western Railway to Salisbury and thence by gig to Amesbury. Carlyle had not slept the night before and claimed in his letter that he had been obliged by Emerson 'to talk all the way'. Still, they rubbed along 'happily enough', with the conversation covering the following topics. Visiting Americans, and what they like to do and see when they come to London. Carlyle's dislike of blather about high art and antiquities – 'he wishes to go through the British Museum in silence, and thinks a sincere man will see something, and say nothing.' Carlyle's further sharp dig at Emerson that Americans 'dislike the coldness and exclusiveness of the English, and run away to France, and go with their countrymen, and are amused, instead of manfully staying in London, and confronting Englishmen, and acquiring their culture, who really have much to teach them'. Emerson made a dignified prophetic riposte to this. Yes, he knew he was easily dazzled, and yes, everywhere he went he found 'proofs of sense and spirit, and success of every sort', achieved by people 'as good as they are handsome'. But he also knew that as soon as he returned to Massachusetts, he would 'lapse into the feeling, which the geography of America inevitably inspires, that we play the game with immense advantage; that there and not here is the seat and centre of the British race; and that no skill or activity can long compete with the prodigious natural advantages of that country, in the hands of the same race; and that England, an old and exhausted island, must one day be contented, like other parents, to be strong only in her children'. To which Carlyle seems to have offered no answer. And Emerson was right.

From the George Inn at Amesbury, where they feasted on 'a wretched dinner of whale-blubber mutton and old peas', they set out, so Carlyle narrates, 'in the gray windy evening . . . to walk to Stonehenge over the

---

*Although curiously the journals – so detailed and documentary in other respects – record very little about this episode, most of which he must have recreated for *English Traits* from memory.

bare upland; found it; saw it – a wild mournful, altogther enigmatic and bewildering sight – dreadfully cold too (in my thin coat)'. He settled in a nook away from the blast and lit a cigar, reflecting further on the 'dark, meaningless, gigantic dislocated stones; of which no creature will ever tell us the meaning . . . the prey now of Pedants and doleful creatures whose whole element seems one of emptiness and error!'. Emerson took a brighter view of the situation, observing that 'within the enclosure, grow buttercups, nettles, and all around, wild thyme, daisy, meadowsweet, goldenrod, thistle and the carpeting grass. Over us, larks were soaring and singing . . . we counted and measured by paces the biggest stones, and soon knew as much as any man can suddenly know of the inscrutable temple.' The atmosphere of the place kept Carlyle 'subdued and gentle', Emerson recalled. 'I plant cypresses wherever I go, and if I am in search of pain, I cannot go wrong,' he muttered psalmodically. 'The spot, the gray blocks and their rude order, which refuses to be disposed of, suggested to him the flight of ages, and the succession of religions.'

As twilight thickened and rain began to fall, they walked the two miles back to their inn. It had the recommendation of Dickens and Forster, but the place had seen better days. Writing to Jane from 'a most lonesome and rather dilapidated bedroom', Carlyle continued to moan. 'We got Tea, the worst in nature, without cream . . . The place is one of those Coach villages which have been ruined by railways; once the great road from Exeter to London, 12 coaches a day . . . now left sad and silent, the big inn rotting and not even milk to be had.' The next morning they returned to Stonehenge in the company of an antiquary acting as a guide, before taking a dogcart across Salisbury Plain to Wilton, ancestral home to the Earls of Pembroke, where they viewed the treasures and were given a replenishing lunch of 'bread, meats, peaches, grapes and wine' by the housekeeper. On to Salisbury and the cathedral, and then by train to Bishopstoke where they were put up for the night by Arthur Helps, a senior civil servant and bellettrist.

The following morning it rained hard and the three men spent the time sitting in Helps's study, 'disagreeing to the utmost, amicably'. What was the theory, the *idea* behind American society? the Englishman asked. Emerson rose to the bait. 'I bethought myself neither of caucuses nor congresses, neither of presidents nor of cabinet-ministers, nor of such as would make of America another Europe.' Instead he 'opened the dogma of no-government and non-resistance, and anticipated the objections and the fun and procured a kind of hearing for it'. Then dinner was announced. 'As I had just taken in the conversation the saint's part,' Emerson wrote, 'C. refused to go out before me – "he was altogether too wicked". I planted my back against the wall, and our host wittily rescued us from the dilemma, by saying he was the wickedest and would walk out first.' Later that day they visited Winchester Cathedral, where Carlyle, in almost maudlin mood, took hold of the hands of the marble effigy of its architect William of Wykeham, 'and patted them affectionately, for he rightly values the brave man who built Windsor and this Cathedral and the School here, and New College at Oxford'.

Back home in Chelsea late that night, he wrote a mellow letter to a friend describing Emerson as 'a man of genius and worth in his American way; somewhat moonshiny here and there in the results he arrives at, but beautiful in speculation if you leave practice out'. In the words of Professor Joseph Slater, editor of the definitive edition of their correspondence, all the tensions and polarities between two men so near in philosophy yet so distant in temperament 'were somehow muted by tolerance, by good humor, perhaps by the thought that this too was a sort of farewell party. The Stonehenge trip was a recapitulation and a coda; it was also a resolution of discord.'

Why? Perhaps primarily because Emerson had in the course of this English tour become less deferential to Carlyle and grown more forceful, confident and even provocative in the expression of his moonshiny views. He knew he had nothing to learn from Carlyle now ('every hero becomes a bore at last') and felt assured from the latter's failure to refute some of his propositions that he had the best of their argument. He knew too that the United States of America, travelling light through wide-open spaces with democracy and individualism as its gospel, were ultimately on the winning track, while Carlyle sat Canute-like in a civilisation top-heavy with tradition and class, vainly urging tides to turn back. Emerson was not one for petty triumphalism. He found plenty to admire in England and the English: but they could no longer faze him by waving the primogeniture of history in his face. And Carlyle, like all bullies, intellectual or otherwise, was more inclined to respect a strong and combative opponent than to indulge a weakly agreeable one.

Besides, Emerson had also gathered his own band of disciples, earnest young men who looked westwards for hope and who had assembled at that dank soirée in Mrs Massey's Mancunian parlour. One of their number, Henry Sutton, wrote *The Evangel of Love*, a non-denominational theological tract which quivers and quakes with Emersonian rhetoric – 'Every man his own priest; his own church; his own Delphi. TRUST THYSELF: that is almost, in these times, the first of Christian necessities' – as it looks to the truth that runs through all religions – 'Pagan, Mahomet, Jew, Papist, Episcopalian or Dissenter: all are to be embraced in the arms of your affection.' Through the 1850s and 1860s Emerson's influence on certain wings of English thought became ever more diffuse: scholars have found traces of it in John Ruskin's criticism and Charles Kingsley's novel *Alton Locke*, while Matthew Arnold wrote a laudatory sonnet on the flyleaf of a volume of his essays:

> . . . Strong is the soul, and wise, and beautiful:
> The seeds of godlike power are in us still:
> Gods are we, bards, saints, heroes, if we will . . .

'His influence has been as great in other than literary directions,' believed one of his first biographers, Moncure Conway. To illustrate which,

> when [Emerson] was last in England [in 1873], a philanthropic man, a Lord Mayor, asked to be introduced to Emerson, because, when he was a poor youth, the essay on Self-Reliance stimulated his energies and gave him his start to success. The late Dr Lankester, coroner of London, similarly regarded Emerson as the chief influence in his life, and when he died there was found in his pocket a well-pencilled copy of the Essays, which had been his companion through many years. Other similar instances have been related to me.

But Emerson exerted his most profound spiritual impact on that most pathetic and lovable of Victorian poets, Arthur Hugh Clough – an impact made all the deeper by Emerson's reciprocal sense on his return home that exposure to the younger man's 'genius' was 'the most real benefit I have had from my English visit'. From the start, despite the sixteen years between them, they were well-matched. Clough knew something of America at first hand and friendship with a Yankee would not have been hampered by the usual prejudices: born in 1819, he spent much of his early childhood in Charleston, South Carolina where his cotton-merchant father had business interests and where he had seen the realities of black slavery for himself. Back in England he became the star pupil of Dr Arnold's Rugby* and looked set to rank as one of the outstanding figures of his generation, as intellectually talented as he was morally virtuous. Gradually, however, a disease which would prove terminal set in: religious doubt – or, more specifically, the inability to decide what it was that he believed in.

Symptoms had already surfaced in 1848, when he first met Emerson. He was then a young don at Oriel College, Oxford, worrying about his *mauvaise foi* in subscribing to the Thirty-nine Articles of the Church of England (a condition of university Fellowship) and the implications of the Tractarian controversy (which had already led John Henry Newman back to Roman Catholicism), as well as his political stance (he had radical sympathies) and the itch of sexual desire (a bachelor state being another condition of Oxford Fellowship). Many others also suffered from Clough's queasiness and panic at all this. Ten years previously Carlyle had seemed to point a way through the maze of sect and dogma towards some clear, open moral terrain; but now he had become too hot-blooded, too rhetorical and reactionary, too cussedly oppositional, too damned grumpy, to serve as a convincing or even encouraging guide. Clever young men began to turn instead to Emerson, whose belief that the truth which an individual intuits through nature is stronger than any creed or church transcended the brambles and hedges, and rose into cloudy regions of cool simplicity and calm.

Clough first met Emerson in April 1848, when he invited the American to spend a few days with him in Oxford. Emerson accepted and the visit was a huge success. 'Everyone liked him,' wrote Clough to Dr Arnold's younger son Tom, 'and as the orthodox had mostly never heard of him, they did not suspect him. He is the quietest, plainest, unobtrusivist [sic] man possible – will talk but will rarely *discourse* to more than a single person – and wholly declines "roaring".' For Clough, stifled by the Oxford Establishment and its theological nit-picking, it was his openness of mind and spirit that he found so exhilarating. 'There is no dogmatism or arbitrariness or positiveness

---

*See p. 179 for an example of its moral ethos.

about him,' he continued to his brother, and he was 'much less Emersonian than his Essays'.

Emerson was looking for someone to accompany him to Paris. Tennyson had rejected an overture, but Clough accepted with delight: it was a pretext to leave Oxford that he had long been awaiting. They did not travel or lodge together, but Clough was, as Emerson put it, 'in Paris, my chief dependence at the dining hour & afterwards'. The turmoil of the new republic and the stirrings of socialism and communism preoccupied them, but they also visited the theatre, where they both thrilled to Rachel's acting in plays by Racine and discussed another ascendant social question – the position of women. Clough's diary gnomically records talk with Emerson, 'de sexualibus (of sexual matters)'. What does this imply? Emerson's journals only mention the prevalence of posters offering 'La Guerison des Maladies Secrètes (the cure for secret – venereal – diseases)' and the way that Clough talked 'so considerately of the grisette estate'. Had the young man resorted to a prostitute, one wonders, and did that add to his maelstrom of guilt and anxiety?

Having returned to London, more than ever determined to quit Oxford and the Church of England for good, Clough attended Emerson's guinea lectures in Portman Square and saw him regularly through the weeks preceding his departure. On 15 July he went to Liverpool to bid him farewell. The story goes – although neither party mentions the exchange in his letters or journals – that as the ship was about to set sail, Clough berated Emerson. 'You leave all of us young Englishmen without a leader. Carlyle has led us into the desert and he has left us there.'

'That is what all young men in England have said to me,' Emerson replied. Placing a benedictory hand on Clough's head, he left him with a mission. 'I ordain you Bishop of England, to go up and down among all the young men, and lead them into the promised land.'

Clough's failure to meet that challenge became one of the small private tragedies of the Victorian era. Emerson would remain hugely admiring of Clough – of his subtle but powerful satire of contemporary manners and morals, The Bothie of Tober-na-Vuolich, he wrote, 'I do not know of a poem more impregnated with the nineteenth century or fuller of tender force and shy, delicate humour' – but their only other meeting was problematic. In 1852 Clough fell in love with Florence Nightingale's cousin. Unable to find a remunerative teaching job which would allow him to marry comfortably, he solicited Emerson's help in finding some profitable work as a tutor in New England. Emerson was as ever obliging and encouraging. 'Come out and spend two or three months here in my house,' he replied. 'I will defend you from all outsiders, initiate you step by step into all the atrocities of republicanism.' So Clough crossed the Atlantic, and found bits of work and lodgings in Boston – the few days he spent with Emerson at Concord convinced him that he was better out of the way of Lidian's disconcertingly Swedenborgian temperament and erratic housekeeping. Nor were his conversations with Emerson quite what they had been four years previously: he still found him 'the only profound man in this country', beyond compare for 'real solidity of intellect', but to Carlyle he wrote that 'I find him altered from what he was in England – whether the effect of time or difference of place, I don't know. He seems to have much more of a made-up mind than I thought he had then – with plenty of common sense for all the ordinary matters of New England life.'

Lured back to England by a dull, safe civil service job, Clough married and had children, and occasionally wrote to Emerson. The remainder of his life was not happy. Nervous stress and depression continued to debilitate him. He died in 1861 at the age of forty-two, having attempted to subsume his own mental vacillations in devotion to the practical cause of his briskly purposeful cousin-in-law, Florence Nightingale. Something had gone terribly wrong – and although he had written some of the most exhilaratingly witty and original poetry of the century, Clough's friends and family could only mourn a sense of tragically wasted possibility. Emerson wrote to his widow that 'he interested me more than any other companion, when I first knew him, in 1848, by his rare freedom & manliness . . . his own frank entertainment of any good thought & this intellectuality seemed so little English – that I wrote home to my friends that I had found in London the best American'. He made virtually no mention of the sojourn of 1852–3. But in the Clough of 1848, one might say, Emerson found the Carlyle that he had dreamed of.

Emerson returned home at the end of July 1848 and immediately became a family man again, attending to his neurotic wife, small children and property, with his customary and reassuring air of gentle patience. Yet the experience of his English visit took time to assimilate and it was only in 1852 that he was able to begin weaving together the hundreds of relevant entries jotted in his journal into the coherent volume which was published four years later as *English Traits*. Divided into nineteen chapters* and based on the idea that the British genius was the result of a 'lucky fit' of race and place, this is in many respects a conventional book, following a format and itinerary familiar from many other such travellers' tales, and notable more for its easy, ancedotal tone, filtered from the experiences recounted above, than for any great depth of analytic insight. For a true account of Emerson's visits to England, turn to the journals.

Thus tempered to popular taste, *English Traits* proved a tremendous success, selling 5000 copies in its first three months on sale in the USA and 24,000 in Britain. Reviews were generally appreciative, despite the odd burst of knee-jerk Podsnappery ('if you don't like the country, d—n you – you can leave it,' spluttered the arch-conservative *New Quarterly Review*, despite the fact that Emerson plainly did like it and had gone home years ago). Carlyle, perhaps surprisingly, perhaps guiltily, was warmly enthusiastic, apparently untroubled by being characterised in its pages as someone 'driven by his disgust at the pettiness and the cant, into the preaching of Fate'. 'Not for seven years and more have I got hold of such a Book,' he wrote to the author in congratulation, '[a] Book by a real man, with eyes in his head; nobleness, wisdom, humour and many other things in the heart of him.'

For more exigent tastes, however, the flavour of *English Traits* was too anodyne. Clough, for instance, wrote to Emerson, 'I think you praise us too highly – I was anxious for more rebuke – and profitable reprimand'; or the novelist Nathaniel Hawthorne, then the American Consul at Liverpool, who was spot-on in his view that 'it will please the English only too well; for you give them credit for the possession, in very large measure, of all the qualities that they pride, or value themselves upon; and they will never comprehend that what you deny is far greater and higher than what you concede'. But now it was for

---

*Namely: 'First Visit to England', 'Voyage to England', 'Land', 'Race', 'Ability', 'Manners', 'Truth', 'Character', 'Cockayne', 'Wealth', 'Aristocracy', 'Universities', 'Religion', 'Literature', '*The Times*', 'Stonehenge', 'Personal', 'Result' ('England is the best of actual nations . . . the American system is more democratic, more humane; yet the American people do not yield more inventions or books or benefits, than the English'), 'Speech at Manchester'.

others to take up the debate between the Old and New Worlds. With the breakdown of shaky compromises between Northern and Southern states, the Union was driven to Civil War and Emerson had to turn his attention to bloody and brutal conflict, which the hopeful precepts of Transcendentalism could not resolve.

In 1872, after the fighting was over and a new iron had entered America's soul, he returned to Europe for a third and final visit, this time accompanied by his daughter Ellen (Lidian stayed in Concord, supervising the rebuilding of their fire-damaged home). He was now positively famous in England, but his memory was beginning to fail and he treated his two months' stay as a purely private visit, without any professional commitments. His yearning for mental stimulation had subsided: although he heard Ruskin lecture and breakfasted with Gladstone, contact with English notabilities no longer meant much to him. He also met Carlyle once more: it was an insignificant encounter. Over the twenty-five years since the trip to Stonehenge their philosophies had drifted irreconcilably apart. On the matter of the American Civil War, they agreed to disagree, the ever-tolerant Emerson shrugging off Carlyle's blackly reactionary attitude to the Slavery Question as 'no more than could be expected' from someone who 'purposely made exaggerated statements merely to astonish his listeners'. The frequency of their correspondence had dwindled too, and increasingly they exchanged only pleasantries and photographs. Talk of Carlyle visiting America to see it for himself came to nothing.

In Emerson's papers of 1870 there survives a fragment of a letter in which his patience with Carlyle's increasingly insane published fulminations against the 'moonshine' spouted by 'the friends of humanity' briefly snapped. 'How can I write to you? Your mood is not mine & you choose to sit like destiny at the door of nations, & predict calamity, & contradict with irresistible wit your own morale, & ridicule shatter the attempts of little men at humanity & charity & uphold the offender.' But he must have thought better of sending this, because no such excoriation ever arrived in Cheyne Row: they were both old men now, losing their minds, and neither had the inclination to fan new flames from the ashes of the past. Carlyle died in 1881, raging to the last. Emerson died a year later, at the ripe age of seventy-nine: aphasia had robbed him of virtually all his faculty of language, but his deathbed found him quite serene and prepared for whatever might come after.

Most nineteenth-century American visitors came to England with a score to settle. Humiliated by the patronising likes of Fanny Trollope and determined not to succumb to what Australians today term 'the colonial cringe', they could be aggressively defensive, even crowing – and thus the loud, vulgar Yankee, throwing his or her weight around and generally behaving in a brazen fashion, becomes a stock figure of *Punch* cartoons and the Victorian novel. It was as though the New World had an invisible war to win. In Hawthorne's view there was 'an account to settle between us and them for the contemptuous jealousy with which (since it has ceased to be unmitigated contempt) they regard us; and if they do not make us amends by coming humbly to ask our assistance they must do it by fairly acknowledging us as their masters'. Over the next century, until the aftermath of the Second World War and the Marshall Plan, such sentiments ripple through the American attitude, resonating through the work of writers as disparate as Mark Twain, Henry James and Edmund Wilson.

For Emerson it was rather different. Yes, he had a great sense of America's destiny and yes, he found the English swagger daunting. Yes, as Henry James Sr graphically put it, he was 'a man without a handle'. But he always knew who he was and where he belonged – no man more so – and therefore he could travel light, without encumbering baggage or a preconceived agenda. In his lack of prejudice, he stands as the ideal visitor: widely curious, open to the new, and ready to take both places and men as found, not as presumed – unlike Hippolyte Taine, the French intellectual whose *Notes sur l'Angleterre*, published in 1872 and based on his visit of 1861–2, is comparable to Emerson's *English Traits* in scope and aim. But Taine's obsessive rationalism led him to see everything in terms of scientific cause and effect. He piles on the statistics, balancing the advantages of (a) against the perils of (b), and draws eccentric conclusions, such as that English women have long teeth because they eat so much meat. Emerson was more intuitive, more poetically subtle and supple of mind. He did not aim to construct a great synthesising statement, nor was he much concerned with facts and figures. He preferred surprises, like the sight of the clergyman changing his shoes on the train. He was, as Clough had put it, Emerson before he was Emersonian.

The purpose of his visit to England was not missionary. He lectured when he was asked to, as a means of making money as much as from any desire to impart or impose his wisdom. While he was here, the term 'Transcendentalism' probably never passed his lips – certainly the journals of the period make no mention of it. In his heart, he had crossed the Atlantic for personal reasons, poignant ones. He was lonely. He wanted to make friends. He needed conversation. And in unexpected places he found them.

CHAPTER 4

The Psychic Cloud: Yankee Spirit-rappers

As he probably would have wished, Emerson's visit left its mark on lone individuals, not masses or institutions. For all the respect in which the man himself came to be held among freethinkers, the philosophy behind his teachings never significantly established itself across the Atlantic. Transcendentalism as a creed was too generous and optimistic, as well as too vague and democratic, for the middle classes of Victorian England, a species who preferred to swallow their religion straight – either without sugar (if evangelical and severely practical) or with (if moderately Anglican and reasonable). It was one thing to acknowledge that Emerson was a nice and even, for a Yankee, good fellow; quite another to believe that what he wrote held theological water. Better to stick with the Ten Commandments and get about one's business.

Yet that is not quite the full story. Shortly after Emerson returned home, a dubious offshoot of Transcendentalist thought did manage to slip through the side door and penetrate the thick-skinned British mass consciousness. What this mysterious visitor offered didn't come in the guise of religion – it wasn't even entirely respectable – but, in a country renowned for its scepticism, it has commanded ever since a remarkable level of devotion and fascination. It was most commonly called spirit-rapping, and it is a very rum business indeed.

Spirit-rapping may have been to some extent a 'pastime' (as the historian of the occult and supernatural Brian Inglis rightly insists), but it was also a phenomenon born of an age redefining the foundation of its beliefs. The mid-nineteenth century was not a time in which anything could be comfortably believed. God was plainly sickening, according to reports from some quarters, but elsewhere strenuous evangelical efforts were being made to keep him alive: the prognosis was uncertain. Other educated people felt themselves, as Matthew Arnold put it in his 'Stanzas from the Grande Chartreuse',

> Wandering between two worlds, one dead
> The other striving to be born

By which the poet meant that the 'secular' explanation of the natural world – as set forth in quantum physics, evolutionary theory, relativity and so forth – was not yet clearly fixed or fully understood, while the old orthodoxies – Virgin birth, the miracles of Christ and the Genesis account of creation – were looking increasingly fabulous and unlikely. The stronger minded kept a firm grasp on the idea that the ethics of Christianity were its bedrock, but ordinary folk needed matter with which to satisfy the cravings of their baser imaginations. So somewhere in the narrow interstices between science and superstition, on the rich soil of human credulity, spirit-rapping sprang up and flowered.

It may have been a craze, a vogue and a delusion, but it was not without some sort of historical substance. Spirit-rapping should be regarded as a manifestation of the venerable and ramifying tradition, virtually universal to all cultures, which holds that certain men and women are singled out by a special capacity either to communicate with invisible forces or to be possessed by them, and that this capacity affords them wisdom: shamanists, the oracle at Delphi, the Biblical prophets, the witches and wizards of the Middle Ages, the fashionable clairvoyants of Georgian London, the revelations of Swedenborg and Blake are all kin to the spirit-rappers.

What was new in the late eighteenth and early nineteenth centuries was the possibility that such powers might be verifiable according to the logic and laws of Newtonian science rather than the result of divine sanction (or curse). Mesmerism, for instance, was based in the notion not of heavenly powers but of a pervasive fluid which could be tapped by magnetism (its life-giving qualities are parodically commemorated in the Act One finale of Mozart's *Così fan tutte*). Trances, hypnotic or somnambulistic, were also thought to be induced by 'odic force' – a blue and yellow charge contained in the body, the effects of which could be communicated through the ends of the fingers (hence the archetypal magician's pose). Angélique Cottin, the fourteen-year-old French girl who in 1846 was observed to repel furniture simply by touching it, would have been burnt at the stake in 1646; two hundred years later she was regarded as an exemplar of a medical condition in which 'a redundancy of electricity congregated upon the involuntary nerves'.

America had its share of all this too, from the witches of Salem and the ecstatic spirit communings of the Shakers to the sideshow of

Andrew Jackson Davis, the celebrated 'Seer of Poughkeepsie', an illiterate who turned sonorous scholar and prophet when he 'went under'. But something new in the history of mediums began in the winter of 1848, when the perfectly ordinary Fox family moved into a perfectly ordinary house near the town of Rochester in New York state and fell victim to a poltergeist of the aggressively banging and clattering type familiar from report since the early Middle Ages. As so often, it was children who intuited what was happening and how to deal with it: the Foxes' daughters, Margaretta and Catherine, aged fifteen and twelve, knew the source of the trouble to be an unquiet ghost and began to play games with it. When they snapped their fingers the ghost rapped in response. Soon they were communicating yes and no, and the letters of the alphabet, and eventually they built up the tale told by a pedlar murdered in the house and buried in the basement (which was waterlogged and not therefore open to inspection).

But it was what emerged next that caused the sensation: the sisters were not dependent on the poltergeist, but appeared to hold the power to produce or provoke rapping noises wherever they were, along with other effects, such as the moving of furniture, especially tables, and the playing of musical instruments by invisible agency. This was a previously unrecorded phenomenon. Although the spontaneous movement of inanimate objects was a defining mark of the existence of a poltergeist, never before had it been observed that the motor was the force of a living individual. A committee of local ladies searched the girls and found no evidence of trickery, but the almighty dollar soon got the better of them and they allowed their dubious abilities to be touted around as entertainment: in 1850 they established themselves in a Manhattan hotel and began charging for visitations.*

---

*In November 1852, Dickens's magazine *Household Words* published an article , 'The Ghost of the Cock Lane Ghost', in which one Mrs Culver, a relative of the Fox sisters, announced that she had been privy to their fraudulence. 'The raps are produced by the toes,' she said. 'Catherine told me to warm my feet, or put them in warm water, and it would then be easier work to rap; she said that she had sometimes to warm her feet three or four times in the course of an evening.' The method enabled her to produce as many as 'a hundred and fifty raps in succession . . . Catherine told me how to manage to answer the questions. She said it was generally easy enough to answer right, if the one who asked the questions called the alphabet.'

Thirty-six years later, Catherine Fox herself recanted, admitting that she had learnt a trick of cracking her knee joints to make the rapping sound and calling the whole thing 'the greatest rubbish of the century'. But she was by then a confirmed alcoholic and her confession does not suffice as an explanation.

Over the next few years their previously unheard-of feats were repeated and surpassed, mostly by outright charlatans. 'Scarcely a village can be found which is not infected with the delusion,' sighed a disapproving Methodist newspaper *The Olive Branch*, and by 1853 it was estimated that there were 30,000 people in the USA claiming the same sort of powers as those displayed by the Fox sisters. As the press fuelled the craze with ever more extravagantly tall stories, it diversified. Few remained content with tilting tables or speaking in alien voices. Extra dramatic effects, like the ringing of invisible bells or the vision of disembodied luminous hands, intensified the atmosphere. Healing mediums caused palsy to be stilled, blind eyes to be opened and the effects of poison to be reversed. Other miracles were more artistic in nature: several ladies were guided by the shade of Mozart to tinkle on the piano or to paint with the hand of the Italian masters. Miss Lord of Portland, Maine, was possessed by an Indian spirit, name of Black Hawk, who played musical instruments and spoke impeccably broken English. Mrs Burbank Felton specialised in communicating other-worldly solutions to legal quandaries. All over New England, tidings of comfort and joy were received from the rapping spirits of celebrities ranging from Jesus Christ and John the Baptist to Benjamin Franklin and Percy Bysshe Shelley.

William Howitt, a British historian of the supernatural writing in 1863, sought an explanation in the highly strung, earnest intensity and susceptibility endemic to New England, which Henry James would analyse so perceptively in his novel *The Bostonians*: 'The Americans are conspicuously a more nervous and excitable people than we are. They have grown up rapidly under new climatic influences, new blendings of blood and international idiosyncracies ... their minds like their institutions have shot up with a rapidity of growth resembling that of tropical jungles, and have, in consequence, greater openness and receptivity.' England's 'denser atmosphere, less electrical and magnetic in its character' was 'less favourable to the transmission of spiritual impressions.'

The Americans preferred to interpret the marvel theologically. America was under a divinely sent psychic cloud, which hung like a blessing over the young nation. The spread of mediumship was evidence of a 'rainbow bridge' connecting heaven and earth, the quotidian with the hereafter, and it confirmed America's status as a

New Eden whose inhabitants were, in the words of Uriah Clark's *Plain Guide to Spiritualism*, 'immortal, ever-progressive beings, who through eternal ages must grow in goodness, wisdom and glory above our highest conceptions'. These were Emersonian sentiments, but Emerson disapproved violently of what amounted to a quick-fix Transcendentalism which mistook a mere frisson for ultimate wisdom. His belief that every man could by meditation come to apprehend the immanent over-soul of existence was not to be confused with what in 1856 he described in his journal as 'dunces seeking dunces in the dark of what they call the spiritual world, preferring snores and gastric noises to the voice of any muse'. But confuse the dunces it did, the awestruck Abraham Lincoln not least.

Of all the American progeny of the Fox sisters, none remains more impressive and mystifying than Daniel Home (pronounced Hume). His spirit-rapping became one of the wonders of the age, combined as it was with the ability to levitate and elongate himself, and a staggering capacity to sit alone in the middle of a room and set all its contents humming and dancing. His reputation was further enhanced by his eschewal of the stagey darkness and spooky silence in which most of his colleagues insisted on operating and his readiness to perform in a half-light, as well as his refusal to charge a fee for a seance. Home did not invariably sink into a trance and the identity of the spirits that attended him was often vague. He made no claim to impart wisdom or even information: his fate was to be the passive recipient of forces beyond his control. 'He was nothing but the instrument of the phenomena and had never pretended to evoke spirits or exercise any influence over them,' explained his second wife in her memoir *D. D. Home: His Life and Mission*. 'He exercised no more volition in the matter than a [telegraph] wire.' The antics which surrounded him might seem meaningless, but nobody ever decisively caught him out.

Leaving aside the source and nature of his abilities, his life and his personality remain curious. Born in 1833 near Edinburgh, he liked to claim (with no justification) that his father was the bastard son of the Earl of Home and later gave himself the Earl's middle name of 'Dunglas' to make this more plausible. The significant side of his ancestry, however, was his mother's: she came from a Highland family which had for many generations claimed the power of foretelling death. For unknown reasons, as an infant he was taken away from his beloved mother and adopted by his maternal aunt, who in 1842 emigrated with him to Connecticut. A nervous and delicate child, he suffered from consumptive symptoms and a tendency to fainting. His nature was artistic and sensitive: he played the piano, sang, recited and sometimes saw things that were happening far away. At the age of thirteen he had one such vision, which confirmed that he had inherited his mother's second sight. A school friend appeared at the foot of his bed and then made three circles in the air – he had died, it transpired, three days earlier. His aunt, a strict Presbyterian, tried to put a stop to such nonsense, but in 1851, when he was seventeen, his mother died and the house duly erupted in fashionable raps and judders. 'Yours is a glorious mission,' the spirit of his mother had told him. 'You will convince the infidel, cure the sick and console the weeping.' But Home's aunt decided that he was in league with the devil, threw a chair at him and called in the minister for an exorcism. More raps and judders ensued, and Home was thrown out into a world that could scarcely have been more ready to welcome him.

Friends gave him lodging and he proceeded if not to convince the infidel, then to confound the sceptics. His mere presence – tall, pale, spindly, boyish and dandified, with grey-blue eyes, long bony hands, large sharp teeth and a soulfully morose expression – was arresting. In manner he was gentle, complaisant and somewhat too ingratiating, but there was something palpably sinister about the way he could step into a room and charge it with a dense, queasy atmosphere, even before the seance had formally begun. He did not require the joining of hands or insist on the cover of darkness. When his powers were operating at full strength the floor would vibrate, causing furniture to rear up like a frightened horse. Such things were beyond mirrors, beyond illusion, and they occurred without any special stimulus. Two clear-thinking, unbiased Harvard professors watched how, in a well-lit room, he sat calmly on a chair and put a table some feet away under his influence. Having rocked and skidded about, it then 'poised itself on two legs and remained in this position for some thirty seconds, when no other person was in contact with it'. The Harvard report concluded with what would become a familiar verdict on Home's activities: 'We were constrained to admit that there was an almost constant manifestation of some intelligence which seemed, at least, to be independent of the circle . . . we know that we were not imposed upon or deceived.'

Being vain and snobbish, and dependent on patronage rather than vulgar dollar bills for his 'services', Home worried continuously about people's opinion of him. Perhaps as a way of giving his spiritual gift respectable scientific status, he planned to train as a physician, but his tubercular condition prevented this. Anxious not be seen as a diabolist or a careerist, he claimed to have a mission which put him 'at God's disposal', although it is hard to see that anything for which he was responsible ever did anyone any quantifiable good. And it was for the purely selfish need to relieve his lungs (or so he wrote in his autobiography, although it is difficult to see why smoggy London should be recommended to a consumptive) that he left America in 1855 and made his way to England.

He was not the first spirit-rapper to cross the Atlantic. That distinction belonged to Mrs W. R. Hayden, an attractive and genteel young Bostonian, wife to the former editor of a newspaper entitled The *Star-Spangled Banner*. She arrived in London in 1852 and established herself in Queen Anne Street where, so her advertisement announced, 'spiritual phenomena would be forthcoming from 12–3 p.m. and from 4–6 p.m. daily'. Other Americans followed in her wake: for example, a certain Mrs Roberts, 'tall and solemn of aspect', who set up at 1a Devonshire Street. The star attraction of her seances was that favourite spirit personage Percy Bysshe Shelley, whose messages via Mrs Roberts could be guaranteed to contain 'many sentiments of a distinctly religious character'.

In comparison with what came later, Mrs Hayden's seances were modest affairs, in which the number of raps indicated letters of the alphabet, the spirit laboriously spelling out answers to questions. Professor Augustus de Morgan, Professor of Mathematics at University College, tried and failed to catch Mrs Hayden out. The raps were 'clean, clear, faint sounds' he recorded, making the sort of noise 'knitting needles would make, if dropped from a small distance on to a marble slab, and instantly checked by a damper of some kind'. The spirit at that session conveniently turned out to be de Morgan's sister-in-law, who had died seventeen years previously: de Morgan decided not to ask her any questions out loud, but to 'send' them to her mentally. Did she, for instance, remember the subject of a certain letter he had written before she died? The correct answer came back from the raps: chess. De Morgan left, 'perfectly satisfied that something, or somebody, was reading my thoughts'. G. H. Lewes, however, was less than perfectly satisfied. He too privately wrote down questions to the spirit and 'sent' them mentally:

> Did the ghost of Hamlet's father have seventeen noses?
> *Yes*
> Was Pontius Pilate an American?
> *No*
> Is Mrs Hayden an impostor?
> *Yes*

In November 1852 Dickens's magazine *Household Words* published a more detailed account of Mrs Hayden's doings, jointly written by two journalists who had booked a seance together, at the cost of a guinea per head, under the pseudonyms of Messrs Brown and Thompson. For 'Thompson' Mrs Hayden rapped out the word 'mother' – a pretty safe bet – and the uplifting but unspecific 'Dear Son, I am well pleased to see you, I watch over you and God blesses you'. But after that every fact came across totally wrong – the name of Thompson's mother was not Timok or anything like it, and she had died six rather than twenty-three years previously. 'Brown' fared no better. He too was told that his mother wished to speak to him 'from the other side', despite the fact that she was still alive and well. The spirit then informed Brown that her name was Mary, 'falling into a trap which Brown had laid, possibly by dwelling with the pencil over [the letters] M and A and R and Y [laid out on a chart in front of the medium]'. Brown then wrote a question for the spirit – 'How many children shall I have?' – allowing Mrs Hayden to know only that an answer in numbers was required. When '136' was rapped out, Thompson lapsed into 'ill-timed mirth' and the proceedings were brought to a summary close.

Perhaps because of the consequent public exposé, Mrs Hayden returned to America. Later she qualified as a physician and became renowned for her diagnostic gifts, as well as her clairvoyant consultancy with the Globe Insurance Company.

In the years before Mrs Hayden's arrival, intelligent interest in the supernatural in England had focused on the trance states induced by somnambulism and hypnotism. These went under the catch-all title of 'mesmerism', although they had little relation to Anton Mesmer's original theories of animal magnetism. The more rigorous investigators classified somnambulism and hypnotism within the science of 'electro-biology', which explored the still intriguing notion of a living organism's electrical or 'odic' properties. The majority only saw dark forces at work: men were invariably the entrancers, women usually the entranced. From this period dates the image of the dark and swarthy hypnotist with piercing eyes, vatic beard and libidinous propensities who made 'passes' – 'hot', 'magnetic', 'stroking' passes – over a subject and made her an instrument of his will, transferring thoughts and commands from his active mind into her passive body. Certain 'sensitive' subjects became more than their master's marionettes, however – sent under, they also released in themselves the facility to receive, like a radio or television, communications from above and beyond and far away (Oliver Twist has just such a 'mesmeric' perception of Fagin and Bill Sikes while lying in his sickbed at Mr Brownlow's). Medical men also keenly explored the applications of such trances to anaesthetic ends and it was even suggested that hypnotism could be used to reform criminal temperaments. Wilberforce, Gladstone, Dickens, George Eliot, Faraday and Darwin were among those convinced, and in 1844 Harriet Martineau went so far as to claim that she had been cured of a terminal cancer by hypnotised auto-suggestion. But the overnight Yankee sensation of spirit-rapping would divide opinion more.

Arriving in London, Daniel Home was accommodated at Cox's Hotel in Jermyn Street – its owner being a votary of the spiritual world, all charges were waived. With the help of some introductions to well-connected Americans based in England, Home proceeded to launch himself in high society with a series of seances involving spectacular displays of his powers: Lady Waldegrave, Baroness Grey de Ruthyn, Lady Combermere and the Marchioness of Hastings all took him up and in, as did the novelist and politician Edward Bulwer-Lytton, a keen Rosicrucian and disinterested student of the blacker arts, who regarded Home's powers as the 'scientifically' deducible result of a 'preponderance of the electric fluid'. Other fine minds took a similar line: the eminent physicist Sir David Brewster, inventor of the kaleidoscope and a pioneer in the study of optics and electricity, went so far as to conduct a formal examination of the case. Brewster took a predetermined view that to talk of spirit-rapping in terms of supernatural agency was tosh unworthy of an enlightened age; what interested him was the possibility of putting paid to the whole business by establishing some grounds of rational explanation. Michael Faraday, doyen of the Royal Institution and a genius in the field of physics surpassing Brewster, as well as being a profoundly religious man, had already written a letter to *The Times* asserting that the movement of tables which occurred in seances could be caused by the ordinary pressure of fingertips on their surfaces. But as Brewster was forced to observe, this scarcely accounted for the fact that Home never touched any of the furniture he apparently propelled – whatever it was that caused the rumpus, it had nothing to do with his fingers. And meeting the spiritualistically inclined Earl of Dunraven one day on the steps of the Athenaeum, Brewster told him that what he had seen of Home was 'quite inexplicable by fraud, or by any physical laws with which they were acquainted'.

Yet when the story found its way into the newspapers, via a letter that Home had written to a friend in America, Brewster insisted that it was all a matter of theatrical illusion, effected by 'mechanical' means – what those were he could not say, but he had witnessed enough 'to satisfy myself that they could all be produced by human hands and feet, and to prove that some of them, at least, had such an origin'. Others present at the seance publicly repudiated this, affirming that Brewster had, at the time, been utterly baffled by the goings-on and that Home simply could not have conjured them up. It looked as though Brewster had cynically decided to lie in order to save natural science's skin.*

The views of other pillars of the intelligentsia were split, not altogether predictably. Dickens, for instance, intensely interested though he was in mesmeric hypnotism, turned down Fanny Trollope's invitation to one of Home's seances. As he explained to her in June 1855, 'I altogether want faith in the thing. I have not the least belief in the awful unseen world being available for evening parties at so much a night. And although I should be ready to receive enlightenment from any source, I must say that I have very little hope of it from the spirits,

---

*And this was indeed confirmed in 1869 when Brewster's daughter published his letters in a pious volume entitled *The Home Life of Sir David Brewster*. To a friend he had written at the time that the seance had included 'unaccountable rappings', the levitation of a heavy table 'when no hand was upon it', and a bell which floated through the air and placed itself in his grasp.

who express themselves through mediums, as I have never yet observed them to talk anything but nonsense.'

But Thackeray, Ruskin and Emerson's friend Richard Monckton Milnes felt otherwise, recording their astonishment at what they saw with their own eyes, and Bulwer-Lytton and his son Robert continued to investigate. It was the latter who introduced Home to Robert Browning and his wife Elizabeth, visiting England from their home in Florence, where discussion of the spiritualist question was much in vogue among the expatriate Americans and British. A meeting with Home was arranged, at Elizabeth's request, *chez* his devotees Mr and Mrs Rymer of Ealing. There they witnessed a table rearing up of its own accord without its cloth or ornaments sliding off; an ectoplasmic hand which touched Browning 'with a soft and fleshly pat' and another which picked up a garland of clematis and placed it on Elizabeth's head. Then an accordion levitated itself and began to play, before Home went into a trance and began to speak gibberish in the voice of the Rymers' dead son Wat. 'These hands seemed to Robert and me to come from under the table,' wrote an enthralled Elizabeth, 'but Mr Lytton saw them rise out of *the wood of the table* – also he tells me . . . that he saw a spiritual (so called) arm elongate itself as much as two yards across the table and then float away to the windows where it disappeared.' On reflection, Browning decided that the occasion had been a charade, concocted in the half-light out of 'cheat and imposture' and that Home was nothing more than a highly skilled puppeteer. But Elizabeth, a religious freethinker who had recently been hypnotised into a magnetic trance, was deeply stirred by what had happened. She wrote to her sister Henrietta in dismay that Home had become

> a tabooed subject in this house – Robert and I taking completely different views, and he being a good deal irritated by any discussion of it . . . I think that what chiefly went against the exhibition in Robert's mind, was the trance at the conclusion during which the medium talked a great deal of much such twaddle as may be heard in any fifth-rate conventicle. But according to my theory (well thought out and digested) this does not militate at all against the general facts . . . To me it was wonderful and conclusive.

Browning would have none of it. Obscurely jealous, he flung the numinous garland, which Elizabeth had taken as a souvenir and hung on her dressing-table mirror, out of the window and demanded that the Rymers should arrange another seance at which he might make more searching inquiry. Just now, they replied, that would not be convenient: Home was ill, as he often was. But a few days later Home and the Rymers paid an unexpected call on the Brownings. There was much embarrassment as the poet declined to shake hands with the medium, huffing at the way his request had been turned down. 'If you are not out of that door in half a minute,' Browning roared, 'I'll fling you down the stairs.' 'Oh, dear Mr Home, do not, do not blame me. I am so sorry, but I am not to blame,' pleaded Elizabeth, according to Home's memoirs, as Browning became 'pallid with rage . . . his movements as he swayed backwards and forwards on his chair [being] like those of a maniac'.

Home gathered his dignity and made for Italy, at which point his story becomes decidedly rum. In Florence he moved among the expatriate colony. Elizabeth Barrett Browning, one of their number, heard reports via the (aptly named) American sculptor Hiram Powers of ever more Gothic manifestations inspired by Home's presence: the Countess Orsini's grand piano floated into the air while she was playing it; ghostly monks invaded his seance in an old convent, creating mayhem and tearing scandalously at the ladies' skirts; a long-dead murderer, talking Italian, materialised as a hand with parchment-skinned fingers. Amid all the furore, Home fell ill and went to recuperate in the home of a titled English lady separated from her husband. This was Home's first crucial mistake: it was one thing to raise spirits from the dead, quite another to offend against the decencies of married life, and from this moment on a distinct, if indefinable, aura of sleaze hangs about his behaviour and motives.

Protestant societies were accustomed to the idea of individuals communicating directly with the other side, but in Catholic countries such bypassing of the laws of the established church and ordained priesthood was liable to be interpreted as sorcery. Home was quietly warned by the Minister of the Interior to watch out. He did so, but he could not stop the spread of tales of how he had illicitly charged the making of an expensive greatcoat to someone else's account and how Mrs Trollope now cut him because of 'some failure in his moral character'. Elizabeth Barrett Browning defensively regarded such matters as subject to 'an enormous amount of exaggeration' and decided that 'although Home may have been blameable, and gave sign of a vulgar yankee nature . . . there was nothing at all of the criminal character which we all supposed here'.

But something was going on, as evinced by his brush with material death when some unidentified entity stabbed him as he made his way back to his lodgings one night. When he recovered he announced that the spirits had informed him that he was not a worthy vessel and that his powers would desert him for a year. (Was the cause of this simply nervous exhaustion, one wonders; or could he have been the victim of some sort of blackmail or intimidation?) He went on to Rome, where he peremptorily converted to Catholicism and was granted audience with a sympathetic Pope Pius IX. In Paris, his powers returned, with loud rappings on the appointed stroke of midnight, and he became more than an object of fashionable curiosity – historians have even compared his brief period of influence at the court of the Tuileries to that of Rasputin at Tsarskoe Selo.* More success at the most exalted social levels greeted him in St Petersburg, where he married the beautiful seventeen-year-old heiress Sacha de Kroll and assured himself a comfortable income which relieved him from reliance on charitable donation and hospitality.

Back in London in 1859 with his wife and baby son Grisha, Home found lodgings in Sloane Street. Once again titled hostesses vied for his attentions, with Sacha's charms making him even more of a social catch. Shelley's daughter-in-law Lady Jane was fascinated and Lady Palmerston, Lady Pollock, Lady Compton, Lady Loftus Otway, Lady Helena Newnham, Lady Egerton of Tatton and the Duchess of Sutherland extended their patronage. But his closest alliance was with Susanna Milner Gibson, wife to the President of the Board of Trade and the mourning mother of a dead son. She was a kind, impulsive and somewhat dizzy creature, who had previously involved herself with the plight of political refugees like Mazzini and Kossuth, and was much gossiped about. Now her mansion in Hyde Park Place became the venue for a series of Monday seances, which attracted dignitaries, celebrities and the press even as they repelled her poor mortified husband. 'Well, my dear, at it again, I see,' he would groan if he

---

*Home's fall from the favour of Napoleon III and Eugénie in 1857 was much gossiped about. See Horace Wyndham, *Mr Sludge the Medium* (London, 1937), Chapter 5: 'Phenomena in Paris'; and also p. 146 for the explanation of the court physician Dr Barthez.

inadvertently opened the door on something spiritual and tremendous. One day he was obliged to report to the House of Commons on his role in the progress of a treaty betweeen England and France. 'I have been a medium—' he thoughtlessly began his speech, before being drowned by laughter from the benches.

It is from this period that some remarkably detailed and circumstantial accounts of Home's performances date: one which caused a great stir appeared anonymously (it was actually written by Robert Bell) in the new *Cornhill* magazine, edited by Thackeray, entitled 'Stranger than Fiction'. Apart from the usual rocking tables, moaning accordions, tinkling bells and moving hands, it also contained this memorable description of a levitation:

> Mr Home was seated next to the window. Through the semi-darkness his head was dimly visible against the curtains, and his hands might be seen in a faint white heap before him. Presently, he said, in a quiet voice, 'My chair is moving – I am off the ground – don't notice me – talk of something else' or words to that effect. It was very difficult to restrain the curiosity . . . but we talked , incoherently enough, upon some indifferent topic. I was sitting nearly opposite to Mr Home, and I saw his hands disappear from the table, and his head vanish into the deep shadow beyond. In a moment or two more he spoke again. This time his voice was in the air above our heads. He had risen from his chair to a height of four or five feet from the ground. As he ascended higher he described his position, as at first perpendicular, and afterwards horizontal. He said he felt as if he had been turned in the gentlest manner, as a child is turned in the arms of a nurse. In a moment or two more, he told us that he was going to pass across the window, against the gray, silvery light in which he would be visible. We watched in profound stillness, and saw his figure pass from one side of the window to the other, feet foremost, lying horizontally in the air. He spoke to us as he passed, and told us he would turn the reverse way, and cross the window; which he did. His own tranquil confidence in the safety of what seemed from below a situation of the most novel peril, gave confidence to everybody else; but, with the strongest nerves, it was impossible not to be conscious of a certain sensation of fear or awe. He hovered round the circle for several minutes, and passed, this time perpendicularly, over our heads; I heard his voice behind me in the air, and felt something lightly brush my chair. It was his foot, which he gave me leave to touch. Turning to the spot where it was on the top of the chair, I placed my hand gently upon it, when he uttered a cry of pain, and the foot was withdrawn quickly, with a palpable shudder. It was evidently not resting on the chair, but floating; and it sprang from the touch as a bird would. He now passed over to the

farthest extremity of the room, and we could judge by his voice of the altitude and distance he had attained. He had reached the ceiling upon which he made a slight mark, and soon afterwards descended and resumed his place at the table. An incident which occurred during this aerial passage, and imparted a strange solemnity to it, was that the accordion, which we supposed to be on the ground under the window close to us, played a strain of wild pathos in the air from the most distant corner in the room.

Punch's understandable but unsatisfactory response was to pooh-pooh 'the Spirit business' as 'an American invention' and, in the vein of robust, philistine scepticism that was its trademark, to make giggling quips about alcoholic spirits and issue mock warnings against the perils of over-exciting the delicate sensibilities of items of heavy furniture. We can assume that this sort of debunking reflects an average middle-class conservative view, but the picture of Home painted in a poem published in the issue of 18 August 1860 was not so much caricature as misrepresentation, which simply did not engage with, let alone refute, the evidence:

> Through humbugs and fallacies though we may roam,
> Be they never so artful, there's no case like HOME.
> With a lift from the spirits he'll rise in the air
> (Though as lights are put out first, we can't see him there)
> HOME, HOME, great HOME -
> There's no case like HOME!
>
> Of itself his Accordion to play will begin,
> (If you won't look too hard at the works hid within);
> Spirit-hands at his bidding will come, touch, and go
> (But you mustn't peep under the table, you know)
> HOME, HOME etc.
>
> Spring-blinds will fly up or run down at his word,
> (If a wire has been previously fixed to the cord).
> He can make tables dance and bid chairs stand on end
> (But, of course, it must be in the house of a friend).
> HOME, HOME, etc.

Home was always sensitive about being associated with frauds or showmen, and readily denounced them. He was disgusted by his fellow Americans, the brothers Ira and William Davenport, who visited London in 1864 under the dubious management of a Revd

Géricault's portrait of
his assistant, Jamar

Horse Frightened by Thunder by Géricault

The Piper
by Géricault

Pity the Sorrows of
a Poor Old Man
by Géricault

Richard and Cosima Wagner in 1872

Hubert Parry as a young man

Edward Dannreuther

Richard Wagner
conducting 'Music of
the Future'; caricature
from *Charivari*, 1869

Slum scene: Dudley Street,
Seven Dials by Doré

The Ship, Greenwich,
by Doré

Engraving of Ralph Waldo Emerson,
after a drawing by S.W. Rowse

Arthur Hugh Clough
by J.H. Bonham Carter

Thomas Carlyle in 1854

Thomas Carlyle with Emerson's
grandson

Stonehenge, around the time that Emerson and Carlyle visited it

One of the splendours of travel by railway: The Great Hall at Euston Station, 1849

A typical Alhambra spectacle: *Ali Baba*

The Russian ballet style: Tamara Karsavina, Koszoff and Baldina,
London 1909

FIREMEN ANSWERING A CALL.

POLICEMAN ON POINT DUTY.

RAILWAY PORTER INDICATING THAT THE LUGGAGE IS IN THE BRAKE VAN

STREET SCAVENGERS STREET SCAVENGING

TICKET COLLECTOR PUNCHING TICKET

DUSTMAN RETIRING EXPRESSING GRATITUDE FOR HONORARIUM.

POLICEMAN EFFECTING ARREST OF BACCHANAL

THOMAS MAYBANK

IT HAS BEEN REMARKED THAT HITHERTO IN THIS COUNTRY THE MASCULINE DANCER HAS ALWAYS LOOKED MORE OR LESS FOOLISH AND GENERALLY TAKEN REFUGE IN FRANKLY ECCENTRIC CREATIONS. NIJINSKY, MORDKIN AND OTHERS HAVE SHOWN US THAT A MALE CAN BE MANLY THOUGH GRACEFUL. THIS DISCOVERY MAY HAVE FAR-REACHING RESULTS, AS DEPICTED ABOVE.

Unexpected effects of the Ballets Russes on British society:
Punch cartoon, 8 November 1911

Jesse Ferguson and Colonel Fay. Claiming to have been authenticated by 'Harvard Professors', they submitted to being trussed up to a state of immobility with yards of new rope and locked into a large cupboard. Inside a central section of this 'portable spirit-room', guitars, tambourines, violins and accordions were placed. When the lights went down, detached hands materialised in the air above the cabinet and soon a series of more or less musical noises, clamorous and spooky, were heard. When the lights went up, the doors of the cabinet were opened and the Davenports were revealed (surprise, surprise) to be still roped within. On occasion they effected Houdini-like escapes from the knots, bringing the whole affair well within the bounds of ingenious illusionism. But the Davenports commanded the respect of *The Times* and Sir Richard Burton (who claimed that the floating hands thrust a cigar into his mouth and pulled at his moustache), on the strength of which they made a hugely successful tour of the variety and music halls. In Liverpool, however, they met with their come-uppance. As usual, a volunteer from the audience was solicited to tie the ropes himself: a burly sailor took up the offer and knotted the brothers up with such naval expertise that the master of ceremonies, Revd Jesse Ferguson, complained that they were being injured and put a stop to the proceedings. At this, members of the audience stormed the stage and discovered that the cabinet contained various suspicious objects, including copies of the musical instruments. A riot ensued and the Davenports were obliged to leave the country. Home was not fazed. 'I have never had anything to do with rope-tying and banjo-playing in a cupboard,' he insisted loftily. 'They are not mediums at all. Surely spiritualism must have fallen very low if a couple of professed conjurers are to be hailed as its exponents.'

The plethora of such acts* meant that Home could persuade himself that Browning's (immensely prolix and tedious) dramatic monologue 'Mr Sludge the Medium', published in 1864, was nothing to do with him and indeed the caricature is gross: Home was certainly never seen to be drunk in charge of a spirit. Nor does Sludge's grovelling confession have the ring of authenticity:

---

*The routine of the Davenport brothers was repeated in London in 1874 by another American, Annie Eva Fay. But the bills for her turn cannily claimed only that she was' an enigma'.

I cheated when I could,
Rapped with my toe-joints, set sham hands to work
Wrote down names weak in sympathetic ink
Rubbed odic lights with ends of phosphor match
And all the *rest*.

But the point the poem develops is the more philosophical one, that in a world full of fantasy and wishful thinking we are all complicit in some form of deception

there's a real love of a lie,
Liars find ready-made for lies they make,
As hand for glove, or tongue for sugar-plum

and have only ourselves to blame if we are ready to believe what we want to believe.

For Dickens, there stood the obvious explanation: Home's fans, like Susanna Milner Gibson, were well known to be credulous and the conditions of Home's seances were 'preposterously wanting in the commonest securities against deceit and mistake'. It is true that Home forbade the taking of notes while spirits were risen, but otherwise this was not a fair accusation. The fact remains that plenty of reasonable sceptics did observe Home in action and were left totally baffled. Like Browning, you could shrug your shoulders and ascribe his art to the Magic Circle's apparatus of mirrors, wires, sleight-of-hand and sympathetic ink. You could opine that he concealed a small squeeze-box about his intimate person with which he produced his soundtrack or put his boots on his hands in order to simulate levitation in the dark; you could fantasise that he used a tiny tame monkey, chloroform, or the machinations of a lady assistant masquerading as a servant. You could follow the far-out scientific jargon of the day and suggest that he charged himself with odic electricity by sleeping with cats. You could even label him an outright trickster: Dr Barthez, Napoleon III's physician, reports in a letter of 25 September 1857 a rumour that 'M. Hume wears shoes that are easy to remove and put on again, and his socks are cut in a fashion that gives his toes freedom. Whenever he wishes, he slips off a shoe and with his naked foot he pulls a dress or jangles a bell, knocks on this side or that, and once the thing has been done, he quickly puts his shoes on again.' Home's own memoirs continue this catalogue: 'a very popular idea . . . is that my legs are so formed as to be capable of elongation and that my feet are like those of a baboon. Many people suppose that when I go to a strange house, my tables have to be sent first . . . that they are always copiously draped and that I take with me wax hands and arms to show at the proper moment . . . others have stated that when I am said to rise in the air, it is only a balloon filled with gas in the shape of a man.'

But none of this amounts to a sufficient rationalisation of the recorded phenomena, and even if you jump one stage further and question the veracity of the records, you can only land on the conclusion of Trevor H. Hall, the most rigorous investigator of our own era, 'that Home's principal secret lay in his peculiar ability to influence his sitters and those with whom he came into contact' – a verdict which continues to allow Home remarkable psychic gifts.

Although none of the dirt flung at him stuck, Home was having a miserable time. In 1862 his wife Sacha died of tuberculosis contracted from her husband: there ensued a nasty lawsuit with his sister-in-law related to the disposal of her property. The wrangling left Home once again penniless, until he wrote – or paid some hack, appropriately enough, to ghost-write – the first volume of a successful autobiography, *Incidents in My Life*. In 1864 he returned to Rome, only to find himself expelled from the city, by order of the Papal police, on the grounds that he practised sorcery. Efforts were made to stir up an international campaign to exonerate him from such charges, to no avail: questions raised in the House of Commons by a sympathetic MP were laughed down, and none of the crowned heads entertained by seances in the past wanted to involve themselves in such a murky cause.

By 1866 Home was again financially desperate. He sought new sources of income in lectures and readings, and briefly took to the boards as a professional actor – a step which had his detractors chortling that he had never been anything else and which certainly suggests a capacity to dissimulate and impersonate. At the Theatre Royal Worcester, he made a modest début as the scheming Chief of Police Fouché in Tom Taylor's *Plot and Passion*, but the response was no more than polite. Then his nerve seems to have failed him. A plan to play Hamlet, a role in which he could have displayed his capacity to communicate with ghosts, came to nothing. It was also announced, twice, that he would play 'for one night only' the part of Mr Oakley in

Colman's hoary old comedy *The Jealous Wife* at the St James's Theatre in Piccadilly. This did not come to pass either, much to the gratification of Charles Dickens, who wrote to Tom Trollope that he had spotted 'an appropriate dirty little rag' of a poster for the event, 'fluttering in the window of an obscure dairy behind the Strand', but believed 'the public to have found out the scoundrel'.

That same year, however, Home made both his boldest bid for a secure position and his silliest mistake. In collaboration with Professor John Elliotson, an esteemed clinical psychologist of University College Hospital, he established an organisation called the Spiritual Athenaeum and became its secretary. Operating from premises in 22 Sloane Street, where Home also lodged, its aim was to uphold standards among the gifted, to host seemly seances ('refreshments at a moderate tariff' also provided), to record and publish accounts of phenomena and generally to advance spiritualism's good repute. In January 1867 it formally opened with an exhibition of Miss Georgina Houghton's drawings, 'executed by herself under the guidance of the Archangel Gabriel' and a lecture given by Mr D. D. Home Lyon.

Behind this additional name lay a rich, pathetic and ridiculous widow of seventy-five. Mrs Jane Lyon was the illegitimate daughter of a Newcastle tradesman. Before her husband, a grandson or some such scion of the Earl of Strathmore, passed over, he had told her that she would outlive him for only seven years. As the deadline approached she became increasingly anxious and sought out Home at the Spiritual Athenaeum. Being innocently snobbish, she was immensely impressed by the pictures of royalties and aristocracy on the walls, and was even more thrilled when (so she would claim) Home managed to communicate with Mr Lyon instantly: 'I live to bless you, my own precious darling I am with you always I love love love you as I alway did,' were the tidings, for which Mrs Lyon gladly paid a £10 subscription to the Athenaeum.

What ensued would be profoundly disputed between Home and Mrs Lyon, and one can only construct one's own narrative from their different accounts. But further seances seem to have brought more encouraging news of Mr Lyon's pleasure in his wife's acquaintance with Home. The table jumped up and down cheerfully as it spelt out that 'Home is to be our son; he is to be our son he is my son, therefore yours' and then advised Mrs Lyon to make over to Home an annual income of £700. Some days later he received a summoning letter from his benefactress: 'I want you to take a nice mutton chop for your breakfast before you come. I write knowing your timidity to come and be made a rich man.'

So the following morning he accompanied Mrs Lyon in a cab to her bankers, where by deed of gift she endowed him with the necessary capital sum of £24,000 and rewrote her will. According to Mrs Lyon, the transaction was completed to the accompaniment of celebratory raps, and Home then went off alone to the Grand Hotel in Brighton and on to Malvern, where he took Dr James Manby Gully's celebrated hydropathic cure for nervous exhaustion.

Back in London, another seance with Mr Lyon revealed his desire that Home should assume his adoptive mother's name. A present of £6,000 followed, along with mortgage securities to the value of £30,000: these were enormous sums, which would have assured Home a lifetime of financial independence. But while he was making further recuperative visits to Hastings, Torquay and Plymouth in the early months of 1867, the worm began to turn in Mrs Lyon. She had taken a violent dislike to Home's son Grisha and reflected that, if she and Home died, Grisha would inherit. Well-wishers reminded her of the scandal in Rome and whispered that she should beware his sorcerer wiles. Another medium, name of Miss Berry, contacted the late Mr Lyon, who now advised her that darling Daniel was 'a swindler. Go to law, and be very firm.' In a sudden access of panic Mrs Lyon demanded cancellation of the deeds and the retraction of her more extravagant acts of largesse. Home attempted to mollify his 'darling mother', proposing to drop the name of Lyon and to return some of her jewels if she would acknowledge his probity in writing and allow him to keep £30,000 for his trouble. This made her even more hysterical, to the point at which she decided to sue. Home attempted to flee the country: he was arrested and locked in the debtors' prison in Whitecross Street.

The ensuing trial in Equity was a sensation. At a court filled in the public gallery with his many enemies and detractors, Home was hissed as a blackguard, but it was the cross-examination of Mrs Lyon's affidavit which provided the high comedy. For all her vigour in the witness box, she did not emerge as a steady character: despite her wealth, she lived in measly lodgings above a stationer's shop in Westbourne Place and had a long history of altering her will – Mrs

Pepper was beneficiary one minute, Mrs Clutterbuck the next. She had loved Home only as a son, out of respect for her dead husband's wishes, and had no amorous or marital designs on him. 'I just put my head to his forehead. That was the only two times. I am not so fond of kissing.' She claimed to be a highly intelligent woman who thought deeply on theological issues and had read Josephus and the controversial commentaries of Bishop Colenso, but having been snubbed by her late husband's noble family on account of her uncut glass accent and illegitimate birth, the focus of her aspirations was elevation to the superior class of person she had seen exhibited on the walls of the Spiritual Athenaeum. 'But she was grievously disappointed with her reception in the society where Home moved, and to which he had introduced her.' Instead, Home had 'entranced' her and she had fallen under his 'magnetic influence'. She had then become the victim of his false pretences and now she wanted her money back. 'Mrs Pepper had been right to caution me and to keep the door locked lest I should be killed in my bed.'

Home denied he had ever put her in touch with her deceased husband and emphasised the cloying nature of her affections, relating how she clucked and fussed about his health, flinging her arms round him with cries of 'it shall be just as you like, darling!' Passages of her wittering letters to him were read out in court – 'heigh-ho for the spirit-land lay down the flesh and be off to the spirit-land lay down your bones and be off to the spirit-land' and so forth. When he described the fond manner in which she gave him his £6,000 birthday present, she screamed out 'False, false, false'; later in the hearing, she began openly contradicting herself, yelling abuse at witnesses and berating the Lord Chancellor like some lunatic Dickensian obsessive.

Whether she was conscious of her lies or not, Mrs Lyon was clearly very distressed and it still looked to the world as though Home had taken advantage of a demented and defenceless old woman. In its issue of 9 May, *Punch* had another go at him:

> Confronted with Home, Lyon's terrors are vain;
> Into fortune he flies, and won't fly out again;
> And with raps' worth as his, 'worth a rap' means worth all.
> For which, on rappees, up-to-snuff rappers calls,
> HOME, HOME, DAN HOME,
> No medium like HOME

He is vouched for by friends, FRSs, MPs,
With Emp'ror and Czar hobs-and-nobs at his ease;
And to show off for shillings he cannot have grounds
Who has still on tap drafts for thousands of pounds
HOME, HOME, DAN HOME,
No medium like HOME.

The judge was not amused by any of it. His verdict emphasised that those who contributed to charitable or religious bodies had no right to ask for their money back when it suited them, and ordered Mrs Lyon to pay both her own and Home's costs. But he then told Home to give the money back, on the dubious legal grounds that Home's reputation as a medium laid on him the burden of supporting Mrs Lyon's gifts and that he had failed to do so. What he meant was that it was impossible to uphold spiritualism's claims in a court of law.

The verdict again made the getting of income a priority for Home. His nerve for the stage having failed him, he resorted instead to the platform and toured fifty cities throughout the kingdom giving public readings. The programme was not spiritualist: Tennyson and Poe provided the elevating parts of the evening, followed by some light comic relief rendered in various dialects – significantly, he seems to have had a gift for doing the different voices. The *Court Journal* was one of many publications to be impressed: 'So great is his versatility that he draws tears in some of his pathetic readings, while in his Irish and American anecdotes his humour is so great that it convulses the audience with merriment.' And after the performance, if some titled lady was so gracious as to take him to supper, the entertainment might be rounded off with a quiet little seance too.

Although Home had been allowed to slither away from the Lyon case, the fracas did nothing to help his reputation or his cause, and his claim to look down on vulgar spiritualist hucksters from the high moral ground in polite society looked ever more shaky. Even his warmest friends and supporters like Elizabeth Barrett Browning had always been compelled to admit that he was not quite the gentleman, although they never make clear precisely in which respects he fell short of that all-important status. Modern commentators such as Colin Wilson have suggested that the hazy nature of the complaints against Home and the excessive hostility that he aroused in men such as Browning may have been connected with smoking-room rumours about his sexual proclivities, perhaps provoked by some effeminate affectations (adorning himself with expensive jewellery, frizzing his hair) about his appearance.

A veiled passage in Dickens's scathing review of Home's autobiography (published in *All the Year Round*, 4 April 1863) insinuates that he 'had lately heard overmuch touching young men of promise in the imaginative arts, "towards whom" Martyr Mediums assisting at evening parties feel themselves "drawn". It may be a hint to such young men to stick to their own drawing, as being of a much better kind, and to leave martyr mediums alone in their glory.' (Dickens confessed in a letter of the same day that he had written this review 'with the terrors of the libel laws before my eyes'). Homosexuality may be the wrong label, but after the break with Mrs Lyon, Home certainly did develop an unhealthily intimate and intense relationship with a young aristocrat, Lord Adare, son of the Earl of Dunraven.

They became friendly at Malvern, where they were both taking Dr Gully's cure for rheumatism. In that salubrious atmosphere Adare witnessed several 'manifestations', at one of which Home was possessed by the spirit of Adah Menken, the American actress celebrated for playing the part of Byron's Mazeppa 'in a state of virtual nudity while bound to the back of a wild horse' and lately dead in Paris at an early age.

Adare was transfixed: he went on to travel with Home to the German spas and then over several months lived with him in hugger-mugger seclusion, both in London and at the Dunraven family seat in Wales. For Home, this hospitality was vital: the Spiritual Athenaeum had quietly closed in the wake of the scandal over Mrs Lyon and he was in desperate need of new patronage. As a result, he was on his very best behaviour and the wonders obligingly came thick and fast. Adare began to write letters to his father, also a keen spiritualist, relating what occurred and, in 1869, the Earl edited and privately printed a volume based on this correspondence entitled *Experiences in Spiritualism with D. D. Home*. Apart from descriptions of seances and spookiness, it detailed a levitation at Ashley Place, which apppeared to take Home in and out of two windows* and two rather gruesome additions to

---

*This episode has remained a focal point of all controversy surrounding Home, with abseiling proposed as one explanation: see Trevor H. Hall, *The Enigma of Daniel Home* (Buffalo, 1984), p. 103–39 for the most rigorous analysis of the texts. Incidentally, Mr Hall is also the author of *The Early Years of the Huddersfield Building Society, 1864–1928* (Huddersfield, 1974).

Home's repertoire – self-elongation (by about six inches) and the ability to handle fire unsinged. News of the book's revelations made a great stir, but Adare soon thought better of its claims, or at least attempted to retrieve all the copies. He married the Hon. Miss Florence Kerr, who probably did not approve, disengaged himself from Home and took little subsequent interest in the occult. Only a half-century later, in 1924, when he was too old to care or resist pressure from spiritualist factions, did he agree to its reprinting.

What made Adare's temporary surrender to Home's influence so striking is that to the world at large he appeared to be an uncomplicated, cheerful, out-of-doors type, keen on shooting and sailing, and far removed in personality from the typical spiritualist devotee. But something in Home's physical presence unmanned him and, together with his friends Captain Wynne, Lord Lindsay and Captain Smith, Adare lived for several months at a time cocooned in what Home's American biographer Jean Burton describes as 'an eldritch world' where 'hassocks stood up and tapped out messages; clocks struck eerily in answer to questions; spirit hands opened desks and rustled papers; strange perfumes filled the air. Folding doors swung unnervingly open and shut. Heavy steps reverberated in empty passages and followed them up stairways.' They were spooked, in other words, to a point at which they could have hallucinated anything that could be seen, felt, touched or heard; but what is even more chilling is to read between the lines how Home played on the young men's exposed nerves and sensibilities. Adare on several occasions fell ill, perhaps under the strain of it all, and his account of Home's hypnotic ministrations at his sickbed, with their eerie erotic overtones, is particularly telling.

> The other night, having been unwell for some days, I went to bed very uncomfortable, and agueish; I could not get warm . . . Home went into a trance, got out of bed, wrapped a fur rug round his middle, then warmed his hands at the fire, and commenced shampooing me over my chest, stomach, legs and feet. He then took off my fur rug, warmed it at the fire, and put it on again, and made passes over my head, retreating as he did so to the further side of the room. He then got into bed and awoke.

And later:

> Home came over to where I was sitting on the sofa, and made me lie full length upon it; by the attitude he assumed I recognised the spirit he

called 'the nameless doctor'. He stood beside me apparently lost in thought for a minute or two, then kneeling down, made me unbutton my waistcoat, and began sounding my chest as doctors do; he then rubbed and patted over my chest, loins and legs. Occasionally turning round as if to seek advice from someone, his efforts were principally directed to my right side, he frequently pointed to it and turned his head as if to call someone's attention to that particular spot. He placed his mouth to my right side and exhaled a deep breath; the heat I felt was something extraordinary.

Small wonder if the Hon. Miss Kerr objected.

In 1870 Home left England for the Continent. When the Franco-Prussian War broke out in September, he attached himself to the press corps following the German army. As well as sending reports to the *San Francisco Chronicle* on the Battle of Sedan and the Siege of Paris, he raised spirits for bored generals kicking their heels at their Versailles headquarters. After a visit to St Petersburg, where he found himself another wife, Julie de Gloumeline, he returned briefly to London. Here a brilliant young physicist and chemist, William Crookes, who had discovered the metal thallium and would shortly develop the radiometer, offered to test his powers. Having established what he insisted were laboratory conditions of objectivity, complete with galvanometer, thermometer and electro-magnet, Crookes invited distinguished colleagues to attend as witnesses, but to a man they declined. Instead, members of his own family and friends of Home made up the audience. Crookes reported the results lyrically in the July 1871 issue of the *Quarterly Journal of Science*. 'I have seen a luminous cloud hover over a heliotrope on a side table, break a sprig off, and carry a sprig to a lady . . . a beautifully formed small hand rose up from an opening in a dining-table and gave me a flower . . . the hand sometimes appears icy-cold and dead, at other times warm and life-like, grasping my own with the firm pressure of an old friend.' There were several levitations – 'he rose eighteen inches off the ground, and I passed my hands under his feet, round him, and over his head when he was in the air' – and appearances of ghostly forms – 'a dark, shadowy semi-transparent form, like that of a man, was then seen by all present standing near the window, waving the curtain with his hand. As we looked, the form faded away and the curtains ceased to move.'

The scientific establishment was appalled – the climate of the 1840s, with its mesmeric currents, had frozen to a tight rationalist orthodoxy. Critics and scoffers sourly pointed out that the presence of friends and family biased the circumstances of the test sympathetically to Home and that the death of Crookes's son predisposed him in spiritualism's favour. Later Crookes would admit that the apparatus of galvanometers and thermometers had not invariably governed the experiments. 'I used jokingly to say to [Home], "Let us sit round the fire, and have a quiet chat, and see if our friends are here and will do anything for us. We won't have any tests or precautions." On these occasions, when only my own family were present, some of the most convincing phenomena took place.'

In any case Home now felt that his time was up and, at the age of thirty-eight, for several reasons, he retired. His health was bad and his powers, he said, were failing – by which he may have meant that he could not compete with the gimmicky new trends in the business arriving from the USA. Spiritually possessed lecturers like the much-married Mrs Cora Lavinia Victoria Scott Hatch Daniels Tappan Richmond gave interminable 'entranced' lectures of profound erudition and wisdom on any subject presented to her by an audience; while in 1876 – before being caught out and sentenced to three months' hard labour – Henry Slade presented spirit messages on a slate and started a vogue for 'automatic writing'. English mediums, on the other hand, developed a taste for materialising palpable, full-dress revenants (usually themselves, swathed in muslin). In 1874 a great stir was caused by William Crookes' sponsorship of a cockney-sparrow teenager from Hackney. Florrie Cook materialised the spirit of 'Katie King' inside a 'portable spirit-room', with a glass portico, similar to that used by the Davenport brothers. Doubtless because of his friendship with Crookes, Home refrained from attacking Miss Cook, but in 1880 she was decisively exposed as a fraud when Sir George Sitwell risked the terrifying injunction that he who touched a materialised spirit would instantly perish, grabbed at Katie and discovered she was Florrie.* Meanwhile, John Maskelyne, a young magician who in 1865 had been appalled by what he considered the blatant trickery of the Davenport

---

*Trevor H. Hall believes that Cook was Crookes's mistress. See 'Florence Cook and William Crookes' in *New Light on Old Ghosts* (London, 1965).

brothers, hired the Egyptian Hall in Piccadilly – where Géricault had shown *The Raft of the 'Medusa'* – and developed a remarkable 'anti-Spiritualist' entertainment, which for several years delighted audiences with its exposure of the tricks of the trade.

Money, at least, was no longer a worry to Home – his second wife was rich and the lawsuit over his first wife's estate was finally decided in his favour. He settled in France, occupying himself with an extensive correspondence with his high-born admirers, as well as writing the second volume of his autobiography and the more reflective *Lights and Shadows of Spiritualism*, in which he railed from a height at the 'brazen and unblushing' impostures of every Johnny-Come-Lately in the business and the 'Punch-and-Judy boxes' on which the materialisers relied. Perhaps it was this sort of talk which endeared him to Mark Twain, who became a cordial friend in these last years, despite – or because of? – his cynical fascination with the wiles and pretensions of frauds and charlatans.

In search of better health, Home travelled throughout Europe, frequenting spas and watering places, where he liked to mingle with grand duchesses and the beau monde. But his slender frame was racked by the inexorable advance of his tuberculosis and his ring-heavy fingers – the diamond setting a gift from the Tsar, the pearl from the Kaiser – now clutched a walking stick. Despite all the succour of benevolent guardian spirits ('I have often seen during the night a light shine round him,' wrote his wife after his death, 'while a hand issuing from a luminous cloud made passes over his face, as if blessing him, and ended by making on his forehead the sign of the cross'), he died in 1886, at the age of fifty-three. Having converted to the Greek Orthodox faith on marrying his second wife, he was buried in the Russian cemetery at St Germain-en-Laye. His tombstone reads

> Born to earth-life near Edinburgh, Scotland March 20 1833
> Born to spirit-life, 'To another, discerning of spirits'
> (1st Corinthians, 12th chapter, 10th verse) June 21 1886

One wonders if he has ever been back.

In the years following Home's withdrawal, what one could call the American school of spirit-rapping became domesticated in British society. Institutions like the British National Association of Spiritualists (founded in 1873) and the Psychological Society (founded in 1875), both of which developed an extensive network of branches throughout the provinces, set out codes of practice for professionals and advised and encouraged the amateurs ('inquirers into spiritualism should begin by forming spirit circles in their own homes, with no spiritualist or professional medium present' and so forth). Two new journals, *The Medium* and *The Spiritual News* were published. To steer scientific investigation and log records of the phenomena, the Cambridge intellectuals F. W. H. Myers and Henry Sidgwick founded the Society for Psychical Research in 1882 'with a single-minded desire to ascertain the facts, and without any foregone conclusion as to their nature'. On another broader social plane, the wonders and mysteries of spirit-rapping and mediumship filtered by the end of the century into lower-middle and working-class culture, with seances and lectures on the subject, of a sober and godly kind, becoming the regular stuff of every Mechanics' Institute and Temperance Hall. Even the attitude of the Church of England softened – in 1881 a debate at its annual congress wound up with a plea to acknowledge 'the truths of Spiritualist teaching, as weapons which we are all too glad to wield against Positivism, and Secularism, and all the anti-Christianisms of this age of godless thought'. Other creeds and causes also linked themselves to spiritualism – the advancement of women, for example, which saw mediumship both as a development of the faculty of 'feminine intuition' and an extension of the spheres of wife and mother.

All this took spirit-rapping far from the private salons of titled folk in which Home functioned most successfully and to which he would have been happy to confine himself. It is this vein of opportunistic snobbery that one finds his most disagreeable quality: his spiritualism, for all the professed Christian piety which framed it, was an exclusive affair and *Lights and Shadows of Spiritualism* turns up its nose at the vulgarity of the newcomers to the field as much as at their fraudulence. How he would have loathed the likes of Mrs James of Sutton, whose ludicrous suburban seance is depicted in George and Weedon Grossmith's comic masterpiece *Diary of a Nobody* (1892):

> The spirit 'Lina' came again, and said 'WARN' three or four times, and declined to explain. Mrs James said 'Lina' was stubborn sometimes. She

often behaved like that, and that the best thing to do was to send her away.

She then hit the table sharply and said, 'Go away, Lina; you are disagreeable. Go away!' I should think we sat nearly three-quarters of an hour with nothing happening. My hands felt quite cold and I suggested we should stop the seance. Carrie and Mrs James, as well as Cummings would not agree to it. In about ten minutes' time there was some tilting towards me. I gave the alphabet, and it spelled out 'SPOOF'.

But Home had departed before the spirits had reached the villas of Holloway and he passed over to the other side with his glamour unsullied by low associations. Today, he remains secure in his reputation as the supreme exponent of his art: it is his bust which presides over the library of the Society of Psychical Research in Kensington, defying the ghost-hunters' theories and explanations as bafflingly as he did a hundred and fifty years ago. Spiritualism's history would look completely different without him. His visit – his visitation – was without doubt the most consequential of any in this book.

CHAPTER 5

Sporting Chances: Australian Cricketers

What picture did a middle-class Victorian have of the natives of Australia?

> The aborigines performed barely half of their duties as men. They partially exercised their dominion over the beasts and the birds – killing, but not otherwise utilizing them. But, although they inherited the earth, they did not subdue it, nor replenish it. They cleared away no useless bush or forest, to replace them with fruits; and they tilled no land, leaving the earth exactly in the same condition that they found it . . .
>
> In process of time white men came to introduce new arts into their country, clearing away useless forest, and covering the rescued earth with luxuriant wheat-crops, sufficient to feed the whole of the aborigines of the country; bringing also with them herds of sheep and horned cattle to feed upon the vast plains which formerly nourished but a few kangaroo, and to multiply in such numbers that they not only supplied the whole of their adopted land with food, but their flesh was exported to the mother-country.
>
> The superior knowledge of the white man thus gave to the aborigines the means of securing their supplies of food; and therefore his advent was not a curse, but a benefit to them. But they could not take advantage of the opportunities thus offered to them, and instead of seizing upon these new means of procuring the three great necessities of human life, food, clothing and lodging, they not only refused to employ them, but did their best to drive them out of the country, murdering the colonists, killing their cattle, destroying their crops and burning their houses.
>
> The means were offered to them of infinitely bettering their social condition and the opportunity given them, by substituting peaceful labour for perpetual feuds, and of turning professional murderers into food-producers, of replenishing the land which their everlasting quarrels, irregular mode of existence and carelessness of human life had well-nigh depopulated. These means they could not appreciate, and, as a natural consequence, had to make way for those who could. The inferior must always make way for the superior, and such has ever been the case with the savage.

Thus the Revd J. G. Wood, in *The Natural History of Man*, a popular illustrated book published in 1870. Its attitude is typical. Most Victorian ethnographers speak of the Aborigines of Australia in similarly head-shaking tones, more in sorrow than in anger, as of children who had failed to reach the mark and remain bottom of the evolutionary class. From the longer perspective of our sophisticated anthropology it is easy enough to judge Wood's mindset as ignorant, insulting and naïve in its facile Darwinian snobbery and sinister in its identification of 'superior' and 'inferior' races. Yet there is nothing wilfully vindictive about it; and we should remember that in Australia itself there were as many white Christian settlers determined to palliate wrongs done to the Aborigines and help them integrate with the brave new world of Empire as there were those who happily kicked them like dogs. The colony's great reforming governor, Lachlan Macquarie, had set the tone and led the way forward, as a letter sent to Westminster in 1814 illustrates: 'It seems only to require the fostering hand of Time, Gentle Means and Conciliatory Manners', he wrote, 'to bring these poor Unenlightened People into an Important Degree of Civilisation.' All over the continent, people of goodwill attempted to embrace their black brothers, ignoring the bar-room prejudice and the succession of newspaper reports detailing instances of their drunken violence. In 1852, for example, a certain Mr and Mrs Pope, farming near Perth, benevolently opened their estate to local natives, treating them as members of their family, providing them with land, seed and cattle, and initiating them into the mysteries of knife and fork. What resulted from this experiment is not recorded, but as we shall see it was far from unique.

Running counter to such hopeful gestures was a slow genocide – not consciously or officially sanctioned, but seemingly unstoppable. Those Aborigines who had not been hounded off their lands fled deeper into impenetrable bush country, falling victim to syphilis, alcohol and a variety of chest infections to which they had no resistance. In the outback, on hard land, farmers shot them like vermin: for every one of their number whose murder reached any sort of court hearing, ten must have gone unrecorded. The statistics are appalling: at the beginning of the century the first British colonists of Van Diemen's Land noted something in the region of 4000 Aborigines; the 1871 census of Tasmania found only ten. The press regularly expressed concern and anger at this ghastly process. 'Have we, or have we not done what we ought to do for human beings of their abject condition, whose country we have seized without remuneration to them, and whose habits in life have in consequence become to a great extent altered?'

This appeared in the Perth *Inquirer* in 1854, the year of Australia's first railway and telegraph lines. What price progress? asked the *Argus* in Melbourne, rhetorically and ironically addressing those who would scarcely profit from its march.

> Listen, dusky fellow-subject, for there comes *Christian* England; the great, the powerful, the intelligent, the good! There comes Christian England, who, if you were strong enough to demand a price for your land would *buy* it from you; but who, as you are few and weak, and timorous generously condescends to *steal* it! There comes Christian England, to absorb your hunting grounds, destroy your game, inoculate you with her vices, and shew her Christian spirit by dooming you to 'extirpation'! There comes Christian England, who carries many hundreds of tons of your gold without setting apart one ounce for you; who hands you over to be contaminated by the worst and lowest of her own people, to be taught their crimes, to be impregnated with their diseases; and who, while rapidly destroying you, cants in her churches and her religious meetings about doing to others she would be done by! Rejoice, you dark-skinned savage, at the advent of your most kind, magnanimous and most *Christian* brother!

As one can sense from this, what saddened such liberals most was the tragic passivity of the Aborigines' demoralisation – an element of what seemed like self-destruction. As the Revd J. G. Wood lamented from his armchair in England, the 'remarkable manners and customs' of the Aborigines were 'fast disappearing together with the natives themselves. The poor creatures are aware of the fact, and seem to have lost all pleasure in the games and dances that formerly enlivened their existence. Many of the tribes are altogether extinct, and succumb almost without complaint to the fate which awaits them.'

One important element in all strategies to save the Aborigines was to protect them from the dire influence of hostile, corrupting or exploitative white men and the temptations they offered. Before integration, there must be isolation. One such exemplary community was run by Matthew Hale, a high-minded Anglican archdeacon from Cambridge. In 1850 he was encouraged by the Bishop of Adelaide to set up an institution for Aborigines in a desert homestead at Poonindie.

With the help of an initial grant from the state of £200, Hale's application of Macquarie's prescription for 'Gentle Means and Conciliatory Manners' made considerable headway, even though the Christian message didn't altogether sink in. By 1853 the grant had risen to £1000 and by 1856, when Hale returned to England, over a hundred natives had passed through its kindly regime, with its classes in husbandry and morality. Idleness being the first sign of backsliding, constructive use of free time was another strand of a Poonindie education. This was fraught with difficulties: perhaps the Aborigines were too listless to indulge in their native games and dances, perhaps they were too shy or too secretive. Hale tried to interest his flock in various respectable activities. The singing of hymns proved predictably shambolic and hilarious, but he did better with another archetypically English pastime: cricket.

One day in 1853 the Bishop of Adelaide came to visit. He was much impressed by what he saw.

> One more incident I may mention in proof of their progress in civilisation; a cricket match played by the Poonindie lads and young men, on a holiday given on the occasion of my visit. I was pleased at watching, with the Archdeacon, two Australian native 'elevens' thus enjoying themselves, and remarked not only their neatness in 'fielding and batting', but what was far more worthy of note, the perfect good humour which prevailed throughout the games; no ill-temper shown, or angry appeals to the umpire, as is generally the case in a match of whites.

Cricket had taken immediate hold in white Australia. The first recorded match took place in Sydney in 1803 and, in the rough-and-ready shape which prevailed before the MCC stamped the pitch with gentlemanly regulations, it soon became the colony's most popular sporting pastime. Apart from the purely local, amateur and schoolboy levels of the game, a number of professional teams toured the country, offering a match as part of a programme of entertainment, which might also include parades, fireworks, athletic competitions, stunts and horseplay. These paid performers were a pretty rough lot, less interested in playing by such rules as obtained than in making an exhibition of themselves.

Managing their activities were enterprising publicans, who ran refreshment tents in the grounds – potentially a highly profitable business. In 1861 a pair of upmarket hoteliers and caterers, Felix Spiers and Christopher Pond, owners of the swish Café de Paris in Melbourne, decided to diversify. In association with the flamboyant comic actor-cum-impresario George Coppin – already famous for importing camels, Turkish baths and roller-skates – they offered Charles Dickens a twelve-month reading tour at a guaranteed fee of £10,000, an astronomical sum symptomatic of the boom mentality which had swept Melbourne during its Gold Rush years. But Dickens said no and the partnership turned their attention to cricket.

What Spiers and Pond eventually presented in 1862 was something calling itself an All-England XI. This wasn't an officially sanctioned selection of the nation's best, simply a team of English players captained by H. H. Stephenson. The cricket they played seems to have been a knockabout business, scarcely notable for its elegant stroke-play. Despite trouble from the mosquitoes, the visitors had much the best of it, but who cared? If a match came to a grisly or early end – as it did when eleven members of a Melbourne XVIII failed to score at all in one innings against the visitors – there were roulette wheels and shooting galleries among the sideshows, and on one occasion the proceedings were enlivened by the ascent of a balloon. With daily attendances running as high as 15,000 at an admission price of 2s 6d, Spiers and Pond ended the tour with a reputed thumping profit of £14,000, on which they hastened to establish themselves in the West End of London.*

The All-England tour raised the temperature of cricket fever in Australia to new heights and many Christian missions emulated the example of Poonindie in their efforts to use the game to bring Aborigines into the fold. They certainly took to the bat and ball quicker than they did to the knife and fork, their native skills and sharp eyesight giving them several enviable advantages in throwing, catching and hitting. But the most remarkable episode in the brief history of Aboriginal cricket originated outside the boundaries of Christian evangelising, at a station called Edenhope, in the scrubby Wimmera region about 200 miles north-west of Melbourne.

Here the depopulation and degeneration were as wretched as

---

*One of their several restaurants, the Criterion, founded in 1869, still flourishes in Piccadilly Circus today, its splendid pseudo-oriental interior and gilded mosaic ceiling meticulously restored.

everywhere else, but relations between the two races were not altogether soured. In 1864, three white children went missing in the bush. When Aboriginal trackers brought them home, they were rewarded with £20, fêted and offered work. Two of them, christened Dick-a-Dick (properly, Jumgumjenanuke) and Red Cap (Brimbunyah), seem to have been the founder members of what developed into a cricket team, assembled by two friendly Wimmera farmers, William Hayman and Tom Hamilton, from inhabitants of the surrounding country. By 1866, in its colours of cream trousers, red-trim shirts and straw hats with blue bands, the team had mastered the art to the point of winning against white Edenhope. Local newspapers praised its efforts heartily and made solemnly approving comments on its collective good behaviour, Dick-a-Dick's avowed teetotalism being singled out for special praise.

Hayman now engaged, as coach, the sympathetic if tragic figure of Tom Wills. A third-generation Australian, son of a wealthy sheep farmer, he had grown up close to the Aborigines who worked on the family estate in Victoria. He was sent to school at Rugby, where he distinguished himself as captain of both cricket and football, but after four years in England he chose to return to Australia. In 1861 he accompanied his father to a new sheep station near Rockhampton in Queensland. Here there was a catastrophe: the Aborigines were not content to yield the land and shortly after Wills's arrival they massacred nineteen white men, women and children as they lay resting in the afternoon heat. Among them was Tom Wills's father. Tom himself only escaped the carnage because his cart had broken down. A furious lynch mob subsequently killed sixty Aborigines in revenge.

For the next two years, in honour of his father, Wills desperately tried to establish the station on a secure footing. In the wake of the slaughters, however, it proved impossible to find labour, and Wills returned to Victoria and played some professional cricket. A man well known for his 'good nature and kind heart', he agreed to coach Hayman's Aborigines because they came from tribes he had known in his childhood and he understood their ways; perhaps he also needed to purge feelings of loathing and revulsion. Besides, he had been a pupil at Dr Arnold's Rugby and imbibed its high principles. Finally, he would pay a terrible psychic price for his remarkable courage: in the mid

1870s, after continuing his career as a cricket coach, he became a hopeless alcoholic and, in 1880, at the age of forty-four, stabbed himself to death with a pair of scissors.

Meanwhile Hayman sent a photograph of the team to Melbourne Cricket Club, in the hope of arranging a fixture – John Mulvaney and Rex Harcourt, to whose fascinating book *Cricket Walkabout* much of what follows is indebted, believe that this was done in a spirit of pure sporting disinterestedness, but at some point Hayman must have realised the commercial potential in what he was nurturing. In any case the match which finally took place in Melbourne on Boxing Day 1866 was sponsored by the publicans Bryant and Rowley. It attracted a crowd of 8000 spectators and it is impossible to imagine the emotions of the Aborigines as they faced that swarm of alien faces. In the event, they understandably played rather badly, despite the sterling captaincy of Tom Wills. Seven players failed to score in the first innings, and they were all out for 39 to their opponents' 101. In the second innings they did rather better, reaching 87. So they lost, but no matter: *The Australian* reported that 'the black fellow has an extraordinary readiness for picking up a knowledge of cricket, however deficient he may be in other respects . . . it is only reasonable to suppose that, if properly managed and instructed, the native race might have been turned to much better account . . . and that instead of dying off from the face of the earth, they might have become civilised and respectable members of society.'

After the match was over there were field sports. One star of the show was the exuberant Tarpot (otherwise Murrumgunerrimin and noted for his endearing habit of turning double-somersaults in the field when a wicket was well taken), who won the crowd's admiration by running a hundred yards in fourteen seconds – backwards. Jellico (Unamurrimin) was interviewed by a journalist and joked: 'What for you not talk to me good Inglis? I speak him as good Inglis belonging to you.' Less plausibly, he was also reported to have announced that the heat in Melbourne was just too much: 'I spoil my complexion. When I go back, my mother won't know me.'

Inevitably, the novelty of it all soon wore thin and further matches in Melbourne proved less fun. Three of the Aborigines' best players went out of action – Mullagh (Unaarimin) injured his leg, Tarpot had a cold and Dick-a-Dick was struck down with measles. But their first flush of success had been enough to attract the attention of a dubious entrepreneur, Captain Gurnett, who proposed to Hayman and Wills the organising of a year-long tour to England. Gurnett would be responsible for all expenses and the necessary arrangements, as well as paying Hayman and Wills a salary and guaranteeing each of the Aborigines a cachet of £50 on their return.

It was an attractive deal, but the Central Board for the Protection of the Aborigines – a government-sanctioned, predominantly Quaker body – got wind of the scheme and demanded bona fide guarantees from Gurnett. Which, being dubious, he was unable to give. There ensued much humming and hawing, all indicative of the conscience of White Australia towards the natives. The Central Board's particular concern that, should the tour flop, the Aborigines might be abandoned in England and left destitute seemed all the more reasonable in the light of the deaths of three team members, Jellico, Watty (Bilayarrimin) and Paddy (Pappinjurumun); access to alcohol seems to have been a contributory factor. There was no doubt that the team was intensely vulnerable to Western civilisation.

After a trip to Sydney (where the Aborigines again attracted vast crowds and lost badly), Wills and Hayman finally broke with Gurnett. But the scheme of an English tour had taken hold, and they now formed their own consortium with several investors and put themselves in the hands of Charles Lawrence. This was an excellent choice. Lawrence was an Englishman who had arrived in Australia as one of the 1862 team and stayed on in Sydney, where he owned a hotel. He was a superb coach and a man of upstanding character. His priority was the fostering of a disciplined team spirit, in the name of which he devised a smart new kit: white flannels, loose red Garibaldi blouse, blue belt and tie, peaked caps with embroidered bat and boomerang, and sashes individually coloured so that spectators might distinguish one player from another. His unfinished, unpunctuated diary also records other morale-boosting measures:

> I took them all to church as I had promised they seemed to like and was
> very attentive and when the collection plate was presented they gave a
> little help. When they came out I asked them how they liked it and they
> replied this way. Music very nice and him talk a lot and get a lot of
> money. I said and what do you think he does with it. Keep it don't he. I
> said no but gives it to the poor people they were quite astounded and said

does he then. Well when we go to church again I will always put my money in the plate which I am pleased to say they did.

On 8 February 1868, despite last-minute huffings from the Central Board, the thirteen-strong team set sail in a wool ship, the *Paramatta*, for the three-month journey to England. Wills did not want to make the trip, so Lawrence became both captain and coach, while Hayman functioned as manager. Everything seems to have been efficiently organised, with the Aborigines travelling in 'intermediate' class, away from the damp and discomfort of steerage, their diet and health carefully monitored. Another unimaginably new experience for these land-bound people was the open sea, but one which they seem to have found exhilarating. 'They very soon lost all fear', wrote Lawrence,

> as they heard the captain pray and said to me does he know Jesus Christ and the little pickaninny you used to tell us about that we saw in the picture and Dick-a-Dick said they kill him. I told him that Jesus was in heaven now and that the captain prayed to him that we should all arrive safely in England nothing seemed now to trouble them for they thought the captain was so good that the ship would never sink I took a good supply of copy books and endeavoured to teach them to write and read I gave them lessons every morning but this did not last long for they soon tired and amused themselves in drawing trees birds and all kinds of animals and anything they could think of Drafts and cards they liked and to play with the children and to get pieces of wood from the carpenter and to make needles and lots of other little things for the ladies one gave them a shuttle to see if they could make one which they did they therefore became great favourites with the ladies and their children always wanted to be with the Blacks.

Early in May, the *Paramatta* docked at Gravesend and the team went to recuperate for a couple of weeks in Town Malling, a village in Kent where Hayman had family connections with a cricketing celebrity, W. S. Norton. The locals were entranced by their visitors and vied to make them welcome. Lawrence, for instance, records three of the team being taken up by the daughters of the village draper. One day he found them 'reclining upon sofas' in their drawing-room, 'whilst the ladies were playing and singing'.

With the help of W. S. Norton, Hayman appointed an agent and fixed a schedule. The arrangements for matches generally involved renting the ground from a club, which in return provided the opposition and took a percentage of the takings. Surviving records indicate that this worked to the satisfaction of all parties: the tour was to prove an impressively efficient and orderly operation, right down to the generation of advance publicity.

In consequence, 7000 people attended the first match against Surrey, at the Oval on 25–6 May. The team had travelled up from Town Malling by train to London Bridge, stopping off for a little presentation, much reported in the newspapers, at the factory of the bat makers E. J. Page, where they were each presented with a cane-handled bat and a copy of *The Cricketers' Pocket Book*. They ran on to the pitch barefoot, hailing their opponents with three cheers and a wild whoop – and lost by an innings and 7 runs. *The Times*'s verdict was snootily dismissive. 'It was apparent to everyone', it crowed, 'that these Aborigines had little or no chance against the cultivated teams which Surrey had summoned to confront them with.' Their bowling was 'second-rate' and their batting 'sadly wanting in power'.

Undaunted by a bad press and crushing defeat, they returned to Town Malling and a few days later drew a match against the socially exclusive More Park Club of Maidstone. Two military bands played, there was a lunch with the local gentry, and the columnists reported 'a more numerous and fashionable attendance than we ever remember'. After a few more such engagements the revered Marylebone Cricket Club opened its gates and the Aborigines were admitted to the sacred greensward of Lord's. Against a team which included an earl and a viscount, the visitors did creditably, scoring 185 in their first innings and losing by only 55 runs. Among the crowd was nineteen-year-old W. G. Grace. 'In strength they were about equal to third-class English teams,' he later grudgingly recalled in his memoirs, although 'it was generally admitted that two players, Mullagh and Cuzens [Yellanach], showed very good all-round form'. Indeed they did: Mullagh scored 75 in the first innings, while Cuzens took six for 65 in the second. *The Times*, however, judged the whole exercise 'a travestie'.

Until their departure in mid-October, the Aborigines played a total of forty-seven matches in forty towns and cities: won fourteen, lost fourteen, drawn nineteen, against seven county teams, fourteen first-rank clubs and twenty second-rank. About half of these were London or Home County, but the team also reached as far west as Swansea and as far north as Tynemouth, travelling mostly by train. They were worked hard: out of the 126 days they were in Britain they were playing for ninety-nine of them, mostly in two-day matches which lasted between 11 a.m and 7 p.m., with only a brief stop for lunch. For people with a generic reputation for shiftlessness and walkabout, they maintained extraordinary discipline – a tribute to Lawrence's captaincy and Hayman's management too – as well as astonishing resilience in the face of a profound disorientation.

The press and public showed uninhibited interest in the Aborigines' physiognomy and behaviour. 'Many and confused were the ideas generally entertained respecting these Aboriginals, both as regards their cricketing acquirements and their physical conformation,' as *The Times* put it. Behind such confusion sat a deeper certainty: the British were superior, not just in terms of knives and forks and clean collars, but of their rung on the ladder of species. Generally received post-Darwinian notions may have accepted a common evolutionary ancestry but also reassuringly emphasised the unbridgeable distance between the White Man who had developed intelligent European civilisation and the Black Man who had remained a naked savage, close to the ape both geographically and biologically: we may have shared fundamental physical characteristics, but not spiritual or mental ones.

As imperialism became more aggressive and exploitative, this naive view would degenerate into a hate-based ideology which sanctioned genocide, but in the nineteenth century the respectable Christian view of race was more smiling and patronising, coloured by the same sort of tolerant condescension shown to small children, obedient servants and household pets. The huge success of *Uncle Tom's Cabin* and support for the Northern cause in the American Civil War (which had concluded only three years earlier) further predisposed sympathies towards the 'darkies'. The worst the team faced was a sort of wide-eyed curiosity and incredulity, as if its members might not be quite human beings of Planet Earth. The Aborigines might well have wondered too. 'I thought to give the Blacks a bath before breakfast,' wrote Lawrence. 'We could hear them saying they will never allow them in as the dye will spoil the bath thinking they were white men and just dyed for the occasion. This idea so impressed the ticket clerk that he w'd not give tickets until he washed and rubbed them with towles [sic] this satisfied him.'

They were not quite the first of their race to visit England. Several individual Aborigines had arrived previously – the earliest in 1793, when Australia's first governor, Arthur Phillip, returned to England with 'two promising young men', Bennilong and Yemmerawannie, who 'had acquired from residing with the Governor, a knowledge of the usages of civilised life, and both were persons of more than ordinary sharpness and address'. Bennilong was presented to George III. 'He adopted the observances of society with remarkable readiness, and behaved on all occasions, while among strangers, with propriety and ease.' Yemmerawannie died in England, but Bennilong returned to Australia, where he stopped playing the game, 'threw off his fine clothes, and the restraints of civilised life, as alike inconvenient and distasteful, and in spite of all persuasions to the contrary, reverted to his old habits and his old haunts'.*

But Aborigines remained a novelty in England and as such they were gawped at. The more educated justified their curiosity as scientific, and wondered about their relative status in the Darwinian hierarchy and the family of races. The *Sheffield Telegraph* reported that the Aboriginal team turned out to be 'a really fine body of men, of superior type for Australians, and in "build" and physique not only far removed from the low, negro type of the *genus homo*, but able "to take their own part" with well-developed Europeans'. Down in Eastbourne, the *Standard* decided that 'the troop, although perfectly black, did not at all give one the idea of negroes, having more of the Malay appearance, or, as we heard several remark, "why some of them are exactly like the pictures of Sikh soldiers." Some of them were very diminutive. Everyone who has had anything to do with them bears testimony to their good behaviour, in fact they are quite the gentleman, their only resemblance to the savage being their taciturnity.' The *Newcastle Daily Chronicle* more blandly complimented them on their 'smart, lively and gentlemanly appearance'.

Sporting Life announced them to be

> the first Australian natives who have visited this country on such a novel expedition [true], but it must not be inferred that they are savages [as opposed to peaceable 'natives']: on the contrary, the managers of the speculation make no pretence to anything other than purity of race and

---

*From H. G. Bennett, *A Letter to Earl Bathurst, Secretary of State for the Colonial Department, on the Condition of the Colonies in New South Wales and Van Diemen's Land* (London, 1820).

origin. They are perfectly civilised [whatever that might mean], having been brought up in the bush to agricultural pursuits as assistants to Europeans [what they endured was more like Southern state plantation slave labour], and the only language of which they have perfect knowledge is English [untrue].'

The only overt incident of what a century later would be described as 'racial discrimination' came in mid-July, during a match in York. The *Yorkshire Gazette* reported that 'apparently due to objections from one or two of the Yorkshire gentlemen, who should have known better . . . on luncheon being announced, the aboriginals found themselves excluded, nearly all the seats being filled. At this they took offence and left the tent, one of them (Mullagh) declaring he would not play again. This untoward event was the cause of much criticism.' A shocking breach of sporting decorum indeed – for as the *York Herald* pointed out, 'Cricket has hitherto owed much of its popularity as a national pastime to the perfect equality on which all who indulge in the game have met at the wickets.'

Far more controversy was provoked by the quality of the Aborigines' play. Whereas *The Times* saw only weakness in the Oval match, the *Sheffield Telegraph* of 26 May noted an extraordinary accuracy and sharpness of eye. 'We take the liberty of assuring those who have been led to believe that the Australians are a set of humbugs that they are very widely mistaken. These men show very superior cricket indeed. Their bowling is dead on the wicket . . . their "return" of the ball is simply marvellous.' Half-way through the tour, the *Yorkshire Gazette* of 18 July demurred: 'It may be stated that they have much to learn ere they become good cricketers, their fielding and bowling is indifferent, their batting (with the exception of Cuzens) devoid of science.'

What nobody could dispute was that the team was immensely amusing – 'The greatest exponents of brighter cricket in the history of the game,' in John Mulvaney's words – and, local or national honour notwithstanding, the charmed crowds cheered them on. 'As each wicket fell, there was loud applause, everyone expressing themselves desirous that the Australians should win,' reported the *Brighton Gazette* of 11 June. Attendances were record-breaking: 'The largest number . . . we have ever seen on that ground at a cricket match,' continued the *Brighton Gazette*. '2300 persons paid for admission during the day, independent of subscribers. There were numerous carriages, full of fashionable company, and a galaxy of beauty and fashion graced the subscribers' marquees. A more animated scene we have never witnessed on that ground. It was thought that the charge for admission would have been a drawback for attendance, but it evidently was not so.'

The Brighton match was played against an exclusively amateur team, 'Gentlemen of Sussex', and the *Gazette*'s account of it is objective and circumstantial. It was a closely fought affair, which the Gentlemen of Sussex only won by 3 runs, and the paper's correspondent was left thinking that it was 'not too much to expect' that, with practice, 'the Aborigines of Australia may bring an eleven in a few years able to compete with our county players'. The overall impression is of the Aborigines' enthusiasm and natural talent, countered by inexperience and absence of finesse and artistry.

Man of the match – for whom a purse of £5 was collected – was Mullagh. He was the Aborigines' 'great man', a fine all-rounder, scoring 22½ per cent of runs and bowling 37 per cent of overs in the course of the tour: a grand total of 1685 runs and 241 wickets. He shone as wicketkeeper, had a strong batting partnership with Lawrence and his high delivery, fast and well pitched, felled five wickets in one innings against the Gentlemen of Sussex: 'Quite good enough to play in any of our county elevens,' was the *Gazette*'s verdict. As his fury at the York lunch-tent incident suggests, he was the most sensitive and perhaps most reflective of the team, taking his celebrity and possible social elevation with poignant seriousness. Other notable players were Cuzens, barely five foot tall but a good bat; Dick-a-Dick, a natural catch; and the erratically inspired Twopenny (Jarrawuk), who broke records against East Hampshire when in ten overs and two balls, he took a miraculous nine wickets for 9, eight of them bowled, and went on to catch the tenth batsman.

Not all the team thrived in the damp climate and sooty environment of Victorian England. Tragically confirming some of the fears of the Central Board for the Protection of Aborigines, King Cole (Bripumyarrimin) died of pneumonic tuberculosis in Guy's Hospital on 24 June, and in August the ailing Jim Crow (Lyteejerbillijun) and Sundown (Ballrinjarrimin) were sent back to Australia. Keeping the players away from the demon drink was another problem – Bullocky

(Bullchanach) was probably the most susceptible, though it was Tiger (Bonnibarngeet) who disgraced himself and his team by being arrested in Sheffield, drunk and disorderly at 2 a.m. – the magistrate let him off with a £1 fine and a caution.

Lawrence later recorded his struggle

> to keep them in order under the influence of alcohol which could not be kept from them as they were every day in touch with lovers of cricket who thought it kind to induce them to drink their health and chat with them until the poor fellows got quite helpless to refuse. When I remonstrated with this friendly treatment of the people they said they were not slaves and should have what they liked as they were in a free country and I must not stop them therefore taking all these things into consideration they behaved very obedient and did their best to help me and was always saying it was the gentlemens fault and would make them drink their health and like children would promise to be better I always forgave them after breakfast and said how sorry I was and that I should have to take them home again if they did not improve but I felt sure they would try but under the influence of drink it was hopeless for each disposion [sic] would develop one would quarrel and want to fight another would sulk others wd play games quite harmless and profess their love for me and would do anything to please me what ever else could I do than forgive them.

A decent game of cricket wasn't all that the Aborigines offered in the way of entertainment. Most of their matches were followed by a third day of Australian and English track and field sports. The latter were 'open to amateurs' and allowed competition with the visitors in traditional events like sprinting, hurdles, high jump, vaulting, 'throwing the cricket ball', 'one hundred yards backwards' and 'water bucket race'. A brass band played, modest prizes (ranging from £1 to a new cricket ball) were offered and a good time was had by all. The Aborigines wore possum-skin, lyre-bird feathers and fur loincloths over their white tights: here their 'great man' was Dick-a-Dick, the most outgoing and immediately lovable of the team, celebrated for his 'really marvellous display of proficiency in dodging cricket balls', according to the *Brighton Gazette*. 'Armed only with a narrow shield, shaped like a canoe, and with a strange club or bat in the form of a letter L, he stood up boldly to be pelted by expert throwers, not one of whom could touch him. . . . His attitudes were all very picturesque and sometimes quaintly droll.' What amazed the crowds about this feat was the insouciance with which he ignored balls 'that passed an inch or two from his head, legs or body' and only bothered to parry those which threatened his person. Dick-a-Dick's apparent impregnability always caused tremendous excitement and at the Oval things got out of hand – the stunt had to be abandoned after riff-raff invaded the ground and started hurling stones and abuse.*

Exhibitions of 'the national games of our brethren of the Antipodes' brought the jollity to a climax. Great journalistic effort was expended on describing the boomerang, an object which the Aboriginal team introduced to the British public. The *Rochdale Observer* called it 'the nearest approach to Paddy's description of the gun that would shoot round a corner'; the *Brighton Gazette* wrote less evocatively of 'a strong, broad, curved lath, convex on its upper and flat on its lower surface'. Charley Dumas (Pripumuarraman) excelled at illustrating its whirring and twirling properties, but its tendency to skim at high speed through the stands made it rather dangerous – several hats were knocked flying, a stray dog at the Oval was almost cut in half by its cutting edge and in Bootle a man's brow was lacerated. Less volatile were the Aborigines' spears, 'natural pieces of sharpened wood, almost as small as an arrow', explained the *Gazette*. Members of the team 'stood at some 80 or 100 yards distant to be thrown at, watching the space in their flight. Some of their spears fell almost at the very feet of them, but they seemed to know exactly where the point would strike and they did not stir an inch.' Lawrence contributed his own somewhat less spectacular trick, catching and balancing a cricket ball on the flat of his bat.

The tour was a considerable financial success. Its account ledger survives, showing a cumulative surplus of £2192 of receipts (£5416) over expenditure (£2415). Deducting the original Australian investment, it is reasonable to assume a clear profit of £1000, shared by Lawrence and Hayman – the players seem to have been allowed prize money and all expenses, plus a final bonus, but no actual wage. Nevertheless, the figures distinctly indicate a novelty which had swiftly worn thin. Attendances started high, with reports of 7000 spectators for the opening day at the Oval, and 3000–4000 in the provinces, but

---

*Dick-a-Dick had a generous nature. He gave all his prize money away, keeping only a Swiss clock which he liked to cradle in his arm. At Dewsbury station, as the team awaited a train, the clock was discovered to be missing and Dick-a-Dick had to sprint back to the hotel to retrieve it. Fortunately the train was late, so there was no real panic.

by the end – admittedly, in mid-October beyond the normal cricket season – they had dropped dramatically.

So the tour concluded mutely. After a farewell dinner at the Railway Hotel in Maidstone (where affable Dick-a-Dick responded to a toast with the visitors' only recorded verbatim remark: 'We thank you from our hearts'), there was a last dismal match at the Oval against Surrey – 'a moderate attendance, the weather being cold, dull and showery,' according to *Sporting Life*, with takings of only £64 as against the corking £603 of their début in May. Some of the players then traipsed down to Plymouth to give a one-day display of field sports. In more bad weather, it flopped. Receipts £15 17s 6d, expenditure £91 3s 2d: time to go home. On 19 October the team boarded the *Dunbar Castle* at Plymouth, arriving in Sydney on 4 February 1869, almost exactly a year after its departure.

And that, sadly, was just about that. The team disbanded or dissipated and the Central Board for the Protection of Aborigines enforced a ban on the removal of any native from Victoria, claiming that 'a sharp change in the climate might injure the health of the players and that they might fall into dissolute habits or be exploited commercially'. So little more was heard of Aboriginal cricket – a sport which could have done more towards integrating Black and White Australia than any amount of Christian schemes and pious words. The team has remained part of the lore of Australian cricket and its achievement is commemorated by a granite slab installed in 1951 at Edenhope, on the banks of Lake Wallace.* But against the friendliness it represented there pulled a stronger undertow of hate and fear, and by the end of the nineteenth century Aborigines were in a more desperate, persecuted and isolated position than they had been in the more hopeful 1860s.

The smaller human postscript to the story is the case of Mullagh, whose hopes of social advancement were falsely raised by his months

---

*The *Daily Telegraph* of 23 May 1997 reported that a scorebook of a match played in August 1868 between the Australians and Scarborough Cricket Club had been 'unearthed'. In the brief flurry of interest this caused, Mr Bill Kneale, the club's custodian, announced that he would try to arrange a return match. But whether he could find an Aboriginal XI of the level of the 1868 team is doubtful. See also a fascinating account of an attempt to bring cricket to the Los Angeles ghetto of Compton, in Edward Smith, 'Boyz with Bats', *Prospect*, March 1999, p. 42–7 of fame. He returned whence he came, the estate of a Mr Edgar near Edenhope, where he worked as a rabbiter and shearer until his death in 1891. In season, however, he continued to play first-class cricket and in 1879 appeared in Victoria's team against an All-England XI captained by Lord Harris. But he was not always treated with the 'perfect equality' that should characterise cricketers: on one occasion, according to A. G. Moyes, 'he went with a team to play at Apsley, another township in the area, and when they went to the hotel for lunch someone without much common sense or charity said "And what about the nigger?" The Captain, who should also have known better, replied "Oh, let him have his dinner in the kitchen. Anything is good enough for the nigger." ' Mullagh refused to eat in the kitchen, but sat outside the hotel in silent protest. 'Anything is good enough for the nigger,' he retorted later that afternoon, having deliberately spooned a dolly catch into the hands of a fielder.

In Edenhope he lived on scrubland, in eremitic solitude. He never married, because he felt himself above the women of his own race, but realised that no white woman, the object of his amorous ambitions, would have him. What damage did those teasing daughters of Town Malling's draper unwittingly wreak?

'It is fair to conclude that the Aboriginals were received on terms as equal as any accorded colonials in Victorian England,' writes John Mulvaney. The judgement subtly begs a question: how equal was that? All the politeness with which the Aborigines were greeted cannot disguise the fact that they were regarded less as citizens of the Empire and subjects of the Queen than as curiosities in the cabinet of exotic races that the Victorian imagination loved to contemplate. There was a long tradition of such imports: in 1810, for instance, Sartje, a woman of the South African Khoj tribe, was brought over from Cape Town and exhibited by Bullock in Piccadilly, much as *The Raft of the 'Medusa'* would be ten years later. Apart from her great facial beauty, this 'Hottentot Venus' boasted enormous buttocks and rumours circulated that her genitals had a peculiar formation. Inspection of her clothed person cost 2s a head: the widow of the showman Charles Mathews memorably evokes the scene:

> One pinched her, another walked round her; one gentleman poked her
> with his cane; and one lady employed her parasol to ascertain that all was,
> as she called it, 'nattral'. This inhuman baiting the poor creature bore

with sullen indifference, except upon some great provocation, when she seemed inclined to resent brutality, which even a Hottentot can understand. On these occasions it required all the authority of the keeper to subdue her resentment. At last her civilized visitors departed, and, to Mr Mathews' great surprise and pleasure [the actor] John Kemble entered the room. As he did so, he paused at the door, with his eyes fixed upon the object of his visit, and advancing slowly to obtain a closer view, without speaking to my husband, he gazed at the woman, with his under-lip dropped for a minute. His beautiful countenance then underwent a sudden change, and at length softened almost into tears of compassion.

'Poor, poor creature!' at length he uttered in his peculiar tone – 'very, very extraordinary indeed!' He then shook hands silently with Mr Mathews, keeping his eyes still upon the object before him. He minutely questioned the man about the state of mind, disposition, comfort &c. of the Hottentot, and again exclaimed, with an expression of the deepest pity, 'Poor creature!' (*Memoirs of Charles Mathews*, London, 1839).

In 1822 it was the turn of a family of Laplanders, displayed against a panoramic view of frozen tundra and surrounded by reindeer and elk; in 1840 came some Red Indians with the paraphernalia of wigwams, tomahawks and war dances; in 1847 they were replaced by a troupe of growling, chattering and occasionally yelling Bushmen who posed on a raised stage; while in 1853 you could choose between thirteen Kaffirs in St George's Gallery on Hyde Park Corner, some pygmies and two 'Aztec Lilliputians'.

Dickens found it all nauseating, though more out of repulsion against than compassion for the exhibits. In the figure of the charitable Mrs Jellyby and her schemes for the natives of Booriboola-Gha in *Bleak House*, he had blown the whistle on evangelical missionary reformers; in a broadside published in *Household Words* of 11 June 1853 he went on to deplore the fashion – first popularised by Jean-Jacques Rousseau a hundred years previously – for sentimentalising the inherent virtues of 'wretched creatures, very low in the scale and very poorly formed'. Why hold them up for public show? 'My position', he wrote, 'is that if we have anything to learn from the Noble Savage, it is what to avoid.' However colourful his habits, he continued (from a position of almost total ignorance), 'he is a savage – cruel, false, thievish, murderous; addicted more or less to grease, entrails, and beastly customs . . . a conceited, tiresome, bloodthirsty, monotonous humbug.'

But the effect of *Uncle Tom's Cabin* and the Black and White drama of the American Civil War (1861–5) combined with the spread of Darwinian ideas (*The Origin of Species* was published in 1859, the climax to half a century or more of biological and geological speculation)forced a new consciousness of race, brotherhood and the Family of Man. Dickens's dismissiveness ('I call a savage a something highly desirable to be civilised off the face of the earth') came to seem merely callous; so did the prurient oohing and aahing of the London public. Since the question of an Englishman's relation to creatures 'low in the scale' had become so much more troubling and serious, the overt exhibition of humans as entertainingly bizarre specimens could no longer be justified. Before this watershed, the idea of the cricketing Aborigines, Blacks competing on equal terms with Whites, would have seemed ludicrous if not blasphemous; now their skills became part of the evolutionary jigsaw and the catchphrase 'survival of the fittest' met the sporting injunction 'may the best man win'.

What makes the visit of the Aborigines even more intriguing a cultural phenomenon is that it occurred at a cusp in cricket's development – the point at which it changed its status from that of an innocent sport to that of a solemn ritual symbolic of nationhood. Before the middle of the nineteenth century, cricket had been simply a game – an exuberant bat-and-ball affair, played throughout the countryside on the basis of custom rather than written rule. Then High Victorian culture ambushed it. First its avatars cleaned up the rules, with the Marylebone Cricket Club, on the basis of its longevity, arrogating a Vatican-like role in legislating and arbitrating. The procedures of bowling, lbw and declaration were fixed and codified. Pitches were rolled and flattened, umpires trained and affiliated, caps and white trousers became the dignified uniform, league tables established a hierarchy which remains fundamentally the same today.

But that wasn't all. Because it involved neither sabbath-breaking, cruelty to animals, nor drink, because it lacked the orgiastic, anarchic potential of a lot of urban street games, cricket was deemed eminently suitable as a recreation for the lower orders. It inculcated great virtues: the individual shining for the greater good of the team, the courtesy of fair play, unquestioning obedience to the umpire's authority. Cricket, in sum, was noble: Christian, gentlemanly and, as one commentator, G. J. Cayley, boomed in 1858, 'a happy and compendious illustration of English characteristics and English social institutions'.

Nothing demonstrates this more poetically than a scene in Thomas Hughes' *Tom Brown's Schooldays*, first published in 1857 and immediately a huge popular success. There is no more morally earnest a novel in Victorian fiction. At heart it is a propaganda tract, preaching the virtues of that sub-section of Christian socialism known as 'muscular' – an adjective which Hughes seems to have been the first to use in a religious context – and putting cricket at the centre of its 'healthy, hearty, happy' mission. The story and Tom's own career at Rugby reach their joint climax with the school's end-of-term match against the MCC, its white summer orderliness standing in a beautiful contrast to the muddy pell-mell of football earlier in the book. Tom captains the home team. His side is batting and, as he sits watching play, he reflects on the scene with his little friend Arthur and a young clergyman master.

> 'I'm beginning to understand the game scientifically. What a noble game it is too!'
>
> 'Isn't it? But it's more than a game. It's an institution,' said Tom.
>
> 'Yes,' said Arthur, 'the birthright of British boys old and young, as *habeas corpus* and trial by jury are of British men.'
>
> 'The discipline and reliance on one another which it teaches are so valuable, I think,' went on the master. 'It ought to be such an unselfish game. It merges the individual in the eleven; he doesn't play that he may win, but that his side may.'
>
> 'That's very true,' said Tom, 'and that's why football and cricket, now one comes to think of it, are such much better games than fives or hare-and-hounds, or any others where the object is to come in first or to win for oneself, and not that one's side may win.'
>
> 'And then the Captain of the eleven!' said the master. 'What a post is his in our school-world . . . requiring skill and gentleness and firmness and I know not what other rare qualities.'

Rugby goes on to lose, because time is up and stumps are drawn before they have a chance to win, 'but such a defeat is a victory' and the honour of the higher sportsmanship satisfied. This was very much the ethos which came to imbue all the major public schools in the second half of the century and their pupils took it out into the world of public service. Cricketing values became the values of the Empire – 'discipline and reliance on one another . . . skill and gentleness and firmness and I know not what other rare qualities' – while the game itself served as a dramatic metaphor, transcending linguistic barriers, of the *Pax Britannica*. 'The central popularity of cricket throughout the Empire', suggests J. A. Mangan in *The Cultural Bond*, 'brought in its wake illusions of social unity which implied that the game transcended normal divisions of class, colour and status while clearly and carefully maintaining social distance within imperial social structures.'*

A great part of the charm radiated by the Aborigines' tour of England stems from its freedom from all this mystique. There is nothing to suggest that the motives of Hayman, Wills and Lawrence were anything other than unpious, humane, decent and practical – there was no element of cruelty or compulsion or exploitation, and whatever profit resulted was entirely respectable.

For players and spectators, the cricket itself wasn't a matter of national or even imperial honour so much as good, clean old-fashioned fun. Before the MCC purified the structure and procedures of cricket, professional teams used to tour England as they did Australia, presenting exhibition matches in which the emphasis was on knockabout entertainment rather than refined stroke play.

---

*Why was India relatively slow to take up cricket? Calcutta Cricket Club, founded in 1792, is the second oldest in the world, but among Indians the game only developed in the Parsee community of Bombay: its first match against the British there took place at the Gymkhana in 1877. Nine years later a Parsee team visited England, where it played in Windsor Great Park against eleven British gentlemen captained by Queen Victoria's grandson, Prince Victor. But the great batsman Ranji (Kumar Sri Ranjitsinhi) played only for England and did nothing to help Indian cricket when he returned to rule the state of Nawanagar. India was not admitted to Test match status until 1932. See Mihir Bose, *A History of Indian Cricket* (London, 1992).

Presumably the strict Hindu abhorrence of handling leather was a major barrier to cricket's popularity. At 'the Eton of India', Mayo College, 'cricket formed half the existence of every boy' (Herbert Sherring, *Mayo College, A Record of 20 years, 1875–95*, London, 1897, vol. 1), but further down the social ladder it met more resistance. In two extraordinary memoirs, *Character Building in Kashmir* (London, 1920) and *Grinding Grit into Kashmir* (London, 1922), that remarkable missionary Cecil Tyndale-Briscoe described – in a picture worthy of Evelyn Waugh at his most farcical – vain attempts to fire Hindu lads in his charge with enthusiasm for the noble game. 'By keeping their hands up their sleeves they had the cloth of their garment between their hands and the untouchable cricket ball. When they had to stop or catch a ball they spread out their garment over their knees or between their legs and thus stopped or caught the ball. So a game of cricket as played by Church Missionary Society boys was a well-conducted comic opera.'

(William Clarke's All-England XI was the most celebrated of such outfits.) The Aborigines fitted that mould both on account of their high spirits and the curiosity of their race and colour – an Aboriginal playing cricket held something of the same novelty interest as a dog singing 'God Save the Queen'. Come the 1870s, there would be much more sensitivity in the matter of distinguishing amateur 'Gentlemen' from professional 'Players' – two different castes whose status was reflected not only in score books ('Mr' or a title prefixing the Gentlemen, the Players recorded only with their surnames), but also in the institution of segregated pavilion entrances and changing rooms. In 1868, however, the Aborigines innocently overrode this nascent snobbery and played as themselves, for pleasure and excitement, not reward or recognition.

The next band of Australian cricketers to appear in England arrived a decade later, in 1878, and reports of their doings were relayed back home in a matter of a few hours via a newly completed telegraph line.* This team was entirely white – entirely British, one might say – although the lasting fame of the Aboriginals meant that up North many fans assumed that it would consist of 'blackfellows'. Its central purpose was to follow up on a victory over an All-England team in Melbourne the previous year. For the Australians, this return match was a speculative venture, each player subscribing £50 towards the costs of the visit and standing to share in any profits accruing. In effect, the team was more like a joint-stock company than a club. Because they did not charge individual fees for appearances, the players could call themselves amateur. This would gall the English.

They travelled across the Pacific to San Francisco, then overland to New York, carrying their entire kit in one huge canvas bag adorned with the painted legend AUSTRALIAN ELEVEN. What happened after they disembarked at Liverpool is one of cricket's great sagas. The terrible weather at the opening match at Trent Bridge, with the

---

* Known as 'the imperial connection', it travelled from London by overland wire to Falmouth, by submarine cable via Lisbon to Gibraltar and Alexandria, overland to Suez, by cable to Aden and Bombay, overland to Madras, by cable to Penang, Singapore and Batavia, overland to Banjoewangi, by cable to Port Darwin and overland to Adelaide. The cost of transmission was 10s a word. See K. S. Inglis, 'The Imperial Connection: Telegraphic Communication between England and Australia, 1872–1902', in *Australia and Britain*, ed. A. Madden and W. H. Morris-Jones (London, 1980).

sweaterless Australians shivering in silk shirts; the loss of the canvas bag; the trip to London and more bad weather at Lord's, thunderous showers alternating with hot sun, the Australians in blue and white caps, the MCC first to bat; the tiny, initially indifferent crowd of 500, which smugly applauded W. G. Grace when he hit a 4 off the first ball and assumed that the match would be a walkover; the first tremor of anxiety when Grace was caught at square leg; and then the sensation – a gangling but sinewy bowler of six foot three, with thick black eyebrows, a hooked nose, calculating eyes, a foot-long moustache and a ferocious expression who within twenty-three balls took six wickets for 4 runs, crowning it with a hat-trick. His name was Frederick Spofforth.

The news hit London like lightning. By the afternoon the crowd had swelled tenfold to 5000 and by the close of play that day the Australians were celebrating a crushing victory, which changed the face of the game for ever. The *Pall Mall Gazette* put the Australians' victory down to luck and a freak, while *Punch* parodied Byron:

> The Australians came down like a wolf on the fold
> The Mary'bone cracks for a trifle were bowled,
> Our Grace before dinner was very soon done
> And our Grace after dinner did not get a run.

But *The Globe* faced up to the bitter fact. 'Seldom in the annals of modern cricket has so small a score been made as by the Marylebone Club yesterday, and never was so severe a humiliation inflicted individually and collectively upon the members of the club. The eleven was as good a one as could be found to represent London and England, and probably as good as the Club ever turned out. Yet its best batsmen were bowled out one after another as if they were novices.'

The Australians went on to tour the counties with huge success: both mighty Yorkshire and Lancashire fell and, not for the last time, England was left wondering why it wasn't any good at cricket any more. From a longer perspective we can see that there were two reasons. First, whatever their financial status, the visitors played in a spirit of ruthless professionalism. The expense of staying in England meant that they were obliged to play almost daily, but equally they refused to start before 12 noon and insisted on stopping by

6 p.m. And they played to win. In the words of H. S. Altham and E. W. Swanton, 'They took their cricket in deadly seriousness . . . keen enough about their success to place it above all the minor distractions that, often in the name of hospitality, threaten the form of a touring eleven.' The politesse, the back-slapping, the delicate business of social deference didn't concern them – they could be good, clean sportsmen without it.

Their other related advantage lay in their attitude to bowling. An English gentleman took a slightly dim view of bowling: his caste wished to excel at batting. It was here that the art of cricket lay, providing opportunities to turn stylish defensiveness to one's ultimate advantage with an elegant minimum of sweaty physical effort. Traditionally, on the village green, the squire would face the bowling of his brawny-armed tenant farmer: that was the image which lay at the heart of Victorian cricket in all its glow of social, moral and spiritual rectitude.

The Australians had no such inhibitions. They attacked, full-frontal, and as Altham and Swanton insist, 'It is no exaggeration to say that this was a real revelation to English cricketers.' Framed by aggressive fielding, Frederick Spofforth was their secret killing machine. 'His delivery is quite appalling,' admitted the *Home News* correspondent, 'the balls thunder in like cannon shot.' He took a total of 326 wickets during the 1878 tour – 5 for 31 against Yorkshire; 8 for 52 against Surrey; 9 for 93 against Lancashire. This was nothing less than revolution and English *amour propre* had to be reasserted somehow – after all, English XIs had been thrashing Australian XXIIs down under ever since 1862.

The solution was simple: 'The Demon' (as he became known) Spofforth was in reality an Englishman and not one tarred by the convict brush, either. Every week, 'Spy' drew a celebrity cartoon in the fashionable periodical *Vanity Fair*. The caption for The Demon's depiction explained that 'Mr Spofforth is Australian by origin and breeding, yet like all the better kind of Australians, he is not distinguishable from an English gentleman. He comes, indeed, of a good English family . . . He is withal of excellent manners, modest and diffident and has become a favourite with all who have known him in England.' *Home News* took the view that Spofforth's genius provided welcome proof that 'our flesh and blood' was 'not degenerating in those far-off lands': a victory for Australia could be celebrated as a victory for the greater Anglo-Saxon race. As a hit song from that summer's smash hit show, Gilbert and Sullivan's operetta *HMS Pinafore*, ringingly proclaimed:

> But in spite of all temptations
> To belong to other nations,
> He remains an Englishman!

Spofforth himself proved not unhappy to accept this accolade. He did indeed come from an old Yorkshire family – so old, in fact, that he liked to claim that Spofforths had fought against William the Conqueror in 1066. His father, a lawyer turned adventurer turned banker, had emigrated to Australia in 1836 and married a New Zealander. Their third child, Frederick, was born in 1853. As a boy, he had watched the All-England XI in 1862 and admired an English professional, George Tarrant, pioneer of 'round-arm' bowling at a time when 'under-arm' was still the general rule. After school, young Spofforth joined his father's bank and Sydney's Albert Cricket Club, before beginning his quest for glory in earnest. Every young Australian at the time was fired by the triumph of the colony's first sporting hero, the sculler Ned Trickett who in 1876 had taken the world championship at Henley Regatta from a pukka Englishman, but what distinguished Spofforth was not so much his brute physical strength or speed as his power of analysis.

'Bowl with the brains,' he would tell those who inquired into his secrets and his years of apprenticeship were largely spent watching from the sideline. At one stage in these preliminary studies he is said to have pestered a university professor to explain to him the pure aero-dynamics of swinging, swerving and spinning the ball; the professor told him it was all an optical illusion and nonsense, but Spofforth knew better. 'His mechanical precision is extraordinary, but his success is due even more to the mental influence he brings to bear on his work,' explained the correspondent of the journal *Cricket* in 1882. 'He has made bowling a perfect study, and we have heard many amusing anecdotes of how he labours to solve what appears to him a difficult problem in the art of outmanoeuvring a batsman. He has completely learned perhaps the great secret of bowling, to vary his pitch without giving the batsman the slightest clue to his intentions.' Such was his mastery that he could throw an egg seventy yards and persuade it to land on its base, its shell uncracked.

After the upsets of 1878 the temperature of the competition between England and Australia rose to fever pitch. A team led by Lord Harris, the great nob of English cricket, visited Australia in 1879 to avenge defeat, but Spofforth again pulled off a thwarting 13 for 110. There was an unpleasant incident in one important match too, when a professional umpire from Melbourne travelling with the English team controversially called a Sydney batsman run out. In the ensuing near-riot, during which Harris was assaulted, members of the English team were said to have shamefully bayed that the protesting spectators were 'sons of convicts' – a label about which the Australians were increasingly sensitive. It was a bad show.

By the time Spofforth and his team returned to England in 1880, relations had soured further. The English now took the line that a team calling itself amateur was in reality professional. This complaint was not unjustified. The Australians charged clubs a high fee for their appearances, and each player netted £750 from his share of the profits on the 1878 tour to England – four times more than Spofforth's annual salary in the bank. 'The Australians have seriously and perceptibly aggravated the symptoms of a commercial spirit in cricket,' *Lillywhite's Cricket Annual* complained. 'If the Australians did not make cricket their profession in their native land, they most decidedly did when they came to this country' and English professionals didn't like it. In the words of W. F. Mandle, 'The profits made by the so-called amateur Australian touring teams incensed the English professional who saw the Australians fêted, and lionized, and made much of, and treated as gentlemen, while he, poor devil, has to touch his hat to "my lord" or any "gentleman player".'

For their part, several of these gentlemen players began to point the Australians in the direction of the servants' entrance. In Nottingham there was a tremendous row when the secretary of the club, one Captain Holden, refused to provide the visitors with a free lunch – a perk to which only amateurs were entitled. After the dust settled, Holden pointedly took out a cigar and loudly asked, 'Will some Englishman give me a light?' One of the Australians angrily retorted: 'I can tell you, sir, I am as much an Englishman as you or any gentleman present: I can trace my family back for six generations and perhaps you cannot do more.'

This confusion between the thin lines separating amateur and professional, English and Australian, was compounded by the bewildering case of Billy Midwinter. Born in Gloucestershire, he had emigrated in 1862 and represented Australia in 1877. He arrived back in England with the Australians in 1878, but after eight games he was netted by that crafty devil W. G. Grace, who decided that it would suit him very nicely if Midwinter played for Gloucestershire, his own county. So Midwinter stayed for five years, playing as a professional for England in Australia on England's 1881 visit. In 1882, however, he decided that he had had enough of England and wished to return to live in Australia and play cricket on its behalf again – which, despite vociferous objections in the colony's press to his 'very slippery character' and dubious loyalties, he duly did.

The official England v. Australia Test series, a manifestation of the MCC's obsession with regulated competition, had been inaugurated in Melbourne in 1877; both sides won a single match. In 1880 the first Test to be held at the Oval was won by England, Grace scoring 152 and Spofforth off with a broken finger. But it was the Oval Test of 28–9 August 1882 that will live, in the words of A. G. Moyes, as 'one of the mightiest battles of cricketing history'. The Australians arrived after an eventful voyage, during which Spofforth was challenged to a duel by a cantankerous Frenchman. Fortunately, the affair had blown over by the time the visitors booked in at their favoured haunt, the Tavistock Hotel in Covent Garden, but Spofforth seemed on edge and off form for the first five fixtures of the tour, taking only eight wickets for a mediocre average of 39 runs each.

Then came the Oval Test. The visitors opened miserably on a wet pitch and were all out for 63 by 3 p.m. But Spofforth then bowled Grace for 4 and went on to take 7 for 46, so the English didn't do much better. The second day of play was tense, brilliant and fought to the death – Grace ruthlessly stumped an Australian who briefly moved out of his ground to pat down the pitch; in any other circumstances, an unsporting act. Like some Homeric hero, Spofforth's hackles rose magnificently. During the break, he stormed into Grace's dressing-room and accused him of being 'a bloody cheat' before storming out again, declaring, 'This will lose you the match.'

One spectator dropped dead from the excitement of the match's last minutes; another left his nails pared to the quick and went on to chew through his umbrella handle. Peate was England's eleventh man and last hope – the scorer could not keep his hand steady to write his name and only managed something which looked more like 'Geese' – but he only lasted three balls. Australia finally won by 7 runs, pandemonium broke out and Spofforth with a match total of 14 for 90, was carried shoulder high to the pavilion, as the English crowd sportingly cheered the visitors to the echo. Afterwards, something (some say a bat, some say stumps and bail, some say a lady's veil) was burnt and its ashes gathered in a cask, which remains the sacred relic and ultimate trophy of cricket played between England and Australia today.

On 3 September the *Sporting Times* published the bat's immortal obituary notice:

In affectionate remembrance
of
ENGLISH CRICKET
which died at the Oval
on
29th August 1882.
Deeply lamented by a large circle of sorrowing friends and acquaintances.
    R.I.P.
N.B. The body will be cremated and taken back to Australia

England put a brave face on it and *Punch* managed another of its jaunty ditties:

> Well done, 'Cornstalks'! Whipt us,
> Fair and square
> Was it luck that tript us?
> Was it scare?
> Kangaroo Land's 'Demon', or our own
>
> Want of 'devil', coolness, nerve, backbone?
> Anyhow, stow nagging!
> Whipt we are.
> Boggling's as bad as bragging:
> England's star
> Seems, to some at least, here to have sunk
> Through that worst of Captains, Captain Funk.

But the lesson's ready,
Dash and skill
Fail without cool, steady
Nerve and will.
That's the best team that calmly pulls together,
Uphill or downhill, fine or dirty weather. . . .

This was Spofforth's triumph, and much Victorian and Edwardian ink would be spent accounting for it. The Demon may not have been the fastest of bowlers, runs the general conclusion, but he was certainly the most terrifying. Simon Rae talks of the way he could ascend to 'a plane of supercharged hostility where few could live with him'. One elderly Lancashire player graphically explained to Neville Cardus what it was like facing him for the first time:

> I were in right form and not afeared of him when I goes in to bat. He'd just taken a wicket, but I walks into th' middle jaunty-like, flicking my bat, makin' rare fancy cuts through th' slips as I went over t' grass. Well, at the Oval, you have to pass t' bowler on the way t' crease, and as I got near Mr Spofforth, he sort of fixed me. His look went through me like a red-hot poker. But I walks on past him along th' wicket to th' batting end. And half-way down somethin' made me turn round and look back at him over my shoulder. And there he was, still fixin' me with his eye.

Even the inimitable Dr W. G. Grace was regularly flummoxed. His encounters with The Demon have something Homeric, in a comic way, about them. There was little love lost between the two men. Grace, ever cantankerous and not always a good sport, drily wrote in his *Reminiscences* that he found 'it difficult to express all one feels about Spofforth', while Spofforth enjoyed recounting the times he had humiliated the great Doctor.*

Grace was not singled out. Spofforth 'seemed to exude a pathological hatred of all batsmen', continues Ralph Barker, 'and even after he had bowled the ball, with rhythmic but deceptive velocity, he did not always feel that he had attacked the batsman enough. Two or three

---

*To *The Memorial Biography of Dr W. G. Grace*, ed. Lord Hawke (London, 1919), Spofforth contributed his favourite anecdote (misremembered, according to Simon Rae in his authoritative biography of Grace). A few years after their first uneventful meeting in Australia, Grace was casually practising in the nets. Spofforth, still an unknown, anonymously sent him down a couple of lollers, someone else sent down a few more, and then 'I sent him down one of my very fastest. He lifted his bat half up in his characteristic way, but down went his off-stump, and he called out in his quick fashion when not liking anything: "Where did that come from? Who bowled that?" But I slipped away, having done my job.'

times in each four-ball over he would follow through up the pitch, seeking the involuntary return catch, closing in on the batsman, hounding his prey.' It was tremendous theatre. Spofforth played the part to the hilt – he loved appearing as a pantomime Mephistopheles at fancy-dress balls – and was chillingly effective. But he wasn't just showing off: as he explained to the *Pall Mall Gazette*, the terror he inspired was vital to his conception of a bowler's first duty 'to lead astray the batsman, to lead him astray by never allowing him to guess what is coming'.

(England's revenge on Spofforth and the humiliations of 1878 and 1882 came half a century later, with the notorious 'bodyline' controversy. In the 1932–3 season, as part of a desperate attempt to stop the unstoppable Australian Donald Bradman, two English players, Harold Larwood and Douglas Jardine, devised a devastating new technique of bowling, backed by a relocation of fielders. Instead of Spofforth's awe-inspiring *terribilità*, it adopted the more directly brutal threat of hitting the batsman's torso or head. The brutal unsportingness of this tactic brought the honour of English cricket low and it was soon outlawed.)*

Spofforth's career was not a long one. On the 1884 tour he took a sensational 14 for 37 in one Test, but elsewhere that season his performance was impaired by the news of the death of his brother and his meeting with his future wife, Phillis Cadman, daughter of a wealthy tea importer. In 1885 he became a bank manager in Moonee Ponds, a suburb of Melbourne;† in 1886 he returned to England to play cricket and to marry, but the dislocating of the middle finger of his bowling hand meant the end of his international career. After two unhappy years back in Australia, he returned to England and took over his father-in-law's tea business in Derbyshire. Like Midwinter, Spofforth now decided that to be born and bred Australian meant nothing at all: as a genuine nationality, the label could be left to the Aborigines. He began to bowl for his new home county, jumping a rule that required two years of local residence by arguing that he had settled in Derbyshire for personal reasons, not as an opportunistic cricket professional. His

---

*See Laurence LeQuesne, *The Bodyline Controversy* (London, 1983)
†Latterly better known as the *dulce domum* of Dame Edna Everage.

attitude was clear-cut. 'Personally, I regard myself as an Englishman,' he wrote, 'but other people seem to take a contrary view.'

In later life – he died in 1926 – The Demon Spofforth became the impeccable Edwardian paterfamilias: a prosperous businessman, aloof and undemonstrative towards his four children, a keen horticulturalist and apiarist, a perpetrator of faintly vicious practical jokes. Perhaps he really was English after all.

CHAPTER 6

The Teetotum Spin: Exotic Dancers

In 1886, the same year that Frederick Spofforth's Test career came to an end, another hopeful young Australian set sail from Port Melbourne. Born in 1861, Mrs Charles Armstrong was the daughter of a prosperous Scots building contractor who had made a small fortune during Melbourne's fabulous boom years as 'the Chicago of the South'. Recently she had separated from her handsome but hopeless husband and decided to leave for England with her baby, chaperoned by her father who had been nominated as Victoria's delegate for that summer's Colonial Exhibition at the Crystal Palace. Strong-chinned and plain-speaking, Helen Armstrong was the embodiment of a recent phenomenon much noted by the new women's leisure and glamour magazines – the Australian Girl. Twenty years previously, Europe had been gossiping about the pert but enchanting American Girl (a breed commemorated by Henry James in *Daisy Miller*); now it was the turn of a tougher, coarser quantity. 'The innate shyness of the English girl has no place in her temperament, nor does she pay much regard to the culture, the self-contained dignity, the gracefulness which sit so easily on the girls of the west. The unrestrained spirit of an independent democracy seems to be ingrained in her.' Thus would the *Sketch* describe the type.

But Helen Armstrong was also exceptionally gifted and extraordinarily determined. Her visit to England was no mere holiday or escape from a mistaken marriage. The fundamental reason for her leaving Melbourne – a town of 'parsons, pubs and prostitutes', as she later acidly described it – was to launch a career as an operatic soprano. To achieve this end, and the glory that went with it, she would have sacrificed anything – even the embarrassing encumbrance of her baby son, who was soon sent back to her husband for rearing. 'I do not think anything in the world could have hindered me from becoming a singer,' she once admitted, and nothing did. Yet she remained loyal to her home town, changing her name to Melba –

Nellie Melba – in tribute to it and unambivalently insisting throughout her forty years of worldwide success that her nationality was Australian. 'I put Australia on the map,' she asserted. There is a grain of truth in the statement.

The story of Melba's rise to fame – of how Sir Arthur Sullivan nearly offered her a place in the D'Oyly Carte chorus, of how she moved to Paris to study with the legendary teacher Mathilde Marchesi, of how Covent Garden at first failed to recognise her – is well known to opera lovers. But the rise was not only professional. 'I'm a damned snob,' she freely admitted and hand in hand with her ambition for a place on the finest opera stages went her craving for a place in the highest social circles. Twenty, even ten, years previously it would have been impossible to have twinned these two spheres – the one debarred the other – but towards the end of the century, in an atmosphere of domestic smugness and prosperity, moral corsets in certain quarters were subtly loosened.

The key which unlocked the doors for Melba was the patronage of Oscar Wilde's great friend Gladys de Grey, sister of the Earl of Pembroke, whose husband Lord de Grey was the Chairman of the Royal Opera's directorate. Gladys de Grey had been overwhelmed by Melba's singing in Brussels and resolved to befriend her. 'You will be under my care and I shall see you do not lack for friends and hospitality,' she wrote to Melba, who was only too happy to be made Lady de Grey's personal project. Thus did an unknown, untried Australian end up at Covent Garden, cast alongside some of the biggest stars of the era. Fortunately, the quality of Melba's singing justified the backstairs manoeuvring required to position her there and, following her triumph in Gounod's *Roméo et Juliette* in 1889, Gladys de Grey threw her a party – 'the first party to which I went after I became a somebody,' gushed Melba later in her autobiography. 'Never shall I forget the succession of women who drifted into that room . . . The Duchess of Leinster, robed in white satin with marvellous sapphires round her neck, holding her head like a queen. Lady Dudley, with her lovely turquoises, so numerous that they seemed to cover her from her head to her knees . . .' etc., etc.

Melba became entirely fashionable. She settled at the Savoy, London's magnificent new luxury hotel, her suite furnished with scented bed linen and a personal telephone. The *Sketch* and the *Star* and the *Era* interviewed and photographed her, Rothschild became her bankers, Escoffier devised Pêche Melba in her honour. Soon she had accumulated enough credit to buy herself a stucco mansion in Regent's Park, which was gutted and remodelled in extravagantly vulgar Louis Seize style. She was always palatial in her tastes, and unashamedly self-important. Prima donnas, since the beginnings of opera in the seventeenth century, had habitually supplemented their operatic incomes by singing for private parties, at which they would be cordoned off from the guests. Not Melba, who only sang at her own parties or gratis as a favour to friends.*

Melba wasn't the first or only visiting prima donna to be accorded such gracious treatment. Lillian Nordica (born Lillian Norton, in Maine in 1857, and a great Wagnerian), the enchanting 'American girl' who preceded and overlapped with her at Covent Garden in the years 1887–93, had also been favoured. It wasn't just that Sullivan's American mistress, Mrs Ronalds – herself a woman who suffered little from her impropriety – introduced Nordica to various members of the Prince of Wales's smart set. Unbesmirched aristocrats opened their doors to her as well: the gracious Duchess of Marlborough, invited her to a house party at Blenheim, for example, and the Duke of Teck rose and went over to speak to her while she was waiting to sing at a private concert.

What boundaries remained? 'Never speak disrespectfully of Society, Algernon. Only people who can't get into it do that,' pronounced Oscar Wilde's Lady Bracknell and her cynical insistence that the superficial maintenance of the proprieties is more important than being truthful, sincere or Earnest makes her a typical voice of 1890s morality: this was a 'society' which had lost faith, even in itself. A visiting diva could flourish in such an environment, so long as she was prepared to play the game of being nominally married. Both Melba and Nordica were generally known to live apart from their husbands, or at least to travel the world unchaperoned and unaccompanied, but nobody inquired too deeply – they were even allowed to pass the Lord

---

*Later in life (she died in 1931), Melba would become positively obsessed with her quasi-royal status. Melba warrants were handed to satisfactory tradespersons and graded Melba tiepins distributed to those who had served her well. In Australia, she lived near Melbourne in an impressive villa coyly called Coombe Cottage, where she referred to herself, only half-jokingly, as the Countess of Coombe. Significantly, Gladys de Grey's house in Kingston-upon-Thames was also called Coombe.

Chamberlain's *cordon sanitaire* and sing for Queen Victoria at her Command Performances in Windsor Castle.

The sin was to be found out, and in 1891 Melba committed it. Her romantic involvement with an aristocrat nine years younger than herself reached the gossip columns in Paris – Melba later claimed that their source was a rival American soprano Emma Eames* – and the smoking rooms of the London clubs. The level of interest in the affair was hardly surprising since the aristocrat in the case was no less a noble personage than the duc d'Orléans, Pretender to the throne of France, whose name soon reached the ears of Melba's abandoned rogue of a husband Charlie Armstrong, in Australia. Scenting possibilities, he sailed to Europe, threatened a duel and ended up serving English divorce papers on the duc, naming him as co-respondent and suing for half a million francs in damages.

A year later, presumably after much legal wrangling, the case mysteriously vanished from the lists before it came to court: there seems to have been a settlement, in which Armstrong promised to lay off in return for an income and custody of his and Melba's son. Her sub-sequent amours – legend suggests them to have been many – were conducted with impenetrable discretion. Duchesses continued to look on her kindly, and her artistic reputation and pull at the box office suffered not a jot from the whiff of *scandale* – if anything, it contri-buted to her glamour. Only royalty coolly turned away and there were no more invitations to Command Performances at Windsor Castle (a snub which rankled: many years later, after all was forgiven and she had been awarded a DBE, a close friend casually remarked on her passing physical resemblance to the late Queen. 'Don't say that! I hated the bloody woman,' she retorted).

So the prima donna of the 1890s could do pretty much as she pleased – make a noise in public; say what she liked and sleep where she liked; spend her own money and even tell men what to do. There was no more 'liberated' class of woman in Europe. Yet her position remained highly anomalous. Her statelessness helped: hidden behind the mask of an Italianate pseudonym, constantly itinerant and

---

*Melba never forgave Eames, who may indeed have been guilty of the charge. Encountering her in a hotel corridor in later years, Melba was observed to sweep her magnificently past, uttering a patronising 'Good day to you, Eames', as though the latter were the housekeeper.

polylingual, with a unique earning power, she could easily be granted the moral exemptions allowed a visitor.

Singing also had an ecclesiastical dimension, which helped. In 1849 the pious Swede, Jenny Lind, had visited the Bishop of Norwich and decided that a career on stage was incompatible with a career as a Protestant. Henceforth she sang only sacred music. But later in the century the French-Canadian Emma Albani, a great favourite in Victorian London,* was able to combine opera and church without feeling compromised – although, as she told the *Sketch* in 1893, 'she would never think of wearing a low [necked] gown when singing the sacred themes of oratorio'.

For the prima donna's sister-in-art, the ballerina, it was harder to maintain dignity. The taboo against a woman raising her voice was easier to break than the taboo against her displaying her legs, even if prophylactically, encased in white tights and satin slippers. The only possible interpretation that could be put on such exposure was that of unequivocal sexual provocation, a danger from which Victorian society was anxious to protect itself, yet a charge which nobody could altogether make stick.

At the centre of the problem sat the lowest caste of theatrical life, the native-born ballet girl, who struggled to hold herself at the level of respectability granted a flower-seller. And the corrupting influences were not only male. According to a moralist in the magazine *Truth*: 'It is not so much the stage itself which is a bad school for the morality of ballet-girls, as the room in which they are herded to dress together – the language of Billingsgate is mild in comparison with that in which some of these young ladies indulge in this common room.'

The ballet girl's situation was aired at intervals in the press. In 1859 there was widespread reporting of a legal case involving a ballet girl called Jane Newell who had attempted to improve on her near-starvation wages of 9s a week by prostituting herself. Amid a lot of tut-tutting, the *Era* reminded its readers that although Newell might have been a bad lot (she was accused of false pretences and other minor offences), the ballet girl represented

---

*She sang Elisabeth in the performance of *Tannhäuser* at Covent Garden, which Wagner deserted for the delights of a German restaurant in the Strand. See p. 73.

a class of females who, from their exposure to temptation, their hard work, and miserable wages, rather deserve our commiseration and applause than what they often meet with instead, reproach and contempt; for we have good reason for knowing that the ranks of the ballet contain innumerable instances of the most upright moral conduct and filial duty, and it is no less a gross wrong to the body than a disgrace to our nature to condemn the whole for the individual vice or depravity of a few . . .

Five years later, in 1864, *Punch* returned to the theme, printing a presumably authentic letter from 'A Lady of the Ballet'. She claimed to be on a weekly wage of 12s, and detailed her expenditure: pink satin shoes, 'about 5s 6d a pare'; 'Uncumbastabel Tarlatan',which is 'secuer again catch fire, 1s 6d a yard, though as no boddy buys it, it is soled for 10½d, but it looks yellerish not white'; 'Tunget of soder', for washing petticoats, 1s 4d a fortnight, and so forth.

> It costs you see about £1 13s 2d to start any one us ladies desently, and I have told you what a continnuel exspense it is on us. I have not said anything of my own averyday dress, gownd and shawl and boots, which were very quick; and my lodging which I cannot get for less than 2s a week, even in clubbing with another lady. Then, my dear, one must dine sometimes evin if it is exspense, and it dose not do to be exstravigant, but safe a little, as when I am ill and cannot come to the Theatre, the Mananger *dose not pay me, but forfits every night we stop away.*

The following week *Punch* published another anonymous letter, praising the Lady of the Ballet's candour and half-teasingly proposing the establishment of a Home for Ballet Girls, even though

> it would be next door to impossible to get trustees to manage it. What father of a family could undertake the office, without continual torments in his domestic life? . . . Just conceive the pious horror wherewith his wife would shrink and shudder at his mention of that terribly contaminating place . . . I just throw out the suggestion, but of course I don't expect that any one will act on it, for I know that most rich people have far too much morality to think of doing anything for such people as poor ballet-girls, who are supposed to be descended from some of the Lost Tribes.

In 1869 there was another flurry of concern, precipitated by a circular issued by the Lord Chamberlain to all the theatres under his jurisdiction, noting that press reports indicated 'much reason to complain of the impropriety of costume of the ladies in the pantomimes, burlesques, &c.' and politely asking the managers to do something about it. This caused a great stir, but was generally considered ludicrous, since the Lord Chamberlain had failed to see 'with his own eyes what he took it upon himself to condemn' and his authority did not extend over the worst offenders, namely the new music halls. In an article entitled 'Stage Morality, and the Ballet', an anonymous writer in *Blackwood's Magazine* argued against such puny attempts at censorship:

> . . . the scanty drapery of the ballet, for the purposes of art, and art alone, is no offence against good taste or good manners; but if the ballet girl – not for the sake of art, but for the sake of attracting lewd attention – overdoes the scantiness, and betrays the immodesty of her mind by her motions or gestures, she commits an offence and ought to be hissed from the stage which she disgraces.

'Better that public opinion should regulate such matters,' was *Blackwood's* conclusion. Public opinion was difficult to canvass, however, and the ballet girl remained unsure whether she stood to be judged as a misunderstood artist, the victim of unmerited social prejudice or a member of the oppressed proletariat.

To her aid came Stewart Headlam, a man of rare, if faintly batty moral courage. Born into the heart of the Establishment, and educated at Eton and Cambridge, he was deeply influenced by the Christian Socialism of F. D. Maurice and by study of the liturgy of the early church, much of which was ecstatically danced. As a reforming young cleric with a burning desire to work 'in the community', as we would now put it, he first came across ballet girls during his curacy at St John's, Drury Lane. Later he recollected to a journalist from the *Sketch*, in a typically unfortunate phrase (Headlam's conversation was pitted with unintentional *double entendre*, which amused the sceptics), 'I have had intimate knowledge of their way of living, and I think it compares favourably with that of any other class of girls forced to go out into the world to fight for existence.'*

---

*In 1895 he supported a far more unpopular cause – the sodomite Oscar Wilde. Headlam stood bail for him, taking him in his carriage to the trial every morning. Many members of the Church and Stage Guild resigned when they heard of this, but Headlam asserted that he had offered Wilde help on the grounds that every man is innocent until proved guilty. And his compassion extended beyond that: at Wilde's release two years later, Headlam collected him from Pentonville and allowed him sanctuary in his house. Headlam – whose own sexuality does not appear to have been the same as Wilde's – was a true Christian.

In 1879 he founded the Church and Stage Guild. Following Maurice's view that the priesthood should sympathise with working-class amusements rather than excoriate them, this was less a mission to reform the morals of the profession, more an attempt to build a bridge between two antipathetic callings. The whole thing was 'well-intentioned but silly', snorted a columnist in the magazine *Truth*. At its peak in the 1880s, the Guild boasted some 250 members from both camps. The core of its activities was a programme of fraternising meetings and tea parties, sometimes held in Headlam's own house, exquisitely furnished in the Aesthetic style with Morris wallpapers and Pre-Raphaelite painting. 'Speeches are made to convince an unbelieving world that the ballet, viewed as a profession, is in a special manner the abode of all the Christian virtues,' explained *Truth* incredulously. To fit in with the dancers' working schedule, proceedings often did not begin until after midnight – an hour which fuelled further sneers from the cynics.

On one memorably Trollopean occasion, Headlam's Bishop, the relatively liberal Frederick Temple, agreed to meet a representative of the Guild, one Miss Wooldridge, *danseuse*. The Bishop sat clutching a copy of the New Testament as though it were vampire-repelling garlic. What, Miss Wooldridge wanted to know, was the source of the church's antipathy to ballet?

'The dance is too sensual,' complained the Bishop (it being unlikely he had ever seen it).

'Do you mean the dancer or the step?' asked the intelligent Miss Wooldridge.

'I mean, er, flesh-coloured tights, the colour of, er, skin,' whispered the Bishop.

'But, my lord,' insisted Miss Wooldridge, 'some of us play the part of fairies: you wouldn't have fairies surely in a blue skin?'

The Bishop shook his head. 'I don't see why so imaginary a creature as a fairy should not have a blue or black skin.'

Such argument was hopeless. At the end of this unsatisfactory interview the Bishop attempted some kindly reassurance. 'I hope you don't imagine I think any harm of you,' he said.

'I should hope not,' Miss Wooldridge pluckily replied, with an understandable touch of huffiness.

In fact, the Bishop was more concerned for the moral health of the audience than of the performers. 'The ballet does suggest what had better not be suggested,' he wrote to Headlam; it leads young men 'into most disastrous sins of imagination'.

Yet absurd and naive as the Guild may seem to us now, it must have effected some slight shift in public consciousness and contributed positively to the contemporary debate about the morality of the theatre. What makes Headlam himself such an intriguing figure is that his agenda wasn't simply limited to the salvation of the ballet girls. He had made a great study of the history of the dance and, in a much reprinted and publicised lecture of 1894, made the first plea in the English language for it to be taken seriously, with a spiritual dimension. The art of dancing, he believed,

> more than all other arts is an outward and visible sign of an inward and spiritual grace ordained by the Word of God. Do not let there be any confusion between an exhibition of beautiful limbs and pretty faces, he preached, still less between an exhibition of delicately moving drapery or gorgeous brocades. The lovers of dancing want something more; for these things after all, together with the scenery, and even the music, are only accessories to the main thing, to the poetry of vital motion, to the trained, finished movements and steps of each individual dancer in the whole ballet.

Sadly, as we shall see, this high tone was not met by what the West End of London had to offer in the Terpsichorean line. 'There are signs of the ballet being spoilt by its being over-dressed and over-propertied,' Headlam wrote, 'of its sinking into a mere spectacular display.' What he proposed in the way of reform – an academy of dance, teaching according to the classical school of Carlo Blasis; simplicity of staging; criticism informed by erudition and experience; visits to the provinces; an end to the church's prejudices – would all come to pass forty years later, largely thanks to the work of Ninette de Valois.

Meanwhile, the fight was just beginning. 'Among the many libels which I have collected about the ballet,' continued Headlam, 'few are more ridiculous than the sneer I have before me – "that English women may make good and virtuous daughters and wives, but they make very bad ballet dancers".' However, his critics did have a point. At the time he wrote, there were no British ballerinas. Nice girls wouldn't even try and there wasn't much incentive to do so. Dancing on stage was more an act of desperation than a professional vocation. In 1896, volume 8 of Charles Booth's immense survey of the *Life and Labour of the*

People in London records that at the major theatres a member of the corps could expect to earn a weekly wage of between 35s and 15s, depending on her proficiency and personal appearance. This compares favourably with the rates of domestic servants, until one bears in mind the expenses listed by the anonymous *Punch* correspondent thirty years earlier: silk tights, 15s, for example, or slippers lasting only a few weeks, 5s. After such deductions the run of ballet girls did no better than a wash-house attendant, chimneysweep or parlourmaid, and it is small wonder that so many of them doubled up as 'dressmakers or needlewomen, or may have recourse to less reputable modes of obtaining a livelihood'.

But then ballet in London in the 1890s was altogether a debased art. Forget Degas' pastels, or *Giselle*: the romantic refinements of Marie Taglioni and Fanny Elssler had long since passed out of fashion, to be replaced by no-holds-barred, no-expense-spared parade shows in vast vaudeville theatres where the actual dancing was only a minor element of the attraction. 'Ballet is dead and gone,' mourned Dickens in *All the Year Round* as early as 1864 and by the end of the century it was little more than a quaint curiosity, an interlude in a colourful variety show, aimed at passing customers of unsophisticated taste rather than an élite of connoisseurs.

It was also essentially foreign, an exotic import. Ballet was not an art which the English royal court ever nurtured – hence the absence of a Royal Academy of Dancing, only established here after the First World War – and all its artistic development took place in Italy and France, where it was blessed by long-term aristocratic patronage. The height of its brief London vogue in the 1830s and 1840s (when visiting superstars like Taglioni and Elssler, alternating or coinciding with the scarcely less dazzling Fanny Cerrito, Carlotta Grisi and Lucile Grahn in full-length evenings of ballets tragical, comical, historical and pastoral, made it sensationally commercial) did throw up a few pale native-born aspirants, notably the wretched Clara Webster, who died from burns in 1844 after her costume caught fire from the footlights – a common occupational hazard. But with only the equivalents of Mr Turveydrop's genteel dancing and deportment school to provide instruction, no standard or tradition could be established.

Theatrical dancing in Britain was otherwise a more rough-and-tumble affair, folkish rather than formal. It drew on circus stunts and comic turns, on the Harlequinade and pantomime, on clog, tap and Morris routines, and such training as there was tended to be passed through families like (to resort to yet another Dickensian example) the Crummles in *Nicholas Nickleby*. This sort of unpretentious stuff was a regular filler on the music halls' bill of fare and nobody was much fussed about it.

For anything approaching genuine ballet, few significant venues existed. In London – aside from Covent Garden, Drury Lane and Her Majesty's, where a danced interlude in the middle of an opera was customary – there were the Alhambra and the Empire; in Manchester, the Palace of Varieties (the latter, which opened in 1891, was in effect a satellite of the London theatres, renting their productions for brief seasons, as did the Olympia in Paris and the Théâtre de la Bourse in Brussels. Its success was severely limited by the authorities' refusal of an alcohol licence).

The most famous of these was the Alhambra, standing on a site in Leicester Square now occupied by an Odeon cinema. Designed as 'a model of Moorish grandeur' in a style which (according to the prospectus) has 'as yet no perfect exemplification in the metropolis', it opened in 1854 as an exhibition centre, complete with laboratories, lecture halls and an organ – a 'Panopticon of Science and Art', in sum, graced by a Royal Charter requiring its presentations to be 'instructive'. Religious services were held on Sundays. Not surprisingly, it soon failed financially – the organ passed to St Paul's Cathedral – and in 1860 the auditorium was converted into a luxuriously appointed four-tiered music hall seating 3500 and boasting a proscenium stage in place of the organ. In 1864 Frederick Strange, formerly the catering manager at Crystal Palace, took over the lease and added both a magnificent series of forty chandeliers and a 'Torrent Cascade' of 'Real Water'. Strange seems to have been keen on ballet, but was hampered by the peculiar terms of his licence. Intoxicating beverages could be served; music and dancing could accompany them. What could not be allowed was anything approaching a stage play, for such a thing would turn the Alhambra into a legitimate theatre, under the jurisdiction of the Lord Chamberlain. This meant that no narrative element could be admitted to the ballet, a restriction which Strange immediately challenged. The *Grand Oriental Divertissement*, first performed on Boxing Day 1864, featured a 'dagger dance' involving the killing of an imaginary enemy. Seven legitimate theatres, anxious to preserve their prerogatives, accused Strange of a breach of the rules, and the magistrate was obliged to uphold their complaint with a fine of £3 1s, even though the guilty verdict was later reversed on appeal.

Such problems continued to dog the Alhambra. A Parliamentary Select Committee reviewed what was obviously a ludicrous state of affairs: Strange gave evidence, informing the panel of MPs that he had increased the corps de ballet's wages by twenty per cent and that prostitutes – the biggest worry underlying the orderliness of large theatres and music halls – constituted only three per cent of his audience. The Committee recommended a change in the law, but the bill was never drafted and in 1867 Strange was prosecuted again over *Where's the Police?*, for which he was fined £240. (The title suggests that Strange was being deliberately provocative.) Matters finally came to a head, however, over a different episode: in 1870 a tabloid newspaper, *Days' Doings*, published a graphic picture of a performance at the Alhambra of the Parisienne Quadrille, commonly known as the cancan. A police investigation reported that its flashing revelation of female thigh, topped by scanty drawers, was indecent – despite the covering of flesh-coloured hose. The timing of this was unfortunate, as Strange had just applied for a renewal of his licence for music and dancing.

Inevitably, it was rejected – at which point Strange closed down the Alhambra. In order to stop the nonsense and qualify for a new status and licence as a legitimate theatre, he then removed the bar-like arrangement of tables and chairs from the ground level of the auditorium and constructed a conventional stalls area, with serried rows of seats and a ban on smoking and drinking. This had the additional advantage of banishing the prostitutes from an easy cruising ground, and brought the Alhambra a cleaner bill of moral health and an estimated 600,000 visitors a year.

'In days gone by', recorded the *Illustrated Sporting and Dramatic News* in 1880, 'one was supposed to visit the Alhambra disguised as a Californian gold-digger or an Australian stock-raiser or a Cape ostrich-farmer or with a false nose and blue spectacles, *mais nous avons changé tout cela* . . . the Alhambra as a theatre licensed by the Lord Chamberlain is now as decorously conducted as any other dramatic establishment in London.' Unfortunately, such respectability could not save the interior from a spectacular fire, which entirely devastated the interior in 1882. Swift reconstruction followed, however, bringing further improvements to the stage machinery and more Moorish intricacies to the foyers and auditorium. The theatre was now firmly established as a dashing place for the faster sort of young blade, keen for a jolly night out on the town – Jerome K. Jerome's Three Men repair there after their over-eventful boat trip, and they would have been typical in leaving 'after the first ballet' and making for a restaurant. The nightly programme could last up to four hours – the two or three ballets being interspersed with turns of a comic, vocal, acrobatic or magical nature – and only sad, lonely people sat through it from beginning to end.

The Alhambra's direct competition came from the Empire, a smaller theatre which opened on another side of Leicester Square in 1884 (its site is now occupied by a cinema too), decorated first in 'French Renaissance' style, later converted to a mélange of Egyptian, Persian, Indian and Pompeiian. Artistically, it aimed higher than its un-ashamedly crowd-pulling neighbour, with programmes distinguished by poetical recitations and 'Living Pictures', in which celebrated canvases of the Old Masters would be staged as *tableaux vivants*, liberally costumed in flesh-coloured hose. In its first seasons it also made attempts to mount ballet classics like *Giselle* and *Coppélia*, but after these found little favour with the public, it resorted to more glittering novelties.

The Empire radiated an irresistible glamour, which made the Alhambra seem rather plebeian. Royalty itself did not disdain its attractions: in 1889 the theatre hosted a splendid gala evening for the Shah of Persia, escorted by the Prince and Princess of Wales, surrounded by enough dukes and duchesses to have sent even Nellie Melba into a fit of the vapours. The *Star*'s reporter registered the telling implications of the event's social morality. 'HRH [the Prince of Wales] goes oftener to a music hall than the admiring public are aware,' he wrote.

> But Duchesses are not in the habit of frequenting the Empire, not exactly, and hundreds of the high and mighty, and severely proper who were there last night would shudder at the suggestion of an evening there. But there they were, all the Duchesses and nearly all the other distinguished people

in England. Never has there been such a display of diamonds and flowers. The magnificence of the ballet *Cleopatra* was made cheap by the magnificence of the spectacle the auditorium presented.

The Empire's superiority was said to extend even to the class of prostitute it attracted. At the rear of the auditorium of both theatres was a mirrored promenade furnished with crimson settees. Here the women of the town would notoriously wander, awaiting or inviting assignation, and there wasn't much that could be done to stop them doing so. Those punters ambitious for more than a snatched hour of pleasure found it easy to slip into the backstage canteen, where they could preface their seductions by offering to buy coffee for chits of girls from the corps de ballet, shivering in their dressing-gowns. Some struck lucky. The memoirs of musical comedy star Emily Soldene record 'one very tall, elegant girl' at the Alhambra who had obviously graduated to the courtesan class.

> She filled the ideal bill, got twenty-five shillings a week, wore sealskin, sable and magnificent diamonds, came in her carriage and pair, and her footman waited at the stage door with her cloak. She could go into the directors' room without knocking, and sometimes gave His Highness the Maharajah [Dhuleep Singh, an aficionado] a lift. Her portrait as 'Mrs Marini' figured in all the photographers' windows, and taken altogether, she was a very fashionable person indeed. The girls used to coax her and say: 'Hi say, Mareenee, send hus hup er bottle of fizz; won't yer, Mareenee.' And Mareenee, who was charming and splendid and good-natured, did.

A new theatre like Richard D'Oyly Carte's Savoy, opened in 1881 as a home for Gilbert and Sullivan's operettas, made every effort to clean up. No promenade existed there; instead came the innovations of universal individual seating, precluding untoward jostling on benches; higher prices and advance booking; bright electric lighting; sexually segregated floors of dressing-rooms and a ban on unauthorised backstage visitors – all bolstering the possibility that decently married ladies could attend a show without worrying about uncalled-for importunings.

The Empire, however, did not do enough, in the view of one Mrs Ormiston Chant, an American busybody who had taken to reforming the nation's morals after serving as the assistant manager of a lunatic asylum. To her stern way of thinking, the London County Council's force of twenty-three music-hall inspectors (appointed in 1889 and surely a subject for Gilbertian satire) was too *laissez-aller* and in 1894 she mounted a venomous campaign to have the Empire's licence revoked unless it converted its promenade into an area of additional seating. Mrs Chant's prudish Philippics were the cause of much controversy and a certain amount of outright ridicule. The result was a feeble compromise. A canvas screen was hung to separate promenade from auditorium, but its flimsiness invited trouble. In *My Early Life*, Winston Churchill records how as a nineteen-year-old officer cadet at Sandhurst, he participated one Saturday night in a minor riot to rip down the canvas and rid the Empire of this infringement of liberty – his first public defence of the rights of the individual against tyranny, he considered. The management re-erected the screen, the promenaders tore it down again and Mrs Chant eventually turned her attentions elsewhere.

So much for the morals of the audience. What actually happened on stage? We shall never know to what levels of lewdness the lower grade of theatrical establishment sank* – perhaps quite low and certainly drunken, for in 1880 that admirable Ruskinian reformer Emma Cons felt obliged to establish, with tremendous consequences, an uplifting Temperance music hall at the Old Vic ('Abandon Hops, all ye who enter here') – but the ballets at the Alhambra and the Empire were essentially harmless entertainments, which could offend only those who took exception to the Christmas pantomime, dominated as they were by spectacular effects, parades and processions, and peopled by casts of hundreds. 'The English ballet is not content with the primitive simplicity of a drop-scene brush,' complained Revd Headlam. 'It labours with a host of mechanical devices – with extravagant properties, with photographic scenery, with the stratagems of electricians, with all the means that the stage manager can array to dissuade the inner vision from rousing itself. Its aim apparently is to create a diversion for the eye so that the imagination may slumber undisturbed.'

---

*The only verbatim example of an obscene music-hall joke from the Victorian era I have ever found is one recorded by the maverick impresario E. T. Smith in 1866. A comedian walks on to the stage bearing a large clock under his arm. As he turns its key, he leeringly announces that 'this is the way I wind the old woman up on Saturday nights'. See Peter Bailey, *Leisure and Class in Victorian England* (London, 1978), Chapter 7. Vague and tantalising references also exist to an institution called the Judge and Jury Club in Leicester Square, which mounted shows both lewd and nude.

The talents involved in these shows have long been quite forgotten: the names of choreographers (then known as 'ballet masters' or 'dance arrangers') such as Joseph Hansen, Carlo Coppi and Katti Lanner, composers ('music directors') such as Georg Jacobi, directors ('stage managers') like George Edwards, designers ('scene painters') such as C. Wilhelm (William Pitcher) are scarcely recorded in the reference books and there is no reason to think that any of them properly rank with Petipa or Tchaikovsky – it would be another fifty years before they were dignified with the status of 'creative artists'.

Broadly speaking, the style and content of their productions fall into two eras. The 1870s and 1880s were dominated by gentle tableaux, connected by only a thread of narrative. Early in the evening might come a brief comic episode, more dumbshow than ballet, with an intriguing title like *Comeathimifyoucano, Brown, Jones and Robinson*, or *Twiddeltumtwist!* Later came the big attraction, lasting about three-quarters of an hour and generally replaced after a nightly run of three or four months. Fairy-tale subjects were popular (*The Sylph of the Glen, A Strange Dream, The Fairies' Home, The Swans*, the latter possibly inspired by reports from Moscow of *Swan Lake*), as were picture-postcard exhibitions of foreign parts (*The Beauties of the Harem, Hawaia* [*sic*], *Carmen*) and representations of natural phenomena (*The Caverns of Ice, Mammoth Waterfall, Les Fleurs du Jardin*). Fey romantic elements would be incorporated into all these scenarios, framing the *coups de théâtre* (cascades of real live water, ghostly gaseous apparitions, sprays of heavy scent, the Alhambra's famous 'crystal curtain' or 'prismatic torrrent' made from thousands of glass fragments) and transformation scenes. Casts of 200 were usual.

Towards the end of the century tastes changed. The Empire in particular began to feed off meatier subject matter, sometimes peppered with a historical flavour (*Cleopatra, Versailles, Monte Cristo*) and a marginally more adult sense of drama. The other development was a new genre, christened at the time the 'up-to-date' ballet. This seems to have grown up as a result of the wildfire international success of *Excelsior*, a ballet first seen at La Scala, Milan in 1881, which showed a Spirit of Darkness defeated by the inexorable March of Progress towards the latter-day wonders of the Suez Canal and the telegraph. It visited London in 1885, and must have given the city's ballet masters the idea of spinning the theme in a British direction. Dropping pantomime fantasy and flummery, the up-to-date ballet became something between a newsreel and a patriotic pageant, aimed to meet the high water-mark of jingoistic imperialism.

First of the up-to-date ballets was *The Sports of England*, a Christmas show devised by Katti Lanner at the Empire in 1887. According to the researches of Ivor Guest, 'it depicted cricket at Lord's (with female representatives of the MCC and Australian elevens), yachting on the Solent (a *pas de "mal de mer"*), football at Kennington Oval, polo at Hurlingham, hunting at Melton Mowbray, boating at Hammersmith, boxing and Derby Day at Epsom'. The Alhambra soon capitalised on the success of *The Sports of England* by taking an entire series of contemporary themes. Among them were *Our Army and Navy* (self-explanatory); *Up the River* (namely the Thames, complete with a scene of the Henley Regatta); *Chicago* (to celebrate the World Fair of 1893); and *Sita* (set in New York and featuring an airship). Perhaps the most successful of all was the Diamond Jubilee tribute of 1897, *Victoria and Merrie England*. With an original score by Sir Arthur Sullivan, this 'Grand National Ballet' started with 'Britannia sleeping beneath the sacred oak of the Druids', before passing through the likes of Robin Hood and Good Queen Bess to Victoria's coronation and a final march past of 'Britain's Glory', with guest appearances from real military contingents and 'groups, allegorical of British colonies'. It ran an exceptional six months, and was said to have been visited by nineteen members of the Royal Family.

A particularly popular hit at the Empire was *Round the Town*, a 'characteristic ballet' of 1892. Opening with a depiction of the Covent Garden flower market, it revolved round the plight of a destitute woman and her child, a profligate husband, the redemptive ministrations of the Salvation Army and a final tableau entitled 'The Daughters of the British Empire', in which representatives of dependencies from Yarmouth to Burma assembled to receive the benediction of Britannia and her trident. In 1898 some sort of peak – or nadir – of the up-to-date ballet was reached with *The Press*, also seen at the Empire. According to Cyril Beaumont's *Complete Book of Ballets*, this featured three tableaux. The first, drawing on a famous painting of Daniel Maclise, was set in 1471, and showed the English printer Caxton (Mlle Malvina Cavalazzi) receiving state visits from Edward IV (Mr Rockliffe) and the Spirit of the

Liberty of the Press (Mlle Adeline Genée). The second was set in Fleet Street and demonstrated some of the stages in the production of a newspaper. The third was a fantasy of the Hall of the Fourth Estate, in which dancers were costumed to represent a variety of modern publications. 'Father *Times* enters to a march, the *Daily Telegraph* whirls in to a waltz, the *Standard* rises to another march. Then came the Morning Papers and the Evening Papers, who have a difference of opinion which ends with a reconciliation between the *Sun* and the *Star.*' Other titles on parade included the *Sporting Times* (Miss Vincent), the *Golden Penny* (Miss Papucci), *Pick-me-Up* (Miss Gradella), and *The War Cry* (Miss Banbury).

The great majority of the dance within such shows would today be characterised as cheerful summer seaside stuff, perhaps not even that. Dressed *en travestie* as merry men, costermongers or tennis players, the English girls were rarely required to execute more than a hornpipe and mostly confined themselves to a graceful twirl and swirl. 'Frequently the corps de ballet have no room for any more elaborate step than an artless hop and a right about-turn, a kind of convalescent pirouette,' noted an intelligent young aficionado and friend of the Revd Headlam's, George Bernard Shaw, in 1893. Gracing the scene with a display of leg, not a brilliant *entrechat dix,* was the crucial issue, and the choreography made no effort to be inventive or original. It was often more like drill than dance: as the turn-of the-century dance historian J. E. Crawford Flitch explained, 'They marched and counter-marched across the stage, performing a number of evolutions with a kind of military precision. Little more skill was demanded of them than of the banner-bearers at a Christmas pantomime.'

The authentic ballet came in the specific single shape of a visiting ballerina. 'The majority of these are foreigners, because it is said that the English girl will not train with sufficient assiduity,' writes Booth. 'The dancing schools in Milan still supply the English stage with the best dancers, and so maintain the traditions of the past.' More specifically, almost all of them emanated from the school attached to the opera house of La Scala. This establishment was popularly identified as the mecca of the art – rather as the Kirov and Bolshoi are today – and those untouched by its éclat could not expect to command total credibility. As kangaroos were Australian and pyramids Egyptian, so ballerinas were Italian and there was no point in their trying to be anything else.

Nor can they be ranked as great interpretative artists. In the 1870s and 1880s they frequently arrived with their own tailored dance routines and costumes, and space in the scenarios of *The Sylph of the Glen* or *Les Fleurs du Jardin* would be cleared to accommodate them willy-nilly. They sprang no aesthetic surprises. Shaw's critique goes on to bemoan 'the half-dozen *pas* of which every possible combination and permutation has been worn to death any time these hundred years, still calling each hopeless attempt a "variation", and still finishing up with the teetotum spin which is to the dance what the high note at the end of a dull song is to a second-rate singer'.

A ballerina was thus an entirely conventional figure: not only did she come from La Scala and finish with a 'teetotum spin', she also wore white tulle and looked ethereal. Reality could not touch her: she was the dream, the vision, the fairy, the visitor from far away and long ago, floating tremulously on pointe shoes (the corps de ballet wore soft-toed pumps) and using a vocabulary of movement (long, deep arabesques, dazzling brisés, the magical tricks of body control that only girls from La Scala understood) far more sophisticated than that of anyone else on stage.

The stereotype had been fixed by the most famous role in the repertory of Marie Taglioni, still considered the embodiment of the art half a century after she had stopped performing. 'In every successive ballet hailing from La Scala', wrote *The Times*'s correspondent in 1891 while reviewing the Alhambra's *By the Sea*, 'there are traces of *La Sylphide*, if it be only in the conventional appearance of the *première danseuse* in muslin skirts, independently of, and sometimes in flagrant contradiction to, the nature of the theme . . . Miss Emma Palladino duly appears in her muslin skirts to dance her *pas de fascination* upon Margate Sands – the last place in the world where such a costume or such an action could be looked for.'

The part played by the ballerina was thus semi-detached from whatever story or setting was nominally specified. It was not until the more dramatically coherent ballets of the 1890s that she became integrated with the rest of the action, but even then only a leggy girl, masquerading as principal boy, was permitted to handle her amorously (the ballet dancer being an almost exclusively female phenomenon in later nineteenth-century London, with men used only for 'national' and eccentric or comic turns; as *The Times* spluttered on 23 May 1885, 'the male dancer with his *pas* and *entrechats* and stereotyped grin, has disappeared from the English boards, where it must be fervently hoped, he will never again find permanent footing'). Of what she thought about these limited possibilities we know little. Ballerinas lacked the urge to autobiography which impelled their sister prima donnas into print, and many of them had pitifully short careers, followed by long lives of total obscurity. How they came to London, and on what terms, is not altogether clear either; we know that international agents were involved, that (according to Booth) their weekly wage could be up to £20* and that the impresarios themselves toured the great stages and conservatoires of Europe in search of young talent, but there are few details of the process.

So as human beings the visiting ballerinas remain shadowy, two-dimensional figures. Many of them being little more than teenagers, they were often chaperoned by their mothers and probably didn't have much to say for themselves in a frightening foreign capital, but what can be gleaned about them is tantalising. First of the great names of the Alhambra was Giovannina Pitteri, who danced there until 1876. Some suspected her of being pseudonymous – of being in truth a Miss Pitt of Hackney – and insinuated that she was mistress to the theatre's manager Frederick Strange. Others found her a sterling trouper and praised her generous spirit. She was certainly a star in the grand style. Recalling her charms twenty-five years later, Emily Soldene wrote of

> a magnificent creature and great artiste . . . Her hair, naturally dark, was dyed a beautiful gold, quite an up-to-date proceeding then. She had a deliciously white, soft, satiny-looking skin. She told me she bathed in warm milk every day. Her dressing room was gorgeous, decorated with bric-à-brac and silken hangings. She had a French maid and an Englishwoman to wait on her maid, also a toilette set of solid silver, and magnificent presents from many persons, some of them princes.

According to Soldene, she died – as people who bathe in warm milk so often do – 'in poverty and distress . . . while filling an engagement in a low dance house among the sailors of Marseilles. She had spent all her money: the presents were gone, so were the princes.'

---

*i.e. nothing like a great opera diva of the time such as Melba, who could command twenty times that sum for a single performance.

From 1874 she vied with a newcomer, Erminia Pertoldi. They were chalk and cheese, reported the critic of the *Illustrated Sporting and Dramatic News*. 'I should say that Pitteri's style is pure motion, noiseless and perfectly symmetrical,' he wrote, 'while that of Pertoldi, though more vivacious and definitely fascinating, is suggestive of sound. Pertoldi touches the earth, Pitteri treads on the air.' From his 1s seat in the stalls, the young Shaw developed a terrific crush on Pertoldi – one which he soon attempted to immortalise in his apprentice novel *Immaturity*, written in 1879. Coded allusions to 'Terpsichore' in his diary for 1876 and 1877 suggest that they at least met each other and it may be that his description in the novel of the ballerina as a Trieste-born girl, incidentally blessed with a beautiful singing voice, battling 'to uphold the tradition of the grand school of Italian dancing against the British ignorance of it', is based on actual acquaintance, or more.

Immaturity also contains the most detailed account that survives of an Alhambra programme, related in a tone of callow sarcasm, which gives way to purple exultation. Shaw calls the ballet in question ''The Golden Harvest', but this is a misnomer for something called *The Golden Wreath*, first seen in May 1878. The scene is pastoral; village nuptials are in progress:

> The bridegroom was attired in purple knee breeches, a white shirt, and a crimson sash in which was a tiny golden sickle. The bride was covered with a veil adorned with orange blossoms. As the orchestra paused on the chord of the dominant, she threw off the veil, and revealed a light nuptial costume consisting of a waistband and shoulder straps of white satin, to which was appended a skirt of about fifteen inches in length. In addition to the ordinary methods of locomotion, she had acquired the power of walking on the points of her great toes and of posing herself on either one, and spinning herself about without becoming giddy. These feats admitted of but few combinations; and Smith [a thinly disguised Shaw] thought the dancing resulting from them deficient in variety, destitute of charm, and no better than a painful and unmeaning species of gymnastics.

The scene changes to a cornfield. After a lot of reaping and binding, the bridegroom falls asleep against a stack of sheaves. 'The bride presently missed him, and having searched for him on her toes in every place but that in which he was, expressed distraction and ran off. The rest, after kneeling in obedience to the sound of the vesper bell, followed her; and night fell on the scene with tropical suddenness.'

Enter Pertoldi, in transfiguring glory:

The music became hushed and full of mystery. A powerful moon cast a halo on the sleeping figure of the bridegroom, and on the stack which sheltered him. Then the sheaves fell asunder, and a transcendent being, the spirit of the harvest field, appeared, enveloped in the hues of autumn, blood-red poppy lightening into gorgeous orange. Cornflowers and golden ears of wheat were twisted fantastically in her black hair. Her dark bright eyes flashed in the limelight. Smith forgot his surroundings. The audience, the lights, the cigar ends, the unpleasant bursts of laughter from the drinking bars, ceased to colour his impression of the scene. The stage became an actual cornfield to him, and the dancer a veritable fairy. Her impetuosity was supernatural fire; her limbs were instinct with music to the very wrists; that walking on the points of the toes, which had given him a pain in the ankle to look at before, now seemed a natural outcome of elfin fancy and ethereality. He became infatuated as he watched her dancing in wanton overflow of spirits about the field, with the halo of the moon following her wherever she bounded. When she reminded him of her real circumstances by making a courtesy, he was irritated at the tameness of the applause which followed, cursing the indifference of the herd to refined art, and hammering with his walking stick on the wooden barricade against which he stood . . .

So much for Pertoldi. Virtually nothing more is recorded about her and in 1922 Shaw had to write to the aged Stewart Headlam because he couldn't remember her Christian name or find any document which contained it. Like almost all these ballerinas, she came, she danced, she conquered, she swiftly and entirely disappeared. Thus in the 1880s Pertoldi was replaced in the public's admiration by Emma Palladino (admired as a singer as well as dancer) and she in turn gave way to Emma Bessone, another enthusiasm of Shaw's, 'abounding in sensual charm'.

Slightly clearer is our picture of Pierina Legnani (c.1863–1923). She was a pure product of the Italian school, with ten years of tuition at La Scala and a style that radiated glamour but lacked poetry. In 1888 she was picked up for London, where she was contracted for seasons of between three and six months' duration, alternating for the remainder of the next five years between her base in Milan and Paris, Brussels and Madrid. She made her Alhambra début in 1888 as the eponymous Goddess of Peace in *Irene*, a production which had plot of a sort, but was scarcely up to date. Her later successes included roles in *Aladdin* (the Princess), *Don Juan* (Zerlina, 'a giddy girl') and her swansong,

Victoria and Merrie England ('The Genius of Britain'), in 1897. She clearly loved London audiences and London audiences reciprocated. 'Once please them,' she announced in an interview with *St Paul's Magazine* in 1894, 'and they will always welcome you, even when you are old.' Which in terms of a ballerina's lifespan, at thirty-one she was (although a decade or so would neatly be dropped when any interviewer asked the impertinent question).

From 1893 until her retirement in 1901, Legnani made her base in St Petersburg. There she is still commemorated as the creator of the role of Odette-Odile in Petipa's and Ivanov's 1895 production of *Swan Lake* at the Maryinsky Theatre and in particular for the way she brought its Act Three *pas de deux* to a thrilling climax of thirty-two consecutive *ronds de jambe fouettés* (viz. a series of pirouettes in which a raised leg 'whips' the body round without touching earth). This feat caused a sensation in St Petersburg,* where ballet was becoming ossified by the patronage of the imperial court and the long domination of the decorously neat, gentle and lyrical French style of dancing. From the mid 1880s, a new director of the theatre decided that a little bracing fresh air was required and began, like the London managers, to import the flashy Italians with their provocatively short tutus and virtuoso techniques. This meeting of Russian, French and Italian cultures was to cause the greatest explosion of creativity in the history of ballet, but that is a story for later.

Legnani's thirty-two *fouettés* were her party trick, achieved by a combination of blocked pointe shoes, 'spotting' (a method of preventing dizziness by focusing the eyes on a single object) and years of practice. *Swan Lake* wasn't the first occasion she had rolled them out – she had shown London her 'teetotum spin' and nobody had much noticed, as she intimated to the *Sketch*'s interviewer. 'Are your shoes made in a peculiar way to enable you to stand on tiptoe so easily?' he asked.

---

*'The step was not unlike an acrobatic exercise,' recalled the Russian ballerina Tamara Karsavina, then a student, in her memoirs, 'and its presentation savoured of the circus, by the deliberate suspense preceding it. Legnani walked to the middle of the stage and took an undisguised preparation. The conductor, his baton raised, awaited. Then a whole string of vertiginous pirouettes, marvellous in their precision and brilliant as diamond facets, worked the whole audiences into ecstasies. Academically, such an exhibition of sheer acrobatics was inconsistent with purity of style; but the feat, as she performed it, had something elemental and heroic in its breathless daring. It overwhelmed criticism. All the girls, big and small, constantly tried to do the 32 turns . . . one constantly saw turning Dervishes wherever a mirror was available.' From *Theatre Street* (London, 1930).

'Oh, yes; they come from Italy,' was the reply.

'Then she handed me a pretty little shoe, with a narrow sole that ended about the middle of the great toe, and had stiffening in the part of the "upper" which covers the toes . . . "With these I hardly get tired: in fact, in the last tableau of *Aladdin*, I turn thirty-two pirouettes on tiptoe without dropping my foot. Not many dancers can do that." '

But some could: among the front rank of Italian ballerinas the thirty-two was not unique – there is, for instance, firm evidence that Maria Giuri, who danced the title role of *Cleopatra* at the Empire in 1889, was capable of executing them,* and maybe even surpassed them. We shall never know, because (as Headlam deplored) the level of critical discourse was so low in London. Reviewers had no grasp of the technical vocabulary of ballet, let alone the technique, and confined themselves to the vaguest noises of generalised approval. Newspaper interviews with Legnani during her London sojourns detail a certain amount of trivial information about her (the heavy breakfast, with '*café au lait* with yolks of egg in it, and fillet of beef or other solid things', that she took before her two-hour morning class; the formidable aunt who functioned as her duenna; the time she injured her knee and went to Brighton to recuperate – 'I did not look at the place, only at the sea; I used to gaze at the waves and watch them dancing, and I grew so envious'), but never convey any sense of the quality of her dancing. 'Signorina Legnani did two clever pas seuls, in each of which she scored successfully; her work "on the points" being, as it always is, of finished expertness and activity, and her posing being grace itself' – this is as sophisticated as it gets.

Shaw wasn't persuaded that Headlam's attempt to introduce the academic French terms was much use either. Headlam's 'indiscreet revelation of how a critic with no artistic sense of dancing may cover up his incapacity by talking about *ronds de jambe*, arabesques, elevations, *entrechats*, *ballons*, and the like, threatens to start a technico-jargonautic fashion in ballet criticism, and whilst it lasts there will be no abolishing the absurdities and pedantries which now hamper the development of stage dancing,' he wrote in *The World* in 1890.

---

*'Her pirouettes and *ronds de jambe* excited the utmost enthusiasm as she constantly made from thirty to thirty-five without resting on the other foot' – from an Italian critique of Giuri's dancing in 1883, quoted by Jane Pritchard, 'The Empire in Manchester', *Dance Research* (Winter 1995), xiii.2.

There was, finally, no way round it. Ballet had become a dodo and there was nothing or nobody likely to revive it.

Other forms of motion had come into fashion. 'And what do you think of the English dancers and the skirt dancing, serpentine dancing, and high kicking?' the *Sketch*'s interviewer asked Legnani in 1893.

'I have not seen any important English dancers,' she replied tactfully (what she really meant was that English dancers were 'shockingly badly trained', as she told the balletomane Paul San-Francisco many years later). 'The dances you speak of seem pretty, but they are not quite serious dancing. As for the high kicking, why, I can do that; yes, and even the *grand écart* [splits], and I did it here the other night to show I could.'

This 'not quite serious' native school – far surpassing ballet in its popularity and number of executants – can be traced back to one remarkable figure, with some claim to be the great forgotten pioneer of modern dance: her name is Kate Vaughan. Born Catherine Candelin in 1852, she was taught by a Mrs Conquest, 'of the school of Marie Taglioni', and completed her apprenticeship in the music halls, where she appeared alongside her elder sister in the Parisienne Quadrille. She first caught the public's fancy in 1873, singing as well as dancing in a production of Offenbach's *Orpheus in the Underworld*, wearing a long black skirt, gold-spangled black tights and heeled shoes. This was the first of many 'characteristic' outfits she sported in her subsequent efforts to impersonate Old Testament, mythological and historical heroines in dance. The constant element was the respectable mid-calf length of her loose skirts – a departure from the customary tutu and white tights of the fairy chorine, complemented by a style of dancing both decorous and elegant, grounded in a stately waltz tempo and refined classical steps rather than thigh-high pointing and kicking: one John D'Auban, resident ballet master at Drury Lane, seems to have provided the initial choreographic inspiration. Kate Vaughan avoided 'all forced over-brilliancies and distortions, as well as all banal affectation', wrote one critic. 'Whatever steps she may be taking with her feet, or whatever curves she may make with her arms, her body is in repose, as though her limbs were unconnected with it,' explained another. She was subtle and harmonious, she was refined. Hers was not a 'poetic-romantic grace', but rather a 'grace that the audiences would wish to see in their own social surroundings and that would serve the ladies of society and the women of the world'.

This aura of sophistication was enhanced when she took up with the Hon. Fred Wellesley, son of the Earl of Cowley, whom she married (disastrously) in 1881. Smart folk were among her keenest fans – in homage to her capacity to animate biblical veils and classical draperies, Burne-Jones rechristened her Miriam Ariadne Salome Vaughan, and Lady Burne-Jones's memoirs record how her husband and Ruskin fell 'into each other's arms in rapture on accidentally discovering that they both adored her'.

She appeared as a solo turn in music halls and took roles in operetta, burlesque and pantomime at the wildly popular Gaiety Theatre, as well as featuring in some of London's spectacular ballets. For her brief appearance in *Excelsior*, performing a 'Turkish dance' in the Suez Canal scene, she was paid an unprecedented £72 a week – about thirty times what a chorine would earn. And worth every penny of it too, according to the patriotic *Illustrated London News* review: 'Two Italian dancers of the first excellence have exerted themselves with praiseworthy enthusiasm . . . but the public have never shown any marked and strong delight in an exotic entertainment until an English artist and dancer floats on from the wings and tantalises her admirers with scarcely five minutes of the poetry of motion. She does not beat the stage with her feet, she floats about it. With her it is not a dance but a dream.'

Later in the 1880s she tried, with some success, to establish herself as a legitimate comic actress (she died in 1903, divorced and miserable in South Africa), but it was as the originator of skirt dancing that she had her greatest influence, inasmuch as towards the end of the 1880s, as part of that broader cultural loosening-up which was subsequently labelled the 'Naughty Nineties' (a convenient alliteration, but chronologically inexact), a watered-down version of Vaughan's technique became a craze, both professional and amateur. Suddenly, in the words of the *Daily Graphic* of 14 April 1892, 'every lady now seems to think it a duty to acquire the art of . . . skirt dancing'. What was the attraction? Only minimal skills were required in order to master the basic vocabulary: the dainty steps of the gavotte, a waltz turn and graceful deep curtsy. More accomplished votaries, like the Countess Russell and her sister (who performed publicly at charity matinées), incorporated aspects of Spanish dances like the cachucha and fandango, 'and by-and-by', added the *Daily Graphic*, 'we shall doubtless include all the dances of the civilised world in the new drawing-room programme.'

But it was really a bit of a cheat. 'Lissomness cannot always be acquired, but a graceful management of the skirts may be, and while such display adds greatly to the picture which the dancer presents, it also avails to cloke [sic] deficiencies of dancing. This is said to be one of the reasons of its popularity, for provided the steps are not made with positive awkwardness or inaccuracy, the performer is always attractive.' Another reason was that it could be practised without the partnership of the male sex; ladies who lunched could repair for a spot of skirt dancing with no loss of propriety and even put on a show for other ladies of leisure – the *Daily Graphic* of 25 January 1893 reported how the Marchioness of Ripon (mother-in-law of Melba's *soignée* patron Lady de Grey) opened the drawing-room of her home on the Chelsea Embankment to the academy of Miss Florence Bright, whose 'bevy of ten charming young ladies' performed different styles of dancing, arrayed in dresses 'notably graceful and artistic'.

> Miss Bright herself contributed two *pas seuls*, wearing an Empire dress of closely fitting yellow satin, over which from a jewelled girdle fell loose draperies of yellow chiffon. The costumes also in the slow rhythmical 'Titania' dance, performed by Miss Aimée Carlton and Miss Ora Newton were much admired in their delicate shade of heliotrope and short waisted sashes. The same ladies also won great applause for their two Spanish dances for which they wore skirts of yellow satin with black lace flounces, and black Bolero jackets, giving in their latter performances a piquant castanet accompaniment to their steps. An Irish jig was also done by them with sprightly vigour, as well as a more conventional *pas de deux*. Miss Bright showed her further versatility by an effective recitation written by herself and called 'Nita', into which she introduced an illustrative dance, as well as by dancing with much verve and spirit a sailor's hornpipe . . .

In the theatres and music halls it became ubiquitous. Every show of the era contained its quota of frothy petticoats and stockings – London's genteel equivalent of the cancan. The number 'Dance a cachucha, fandango, bolero' in *The Gondoliers* (1889) was Gilbert and Sullivan's tribute to the craze (and its only surviving trace today); Legnani herself condescended to a skirt dance in *Don Juan* at the Alhambra in 1892. At the Gaiety, Sylvia Grey's 'statue dance', modelled on poses taken from classical sculpture at the British Museum, won her the accolade of being the 'High Priestess of Skirt Dancing'. At the Empire a girl from

Nottingham called Katie Seymour was the rage. 'No, I haven't exactly any theory of dancing, and I've never had any regular training,' she told the *Sketch* on 17 January 1894. 'My only teacher is my mother, who taught me a few steps. I've never gone through work like the Italian dancers and I don't really practise; but of course I cannot do all the steps they do. They are wonderful, and sometimes awfully graceful; still, I think they are rather stiff at times and mechanical.' There was no choreographer behind her, she admitted. 'I do that myself at home with a cheval glass. The music gives me the idea.'

The fact was that the great majority of stuff in this line was utter tosh. Shaw found it infuriating. 'Who has not seen a musical comedy or farce interrupted for five minutes,' he complained, 'whilst a young woman without muscle or practice enough to stand safely on one foot . . . clumsily waves the inevitable petticoats at the public as silken censers of that *odor di femina* which is the real staple of five-sixths of our theatrical commerce?' In the words of Crawford Flitch, 'The prettiness of the Skirt Dance as it was danced by Kate Vaughan perished in the contortions that were introduced from the Moulin Rouge.'

Yet it didn't exactly perish. Skirt dancing may have passed out of vogue, but it dropped one of the seeds of the modern dance movement, fertilising with the work of continental hygienists like François Delsarte and Emile Jaques-Dalcroze (whose focus was essentially mystical and therapeutic, rather than theatrical) to liberate Woman's Body Beautiful from the constraints of the corset and empower her to move where the spirit listeth. What actually happened to skirt dancing was more in the nature of a transformation – an extension of its possibilities chiefly wrought, yet again, by visitors to London: in this case two dazzling Americans, Cyrene Soler y Turnour, commonly known as plain Cyrene, and Loie Fuller. In their different ways they ignored the gentility and modesty which governed British skirt dancing and flavoured it with a mystery, sensuality and physical energy it had previously lacked.

Cyrene came of circus stock and had been educated as a contortionist, but her speciality was a personal interpretation of the *chahut*, itself a sophisticated, somewhat sanitised music-hall variant of the orgiastic cancan, which working-class Parisians had notoriously been jiving for fifty years or more. She arrived in London in the spring of 1893 to appear on the bill at the Alhambra and caused a great stir. The press talked euphemistically of her 'naturalistic dancing' or 'fantastic dancing'; audiences were exhilarated and aroused by her thrilling lack of inhibition.

> After the musical introduction she bounds on to the stage, dressed in a silver bodice, with a voluminous skirt of heavy orange, lace relieving the costume at various points. The girl has a little head, with black hair gathered at the back into a knot *à la Grecque*, but on the forehead showing a heavy American bang. Her features are decidedly American . . . but the colouring of her complexion is decidedly Spanish. After some long, gliding steps, the orange skirt begins to mount, showing a foamlike mass of white petticoat and lace; then the petticoats follow the dress, and a pair of long, lithe limbs cased in flaming red tights is seen. She turns and swirls around, glides rapidly to and fro, now dropping, now raising the skirts, pirouettes and then kicks. Skyscraping kicks they are, too – kicks that seem to imperil her dainty nose – kicks that set those two finely shaped legs at almost an angle of 180 degrees to one another. Suddenly, she sinks down, the limbs seem to run away from each other, and you find her stretched out like a fully open pair of compasses. This is what the French call *le grand écart* . . . Then the body swings down, she rests one elbow on her knee, her chin on the elbow, and smiles, in a cute, triumphant way at the audience.

But that was only the beginning. The classical Italians like Legnani could go so far – the high kick, *le grand écart* – if needs be, but Cyrene went further. Cyrene went wild.

> Anon she engages in a madder dance, flings up her legs, as if hoping to wrest them from their sockets and use them as missiles; time after time they touch the little hands that she holds above her dainty head. Then she begins to turn like the Nabis (the dancing dervishes to whom King Saul was really compared when it was asked 'Is Saul also among the prophets?'), her skirts and petticoats begin to fly out, mount till at right angles to her body, then higher, and the long lithe flaming-red limbs appear, and are shown at full length. Suddenly she pauses; the centrifugal force stopped, her skirts sink, then she 'presents legs' at the audience, holding one of them by the ankle with her hand, makes her reverence and vanishes.

Thus the *Sketch* of 5 April described the furore. On the next page Arthur Symons, poet and prophet of the Symbolist movement, as well as a lover of the girls of the Empire and the Alhambra ballets, interviewed Cyrene and assessed her performance. In person he found her unremarkable: a 'little figure' with a 'pretty, serious, piquant' face and a personality marked by 'the simple, natural cordiality which is so delightful a characteristic of the American woman'. But what she did on stage was more striking:

> . . . this extraordinary acrobatic dance, cancan and cachucha in one: a dance which reminds one, now of Otero, now of La Goulue [stars in Paris]; a dance which was spontaneous and triumphant, which did the incredible with ease, which did the splits and the high kick with modesty, which captivated the eye and distracted the intelligence at once. The extravagance of the thing was never vulgar, its intricate agility was never incorrect; there was genuine grace in the wildest moment of caprice, there was real science in the pointing of the foot in its most fantastic flights above the head. A novelty which was really novel and delightful . . .

Yet only three months later Cyrene was old news. To the Gaiety Theatre, direct from her triumphs at the Folies-Bergères in Paris, had come La Loie, the all-eclipsing Loie Fuller, 'clad in a maze of diaphanous draperies which at each gyration seemed to assume a new outline' and so magically illuminated on stage that she seemed to become incorporeal, a nebulous swirl of light. The *Star* of 11 July was overwhelmed at this vision, which first appeared as a divertissement following a show called *In Town* (otherwise notable for the number, 'Daddy wouldn't buy me a bow-wow'). The reviewer continued: 'Words are inadequate to describe the marvellous effects of colour and radiance which followed each other in this bewildering kaleidoscope. Now a prismatic cascade, now a revolving sphere of liquid fire, the dancer crowned each movement with a new delight, and finally sank amid a tumult of applause, the like of which is seldom heard in this undemonstrative land.'

Loie Fuller's act – no, her art – had grown from unpromising soil. Born Marie Louise Fuller in the Midwest in 1862, she was the victim of an interesting medical condition, having 'caught a cold at the very moment of my birth which I have never got rid of'. As 'an infant' she performed as a Temperance lecturer and as a teenager had her first break playing a banjo-strumming waif in a show starring Buffalo Bill. A dumpy, grumpy and chubby-cheeked woman with a booming contralto voice, Fuller had no personal beauty: she was, however, intensely determined, enterprising and readily unscrupulous in pursuit of her ends. Her autobiography, written in French as *Quinze Ans de ma*

Vie in 1908, has emerged as an even more bewildering patchwork of evasions, half-truths and downright fibs than that of her better-remembered epigone Isadora Duncan – for a start, the narrative jumps entirely from 1864 to 1890 without so much as a word of explanation. What is verifiable is that she married a man who turned out to be a crook and a trigamist, and from whom she subsequently had great legal trouble extricating herself and her affairs. Partly to escape him, she came to London in 1889 and attempted to hit the big time. First, she ambitiously mounted and starred in her own production of a two-bit play called *Caprice*. After it flopped and the American author engaged her in a shaming legal muddle over royalties, Fuller was left stranded and penniless. To make ends meet, she returned to work as a chorine at the Gaiety, appearing as a soubrette in a musical comedy called *Carmen Up-To-Data*. Here she learned to skirt dance and must have observed all the little variants that were spicing up its limited vocabulary.

By 1891, Fuller had earned her passage back to the USA, where she proceeded to use her experience in London to reinvent herself. There are several versions of how this happened. The account in her autobiography (in the newspaper interviews she gave the details emerge differently) ascribes it to serendipity: shortly after her return to the USA she was appearing in a play in New York called *Quack MD*. In one scene, the character she played falls under hypnosis wearing 'an old Hindoo costume' made from some shimmering stuff presented to her, so she said, by an enamoured British officer recently returned from India. As she walked entranced across the stage, she lifted her skirts to stop herself tripping up and the Indian silk fortuitously caught the limelight with a ghostly shimmering translucence. 'A butterfly!' someone in the audience shouted out – so she began to improvise a fluttering dance, culminating impressively with her collapse at the hypnotist's feet, 'completely enveloped in a cloud of the light material'. The audience roared. 'Three cheers for the butterfly! Three cheers for the orchid, the cloud, the butterfly! Three cheers!' Back home, she began to experiment with the effect in sunlight, manipulating swathes of fabric on long bamboo batons and creating giant billowing curves and spirals, twice her height, to musical accompaniment. 'I obtained modulations of a character before unknown,' she wrote, and 'reached a point where each movement of the body was expressed in the folds of silk, in a play of colours in the draperies that could be mathematically and systematically calculated'. Her manager advised her to call it 'the serpentine dance' and instantly, she claims, girls were floating around imitating her all over New York.

Phooey, claimed the 'electrical serpentine dancer' Marie Leyton, who had worked with Fuller in London, and – perhaps somewhat enviously – blew the whistle and branded her a plagiarist. According to Leyton, such things had been common in shows long before La Loie had blossomed. Kate Vaughan had danced under coloured limes with luminous paint applied to her costume, Clara Wieland was reflected in mirrors, and the hip-swaying 'Nautch Dance' and its silken semi-transparent skirts had also caused a stir. 'Well, I'm telling you, she saw *The Nautch Girl* [at the Savoy, over the road from the Gaiety, in 1889], and she got Miss Fisher, the costumier here, to make her a dress like it, to take back with her to America for a specialty dance,' Leyton told the *Sketch*. 'Because, of course, you see, she wanted a specialty to take back with her.'

Miss Fisher later confirmed this, reporting how 'before Miss Fuller left for America in August 1891, she called upon her to have some gowns made, and was then shown an Indian dress, which Miss Fisher had made at the wish of Mr Percy Anderson, who required some faithful reproductions of Indian dresses for the production of *The Nautch Girl*'. Miss Fisher 'personally showed Miss Fuller the many forms which the skirt would take when properly and gracefully moved with the hands, and she immediately caught the idea. Miss Fisher was genuinely glad to hear of her success with the many dresses she has since had made on precisely the same lines as the model with which she supplied her, but naturally thinks she should have a little credit in the matter.'

Fuller weathered these attacks on her probity,* because, whatever

---

*Although the rumpus put the entire profession on the defensive. Nora Godfrey, 'serpentine dancer on horseback', felt obliged to advertise that she was compelled 'to state that the whole idea, act and title are my own property' – despite reports in the Paris press of a Mlle Hélène Gérard offering the same trick (*Star*, 15 August 1893). Sadly, the *Oxford English Dictionary* is no help: it does not register the first (or any) written occurrence of the dance connotation of 'serpentine'. Later in 1893, Fuller did manage to patent 'certain new and useful improvements in garments particularly adapted for theatrical dancing . . . the said dress being composed essentially of a long skirt fixed on a circlet adjusted to the head of the dancer and provided with canes or bamboos concealed under its folds'. See Heather Doughty, 'The Choreographer in the Courtroom', *Proceedings of Dance History Scholars*, Harvard University, February 1982.

she filched, she also undoubtedly contributed something uniquely her own. La Loie can't properly be described as a dancer. To each 'dance' she gave a pictorial name – Violet, Butterfly, White, Flame, Lily – and a popular melody such as Gounod's 'Ave Maria' and Chopin's 'Funeral March', but there were few specific steps involved in her act and the music served chiefly to enhance the atmosphere: on stage she did little more than run around, her limbs remaining virtually invisible behind the voluminous fabric, her presence a mere shadowy blur. Where she was most original was in her strikingly imaginative use of the new tool of electric light. Panorama exhibitions and pantomime had already sensed its possibilities – a Broadway show called *Alladin* [*sic*] had used magic lanterns to make fabrics shimmer with oriental mystery, while an *Arabian Nights* had illuminated a steam curtain (or 'Veil of Vapor') with multicoloured lights. But Fuller more boldly treated the stage like a three-dimensional canvas, brushing it with an ever more sophisticated palette of smoked and frosted glass, coloured gelatines and filters, projected through magic lanterns on to backcloths and the rainbow-dyed fabrics which undulated about her person.

Or, as the dance scholar Sally R. Sommer, suggests:

> What Loie Fuller understood was the simplest and most fundamental principle of light; that to be clearly perceived, it must have a screen on which to fall. This was not a new idea, but it was an idea that had not been completely explored. Panoramas, phantasmagorias and magic lantern shows were popular entertainments of the time, but in all of these performances the light fell on a static flat screen. Fuller gave new form and motion to light and projections, not just by moving the light sources (revolving discs in front of changing slide projections), but by moulding the screen itself, shaping it into fantastical three-dimensional configurations.

The precise techniques and formulas were kept rigorously secret – as early as 1893 she patented her technique of 'underlighting', which involved dancing over a translucent glass plate set into a stage trap – and for several years only her brothers acted as her stage and technical managers.

In the galaxy of *fin de siècle* high culture, Loie Fuller was a bright star. Legnani, Cyrene – what they did smelt of the sawdust ring; but La Loie was an artist. Toulouse-Lautrec drew her, Artistes Nouveaux were inspired by her swirling and twirling. She was an Impressionist of dance, she was *la fée lumineuse*, she was *Japonaise*. Her evanescent motions fascinated the pioneers of cinema, anthropologists of primitive ritual, the heirs to Baudelaire's rhapsodies (Stéphane Mallarmé was mesmerised by Fuller and scribbled excitedly of 'visions no sooner known than scattered'). In London, where she followed her début season with visits in 1894 and 1895, she was the idol of young Romantics of the Symbolist and Decadent schools, including Arthur Symons and his Irish flat-mate William Butler Yeats,* embodying not only the ancient mystique of the veiled woman and the visitor from the vague afar, but things even more fundamental to their poetics: individuality transcended, a pure image devoid of meaning, morality or personality, a fluid abstraction of form, a being elevated to a plane of intuitive ecstasy, fuelled with primal, sacramental life force.

She herself meditated pretentiously on the affective powers of colour, light and movement. 'Motion and not language is truthful,' she said – whatever that may mean. With fluttering silk and electric light, she believed she could awaken the spectator's sleeping soul so 'that it may be prepared to receive the image'. Her inspiration, she suggested, was quasi-divine: during an 1894 interview with Mrs M. Griffith of the *Strand* magazine, she claimed that she had 'only revived a forgotten art for which I have been able to trace some of my dances back to four thousand years ago: to the time when Miriam and the women of Israel – filled with religious fervour and rapture – celebrated their release from Egyptian captivity with "timbrels and with dances"'. Phooey, of course, but phooey very much along the lines that the Revd Headlam was simultaneously using in dance's defence.

---

*Solid evidence for this – dates, references in letters – is unfortunately lacking: but Roy Foster, in his authoritative biography of Yeats (*W. B. Yeats: A Life*, vol. 1, Oxford, 1997) states that 'it was probably with Symons that WBY saw Loie Fuller perform, bequeathing him an enduring image' – a reference to lines written some twenty-five years later like

> When Loie Fuller's Chinese dancers enwound
> A shining web, a floating ribbon of cloth,
> It seemed that a dragon of air
> Had fallen among dancers, had whirled them round
> Or hurried them off on its own furious path.
> 'Nineteen Hundred and Nineteen'

Aside from the avant-gardiste likes of Yeats and Symons, she pleased a wider public in London too, not least because she made 'no gesture or movement which would offend the susceptibilities of the most modest-minded of British matrons or maidens'. (Even in Paris, added the *Strand*, Fuller raised the tone of the Folies-Bergères to the point that 'even the most particular Parisian has no hesitation about taking his wife or lady friends there'.) But her very popularity meant that she had difficulty in maintaining her uniqueness. As if Providence were taking revenge for her own unacknowledged borrowings, Fuller failed to secure copyright of her ideas and over the years continued to be pestered by imitators: her biographer Giovanni Lista records, among others, Minnie Renwood Bemis (whom she unsuccessfully sued: the judge ruled that because her dance did not tell a story it evaded the protected category of 'dramatic composition'), Annabelle Whitford Moore, Crissie Sheridan, Alice Lethbridge, the Silbon Sisters, Jenny Mills, Miss Russell, Rose Mountain, Miss Hazell Mabelle Stuart, Teresina Negri, Anne Feyton, Alice Fuller (who posed as her sister), Ida Fuller, Ida May Fuller (possibly the same person, possibly not), Kate Fuller, Mollie Fuller, several Loie Fullers, Mabel Atlantis, Julia Kingsley, Clara Hammer, Grace Hunter, Miss Diana, Miss Kaline and Bessie Clayton – all of them religiously tracing waves and spreading clouds of rainbow-coloured silk in a flattering light. (Not to mention the music hall star Little Tich, who parodied her as Miss Turpentine, swanning around the stage in yards of rapturous muslin and then breaking the sublime illusion by stopping to scratch her leg.)

Other adoring young women, keepers of the flame, allowed themselves to be corralled into La Loie's travelling harem, and ministered to her delicate nerves, troublesome spine and unremitting hypochondria. The domestic regime was puritanical: according to the *Strand*, 'Her rooms boast of no costly luxuries, bric-à-brac, or the thousand-and-one costly trifles which artistes usually surround themselves with . . . she works very hard and has to train as severely as any jockey.' One bright-eyed young American – who had taken lessons with Katti Lanner at the Empire and danced 'in the Ancient Greek fashion lost for two thousand years' at fashionable London *soirées musicales* – could not stand it for long: the incense-charged atmosphere stifled her natural exuberance and she had her own dreams (of a pure and natural classicism focused on the body and soul rather than the skirt and petticoat) to realise. Her name was Isadora Duncan. But that story belongs elsewhere.*

Into the twentieth century, the poor old ballet trundled on as part of the variety programmes of vaudeville and music hall. The new dance of Fuller and Duncan, free of the inexorable teetotum spin, charmed the intelligentsia and the smart set; the sexy *Danse des Apaches*, imported from Paris, in which a sadistic rough beats up his masochistic girl, thrilled more proletarian tastes. In contrast to such modern excitements, white tulle and pointe shoes became ever more marginalised and antiquated – a little chocolate box of nostalgia for one's grandparents. In 1906 Reginald St Johnston could write in his *A History of Dancing* that 'ballet is now a thing of the past, and, with the modern change of ideas, a thing that is never likely to be resuscitated. And in a way it is perhaps as well, for, as I have said elsewhere, a forced and mechanical style cannot contribute to the furtherance of the real art of dancing, and movements such as walking on the extreme points of the toes can only be regarded as unnatural . . . No one', he concluded, 'can really regret the wane of the ballet.'

Even the apparently inexhaustible supply of Italian ballerinas began to dry up – it was the Danish-born Adeline Genée who dominated the Empire between 1897 and 1907. When that theatre's ballet mistress Katti Lanner died in 1908, after twenty years of choreographing shows, an era quietly closed. Such was the dearth of new talent that managements were forced to take their chances on some Russians with unpronounceable names who had suddenly emerged on the market. To the Empire in 1908 came the first of these visitors, the haughty Lydia Kyasht. Her regal stage manner could be hard for a music-hall audience to tolerate – in the course of one of her higher-toned numbers, a slave girl laid a bowl of fruit at her feet: 'Have a banana!' shouted a wag in

---

*Fuller's later career is relatively well documented (her papers can be seen in the Library of Performing Arts at Lincoln Center in New York). Into the 1920s she continued to tour the world with her troupe of girls. She had a close relationship with the sculptor Rodin, but her inclinations otherwise seem lesbian (Queen Marie of Romania was rumoured to be her lover). She died in 1928, having become ever more fat, grumpy and neurotic. Her company survived until 1940 and the Nazi occupation of Paris. See Frank Kermode's admirable brief essay, 'Poet and Dancer before Diaghilev' in *Puzzles and Epiphanies* (London, 1963). For more detail, including discussion of Fuller's brief and ultimately disastrous relationship with Isadora, see Richard and Marcia Current, *Loie Fuller: Goddess of Light* (Boston, Mass., 1997).

the gallery, to the amusement of everyone except Kyasht – but she was clearly a mistress of the old school and her success opened the door to others of her nationality.

By the summer of 1909, Russians were performing all over the West End and the Imperial Maryinsky Theatre of St Petersburg seemed to have assumed from La Scala, Milan, the responsibility of supplying ballerinas to the London public. At the Coliseum, Tamara Karsavina starred; at the Palace it was Anna Pavlova; at the Hippodrome, Olga Preobrajenskaya; at the Alhambra, Yekaterina Geltzer. What they danced was only the silly stuff that audiences had been watching for years – at best, potted versions of the old favourites, to the strains of cheap salon music played by a pit band – but both Pavlova and Karsavina were also part of a touring company of Russian dancers organised by the impresario Serge Diaghilev. It boasted an altogether nobler set of artistic ambitions and had caused a sensation when it visited Paris earlier that year. Diaghilev was to prove as revolutionary in his sphere as Lenin was to be in his – for at a moment when nobody could have expected it, the Ballets Russes not only brought a moribund tradition back to life, but put it in the vanguard of the arts of the first half of the twentieth century.

The Ballets Russes arrived in London in 1911, billed as the Imperial Russian Ballet. Their engagement at the Royal Opera House, Covent Garden – promoted by Melba's patron Gladys de Grey, now the Marchioness of Ripon and herself of partially Russian ancestry – was the centrepiece of a lavish programme of official entertainment celebrating the coronation of George V, and there is a gentle irony in the way that something originally imported to please the backward-looking ranks of the post-Victorian court and aristocracy ended up as a banner for those who sought to smash (or ignore) their forefathers' tablets of moral stone.

But take a broader perspective and it emerges that the high culture of London was poised at a fascinating and crucial moment of transformation. The city's public face may have been basking smugly in the high noon of its status as the greatest empire since that of Ancient Rome, variously celebrated in the work of Kipling, Elgar and Newbolt, and embodied in the stony ugliness of its neo-classical architecture (Sir Aston Webb refronted Buckingham Palace in 1913), but if one looks at the months before and after the Ballets Russes's first visit, it is astonishing to see how many of the first bright sparks of modernism were being struck. Roger Fry's two Post-Impressionist Exhibitions at the Grafton Gallery gave London its first real view of Manet, Gauguin, van Gogh, Matisse, Picasso and Braque. The Austrian director Max Reinhardt – who more than anyone liberated theatre from the Victorian proscenium arch – transformed the exhibition hall of Olympia into the likeness of a medieval cathedral for a wordless 'spectacle play', *The Miracle*. In Bloomsbury, both sexes of a free-thinking middle-class intelligentsia chattered about semen and sodomy as though it were the most normal thing in the world. A young American poet called Thomas Stearns Eliot arrived in London. The spineless, shimmering ebb and flow of Debussy's *Pelléas et Mélisande* and *La Mer* was heard for the first time in opera house and concert hall. In the further reaches of artistic Bohemia, the sculptor Gaudier-Brzeska starved in a garret and another American poet, Ezra Pound, evolved the radical doctrine of Imagism.

To the Russian visitors, however, London initially seemed a hard and grim place, especially after the glitter and glamour of Paris. Karsavina (who later married an English diplomat and settled in Hampstead) reflected wryly in her wonderful memoir *Theatre Street* on the way they were patronised as something like savages – 'my adopted country,' she lamented, 'you are generous and infinitely tolerant to a foreigner, but in your heart of hearts you are mildly surprised every time you see the foreigner using his knife and fork in the same way you do. You readily excuse kinks of alien mentality inexplicable to you, but you don't take a foreigner seriously' – while the company's ballet master, Sergei Grigoriev, recalled how shocked the dancers were

> by the extreme simplicity of the architecture; London houses seemed to us almost excessively plain. We found rooms in the neighbourhood of the British Museum . . . but here again the gardens of the squares were all locked up, and only the residents had keys to them . . . Something we had certainly never encountered before were the curious two-wheeled vehicles, with the driver seated behind his passengers, known as hansom cabs . . . What amazed us above all, however, was the Theatre Royal [viz. the Royal Opera House] in Covent Garden itself. It stood in the midst of a vegetable market and was closely hemmed in by vast mountains of cabbages, potatoes, carrots and all manner of fruit.

Administrative problems and international misunderstandings did nothing to foster détente. The wardrobe staff, for instance, had been held by immigration officers at Folkestone, pending receipt of the proper papers – the authorities were watching for Russian anarchists and communists – with the result that what should have been a splendidly costumed public dress rehearsal, designed to stimulate a premonitory buzz about the show, was performed in unsuggestive practice clothes. It was left to a lavish souvenir programme to fan expectations and stimulate the box office. 'There have been signs and portents for a year or so that we were about to witness something of a revival or even a revolution in the public taste in regard to the classic and beautiful art of dancing,' read its blurb. 'For many moons the sacred lamp became devoid of life. But to their exceeding joy, some three years ago, came some scattered harbingers of the revival in the persons of certain individual dancers brought by those unfailing judges of the public taste, the managers of the variety houses . . . The public came in multitudes, took classical dancers and dancing to its heart, and has insisted upon having them ever since.'

This wasn't what we would now call 'hype'. Diaghilev's timing was perfect and it is no exaggeration to say that ballet in England was reborn on the night of 21 June, when his dancers – a troupe of over a hundred, led by Tamara Karsavina and Vaslav Nijinsky – first appeared at Covent Garden in a programme consisting of three works by Mikhail Fokine, *Le Pavillon d'Armide*, *Le Carnaval* and the 'Polovtsian Dances' from *Prince Igor*. On 24 June Fokine's *Le Spectre de la Rose*, with Nijinsky's miraculous and legendary leap through an open window, was added to the bill. On 26 June an episode of *Le Pavillon d'Armide* was repeated as the climax of the otherwise operatic Coronation Gala, at which the auditorium was decorated with 100,000 artificial blooms (the scent of so many real ones would have induced mass nausea), the boxes, according to a delighted Diaghilev, contained 'almost as many maharajahs' and, according to the *Daily Mail*, 'both the King and Queen freely used opera glasses'. Finally, on the following night, came Fokine's exquisite homage to the ethereal qualities of Taglioni, *Les Sylphides*, with Karsavina and Nijinsky the incarnation of perfumed Keatsian reverie.

By the end of that astonishing week the Russian Ballet had conquered, and it is hard to think of any artistic phenomenon in London's history which more immediately and dramatically altered cultured taste. And it wasn't just the upper-middle classes and their broadsheets which registered it. The *Daily Mirror* of 28 June announced that 'the whole of this crabbed world that waits for joy and lightness is crowding to Covent Garden to forget itself in the Russian ballet'; the *Daily Mail* of 23 June decided that 'the spectacle is little less than a revelation'; while the *Daily News* of 22 June marked the contrast with the vulgarity of the Italian girls and the tawdry triviality of the Alhambra and Empire:

> When the orchestra began the prelude, the audience looked at each other in surprise. They had evidently come expecting the jingling tunes associated with ballet in this country, and found they were listening to a wonderful piece of orchestration, restless, passionate, at times almost poignant, which might have been the prelude to a serious opera. It was the first indication that the ballet, as developed in Russia, is a serious form of art, and not merely a frivolous excuse for showing pretty girls and dresses behind the footlights . . . The glitter of spangles and glare of colour which offend the eyes in most ballets in London were absent and the combination of exquisite colouring, graceful movement, sprightly, but never banal, music, made a spectacle surpassing in artistic feeling and charm anything yet seen in this country.

The Times of 24 June dug deeper into the underlying aesthetic: 'If only for the sake of discipline,' wrote its critic,

> there must be some order in the movements [of ballet]. But this has never been treated in England as the be-all and end-all of ballet-dancing, to which all exceptional allurements must be sacrificed; nor have the ideas expressed been pushed upwards, as the Russian ideas have, into the adventurous realms of artistic experiment. Our ballet-designing [i.e. choreography, a term not widely used at this time] has always been a democratic art, so far as it can be reckoned among the arts at all. Our dancing has been to please the people without calling for any mental exertion on their part.

In Russia, on the other hand, 'the ballet has been essentially an aristocratic institution, maintained by an autocratic government for the use of the cultivated classes. It has not depended for its existence on giving immediate pleasure (the bane of all democratic art), but has been able to follow its own bent.' In other words the paradoxical result of Russian ballet's élitism was a creative licence, released from the necessity of satisfying a paying public.

The Times's critic was less impressed by the technical skill of the dancing – which the Italians had long been demonstrating – than by 'the variety and imaginative quality of those ideas which the dancing succeeds in expressing'. He went on to praise the absence of the 'imitation of actual material movements' and the antiquated vocabulary of mime ('comparable only to the means by which omnibus conductors communicate with each other in the hubbub of Oxford Street'). Instead, he observed, the Russian dancer 'does not so much imitate the movement of a butterfly as the emotional quality of a butterfly-flight . . . so that in their suggestion of things flying, things swimming, things poised, or blown by the wind, the sense of the material passes altogether away'. Enhancing this were 'new harmonies of grouping and of movement, avoiding symmetry, that bugbear of all design', as well as 'restraint in the proportion of contrary or subsidiary movements' and 'restraint of emotion'.

But the majority of the audience, less sophisticated and less demanding, seems to have been enthralled by the sheer splendour of the staging, mounted in a style the like of which London had never seen before. The gorgeous designs of Alexander Benois and Léon Bakst were realised with a boldness and richness far beyond anything seen at the Alhambra and the Empire with their tinselly pantomime garishness, and the 'Russian *mode*' spread to fashion and interior decoration. In the words of Richard Buckle, they 'banished for ever from the dress shops and furnishers the favourite Edwardian colours of white, cream, grey and pale mauve. The windows of Harvey Nichols blossomed in purple and red.' Under the influence of Bakst's creations, wealthy ladies in their waistless Poiret gowns and turbans became ever more Byzantine; that quintessential form of Edwardian entertainment, the fancy-dress ball, was full of impersonations of the characters of Karsavina, Pavlova and Nijinsky, and the more ambitious hostesses hired the dancers themselves to appear as the last word in cabaret turns: Pavlova for Lady Michelham, Kyasht for Lady Londesborough, Karsavina and Nijinsky for Lady Ripon.

Diaghilev's company played in London until the end of July and returned to Covent Garden in the autumn of 1911, the summer of 1912 and the spring of 1913. For the summers of 1913 and 1914 it moved to the Theatre Royal, Drury Lane, under the management of the impresario Sir Joseph Beecham and his conductor son Thomas: here ballet alternated with Diaghilev's newest import, the larger-than-life

Russian bass Feodor Chaliapin, whose mesmerising and terrifying performance in the title role of Mussorgsky's *Boris Godunov* became as celebrated as Nijinsky's in *Le Spectre de la Rose*.

Over these seasons, of between four and eight weeks' duration, the company also introduced London to (among much else, now forgotten) *Swan Lake*, *The Firebird*, *Petrushka*, *L'Après-midi d'un Faune*, *Le Sacre du Printemps*, *Daphnis and Chloe*, *Jeux* and *Le Coq d'Or*. Not all of these were received with equal rapture; even on those sensational opening nights in 1911, a significant element of the audience was shocked by the primitivism and decibel level of the 'Polovtsian Dances' from *Prince Igor*. Diaghilev later recalled – exaggerating, no doubt – that on 21 June they caused 'half the public' to walk out. 'At least a hundred old ladies, covered with diamonds as though they were ikons, went out past me with a look of disgust on their faces.' Covent Garden's business manager was appalled. 'You've spoilt your magnificent opening by this barbarian horror at the end,' he told Diaghilev. 'It isn't dancing – it's just savages prancing about.' *Punch*'s reviewer of 5 July 1911 concurred, perpetrating the unforgivable pun, 'I am half afraid that in this matter of the ballet we Britons never, never, never will be Slavs.'

It could even be argued that what London responded to most strongly about the Ballets Russes were the aspects of its work closest in spirit to the shows of the Alhambra and the Empire. The company's classicist and modernist side certainly met with considerably less enthusiasm than its exotic romantic narratives – supremely the de luxe chocolate box of Fokine's *Schéhérazade*. With Bakst's fabulous scarlet-and-gold decor, a glutinously melodic score by Rimsky-Korsakov, slave girls and sultans, an orgy and a massacre in the harem, it exuded a sensual excitement which didn't fall the wrong side of indecency and rendered it accessible to readers of the more lurid fictions of Anatole France and Marie Corelli. Less to its taste was the painstaking production of *Giselle*, which despite Karsavina and Pavlova's poignant interpretations, seemed dusty and genteel, a faded mezzotint from grandmama's parlour: '*Giselle* is not a work of art, and can never become one,' insisted the *Observer*. *Swan Lake*, amazingly, was judged even more harshly – 'full of padding' (*The Times*), 'the music is of little account' (*Daily Mail*) – and it didn't catch on for another thirty years.

Nor, on the other hand, was the London public readily receptive of the more outré choreographic experiments of Nijinsky. His vision of Stravinsky's *Le Sacre du Printemps* had caused the audience to deliquesce into a riot of booing and catcalling at its Parisian première only weeks before it arrived in London on 11 July 1913. A ten-minute explanatory lecture by a musicologist, before the actual performance, obliged the Drury Lane audience to watch and listen with more respect, but did not intimidate the critics. The 'Polovtsian Dances' may have been excessively noisy, but this was a 'whirlwind of cacophonous, primitive hideousness', spat the *Daily Telegraph*; 'Astonishing ugliness – on stage and in the orchestra,' grunted the *Standard*. Well, yes, retorted Nijinsky in an interview with the *Daily Mail*, but was he 'to be tied down to "grace" for ever'? 'Really I begin to have horror of the very word: "grace" and "charm" make me feel seasick . . . my own inclinations are primitive. I eat my meat without *sauce béarnaise*.' He went on to claim that the generality of the audience had been more 'sympathetic', but that is not the impression drawn from the privately recorded views of its more sophisticated members. Lytton Strachey described the ballet as 'one of the most painful experiences of my life. I couldn't have imagined that boredom and sheer anguish could have been combined together at such a pitch.' While Lady Ottoline Morrell wrote in her journal: 'It is really terrible and intense. Too much of Idea in it to please the public. Too little grace.'

What was that public? A socially complex one: because Lady Ripon had engineered it that the Ballets Russes should appear in the Royal Opera House, Covent Garden (at that time not otherwise a home for dance), London's nearest approach to an official court theatre, it attracted the patronage of high society – royalty, the Lords and Commons, the diplomatic service, the smart set, the fast set, the banking, shipping and press dynasties, the wealthiest arrivistes – to an extent that the demotic and (purely commercial) Alhambra and Empire could never aspire to. This does not mean that high society necessarily liked what it saw: such personages were subscribers, who leased their boxes and dropped into them at certain fixed times, often in complete ignorance of what entertainment they were to endure. But there is some evidence that the Ballets Russes pleased: smart and fast Mrs Keppel, for instance, the former mistress of Edward VII, had Diaghilev and Karsavina to dine at her palatial home in Mayfair (and in an emergency once consented to let them use her drawing-room as a rehearsal studio).

Upstairs, reclining on cushions painted in *bleu Bakst*, her dangerous daughter Violet – later the catastrophic lover of Vita Sackville-West – frolicked with Lady Ripon's daughter Lady Juliet Duff. Visits to the Ballets Russes were a fixture in their calendar of idle engagements.

With more commitment, Bohemia and the intelligentsia queued for the gallery tickets (at prices two or three times higher than at the Alhambra and Empire). On its hard benches sat bearded Vorticists and their molls, art students of the Slade, disciples of Wagnerism – the critic T. E. Hulme noted 'the Egyptian coiffures of the ladies, the waistcoats of poets, the side-whiskers à la Café Royal, the shawls and kissing curls, the nightly kaleidoscopic assembly of creators'. The poet Rupert Brooke claimed to have seen fifteen performances in the summer of 1911: '*Schéhérazade* was thrilling again,' he wrote in July to his girlfriend Ka Cox, with a breathless enthusiasm echoed by so many of the new century's brightest young things. 'Bryn and Daphne, of course, didn't like it. What sloughs they must be, within . . . And now, I'm going once more. On Monday with Margery and, probably, Noel. We feed at 7.15, Eustace Miles. James'll be there, have tickets.'

All Bloomsbury had tickets too. Maynard Keynes escaped from Cambridge and his theory of economics 'to view Mr Nijinsky's legs' (fourteen years later, he would marry a former Diaghilev ballerina, Lydia Lopokova). Virginia Woolf had been delighted by Karsavina at the Coliseum in 1909 and became a great ballet fan: in her letters she refers to the Russians simply as 'the dancers', as if there were no others. On 6 November she took Lytton Strachey to see Pavlova in *Les Sylphides* – 'only the amphitheatre this time; but when they do the other thing [*Schéhérazade* on 21 November, worth lashing out for] we will go to the stalls.'

As the Ballets Russes seasons rolled on, one dancer increasingly commanded awed attention. Much as the ballerinas were admired and adored, it was Diaghilev's reluctant lover, Vaslav Nijinsky, who became the idol of the cult of the Ballets Russes. London, as we have seen, had previously evinced no interest in male dancers. At the variety and music halls they had never been used as more than comic turns or porters standing by to facilitate the ballerina's teetotum spins – ridiculous rather than romantic figures. But Nijinsky's appeal transcended his physical qualities as a performer – his famous jump ('like Shelley's skylark, he seemed to "despise the earth",' sighed the

Daily News), his virtuosity, his chameleon acting. What made him unique, however, was his disturbingly ambivalent sexuality and androgyny. In a culture where masculinity was still strictly – almost legally – delineated and demarcated from femininity, such gender-bending was so shocking, so novel that it could scarcely be acknowledged. But it was felt: nowhere more so than in the final image of his own ballet to Debussy's *L'Après-midi d'un Faune*, first seen in London in 1913, where the eponymous faun, a languorous half-beast, half-human, caressed the nymph's dropped scarf in his crotch with something like masturbatory rapture – 'the little incident that set Paris talking' was how the *Standard*'s review tactfully explained it.

Off stage he could appear a bit of a brute: five foot eight, wiry but not elegant in build, with a small nose, black eyes, wide mouth, narrow chin and huge ungainly hands. In the street he could have been mistaken for a docker or a plumber. His manner was farouche, with something of the faun about it – 'a wild creature who had been trapped by society and was always ill at ease,' as one of Diaghilev's British dancers Hilda Munnings (alias Lydia Munningsova, later Sokolova) recalled. 'When addressed, he turned his head furtively, looking as if he might suddenly butt you in the stomach. He moved on the balls of his feet, and his nervous energy found an outlet in fidgeting. When he sat down he twisted his fingers or played with his shoes. He hardly spoke to anyone . . .'

He appealed, not surprisingly, to motherly types. Kind and generous Lady Ottoline Morrell took him under her wing and he was a frequent guest at her Bloomsbury salon in Bedford Square. Her quaint and wide-eyed memoirs give a vivid picture of his charisma and its poignant, helpless aspect. At first, she writes, she had 'rather pooh-poohed him' because 'most of my friends were such enthusiastic admirers', but 'when I saw him dance I was completely converted'. Although he was 'very quiet and rather ugly . . . very nervous and highly-strung', Ottoline grew 'very fond of the little figure with long muscular neck and pale Kalmuk face' and despite the language barriers her affection was clearly reciprocated. Like so many chronically shy people, he was prone to spasms of alarming and uninhibited frankness. Osbert Sitwell was once present at a soirée at Ottoline's when Nijinsky came up with 'Lady Morrell is so tall, so beautiful, like giraffe'. Diaghilev politely protested against what she might have interpreted as an insult, but

Nijinsky insisted. 'No, no, giraffe is beautiful, long, gracious – she looks like it.'

Ottoline would have been touched by this tribute. She understood Nijinsky's sincerity, for it was a quality she herself suffered from among the cynics of Bloomsbury. 'There were at this time fantastic fables about him,' she continued,

> that he was very debauched, that he had girdles of emeralds and diamonds given him by an Indian prince; but on the contrary, I found that he disliked any possessions or anything that hampered him or diverted him from his art. He was incessantly thinking out new ballets, new steps; also he was absorbed by the ideas of the old Russian myths and religions which he wanted to express in his ballets as he did in *Le Sacre du Printemps*. Such ballets as *Le Spectre de la Rose* did not interest him; he said it was *trop joli* and was rather annoyed when people admired it.

One afternoon Nijinsky and Bakst visited Ottoline 'when Duncan Grant and some others were playing tennis in Bedford Square garden – they were so entranced by the tall trees against the houses and the figures flitting about playing tennis that they exclaimed with delight "*Quel décor!*"'. Dance historians have speculated that this may have been the germ for one of Nijinsky's most mysterious and original ballets, *Jeux* (for which Bakst designed a Bedford Square-like setting and Debussy wrote the score), in which a boy and two girls dressed in tennis whites meet by chance in a garden and flirt inconclusively.

To the incipient homosexual culture of the time Nijinsky was an object of intense fantasy and curiosity. Lytton Strachey had long lusted from afar and, for their first meeting, arranged by Ottoline in 1913, he bought himself a new suit 'of darkest purple'. Nothing much happened during their encounter: afterwards he could tell his friend the painter Henry Lamb only that Nijinsky was 'certainly not a eunuch' and 'very nice, though you won't believe it' (later Strachey sent him a huge basket of flowers, which were presented on stage after a performance). But they could do no more than bow and smile, as 'the poor fellow cannot speak more than 2 words of any human language.'

Not true! Within a few years the poor fellow had gone insane, driven over the brink by the horror of the war and the pressures of his own fame, struggling with his genius, his Tolstoyan dreams of goodness and the twists and turns of his unresolved sexuality. Logorrhoea was one of the early symptoms of his lunacy, and his diary of 1919 raves obsessively about the English:

> I go gloo-gloo like a turkey, but I understand what I'm saying when I go gloo-gloo. I am a glo-bule dog, because I have big eyes. I am a globule, because I like the English. The English are not John Bull. John Bull has a stomach full of money, and mine is full of intestine. My intestine feels very well, because I don't eat much money. John Bull eats a lot of money, and that's why his stomach is swollen. I don't like a swollen stomach, because it stops me dancing. The English don't like dancing, because they have so much money in their stomachs.
>
> If the English are frightened of me and send assassins to Switzerland, I shall knock them down before they knock me down. They'll put me in prison for the rest of my life, because that's what the English want. The English are incredibly wicked . . .

Ballets Russes's last pre-war season closed on 25 July 1914, three days before Austria-Hungary declared war on Serbia. Six weeks later Britain was embroiled too, as a hundred years of the balance of power collapsed. The theatres would do their bit for King and Country, with productions of Shakespeare's *Henry V* and new plays with titles like *On His Majesty's Service* and *England Expects*. But first off the mark was the Empire, which mounted a new patriotic ballet called *Europe*, shown alongside a newsreel film of the German occupation of Brussels.

Had the Ballets Russes been a dream and a chimera? There was a reaction against the dangerous continental decadence which had puffed up art with decadence and pretension: in the words of Samuel Hynes, 'The war against Germany rapidly became a war against modernism.' *Europe* therefore reverted to the 'up-to-date' style popular in the 1890s, its three tableaux featuring an Italian ballerina, Francesca Zanfretta, as Dame Europa, in whose schoolroom breaks out a quarrel between the nations; Dorothy Craske as the hornpiping Jack, 'John Bull's Boy' and Pavlova's pupil Phyllis Bedells as Mademoiselle Paris. *The Times*'s critic thought that a final scene showing 'Britannia keeping watch with her allies' would be 'much improved by the immediate introduction of some figures representing the Colonial and Indian forces', but paradoxically it is the extraordinary internationalism of the piece – devised by Edouard Espinosa, son of the Spanish-born ballet master Léon Espinosa, who had been a resident dancer at the Bolshoi in Moscow before settling in London in 1872 – that one notices.

Throughout the nineteenth century the official top layer of British ideology had become ever more supremacist and racist: we ruled the waves, so Johnny Foreigner had better watch out. Chauvinism and jingoism were behind the propaganda of the war: 'We shall hear no more of the pretty-pretty babblers, with their Bond Street barbarism and their rococo recklessness,' thundered St John Ervine in a diatribe typical of the early phase of the war, published in *The Englishwoman* in October 1915. 'The Vorticists and the Imagists and the Futurists and the rest of the rabble of literary and artistic lunatics provided slender entertainment for empty days; but our minds are empty no longer; and we have no time to waste on monkeys on sticks.' Yet there was another deeper spirit of liberalism in England, which in its small, way the pageant of *Europe* celebrated and symbolised – a spirit which reached out to welcome and embrace the foreign ('and what should they know of England,' as Kipling asked, 'who only England know?'), a spirit of cultural open house, which transcended even the implications of its theatre's name.

We have the visitors to thank for that.

Bibliography

CHAPTER I – THÉODORE GÉRICAULT, PAINTER

On Géricault

Géricault, Galeries Nationales du Grand Palais (Paris, 1991).

Géricault: Dessins et estampes, Ecole Nationale Supérieure des Beaux Arts (Paris, 1998). A magnificent comprehensive catalogue of Géricault's drawings and prints.

Géricault: tout l'oeuvre grave, Musée des Beaux Arts de Rouen (Rouen, 1982).

Brookner, Anita, *Soundings* (London, 1997). Contains an excellent introductory account of Géricault's life and art.

Clément, Charles, *Géricault*, ed. L. Eitner (repr. London, 1973). The first biography and still our main source of first-hand information.

Eitner, Lorenz, *Géricault: His Life and Work* (London, 1983). By far the most authoritative modern monograph and biography.

—— 'Erotic Drawings by Géricault', *Master Drawings*, xxxiv (1996), pp. 375–89.

—— *The Raft of the 'Medusa'* (Oxford, 1972).

Nochlin, Linda, 'Géricault or the Absence of Women', *Géricault*, Conférences et Colloques du Louvre (Paris, 1996), vol. 1, pp. 403–17

Wheelock, Whitney, *Géricault in Italy* (New Haven and London, 1997).

On the 'Medusa'

Barnes, Julian, *A History of the World in Ten and a Half Chapters* (London, 1989).

Eitner, *The Raft*, op. cit.

Nicolson, Benedict, 'The Raft of the Medusa from the Point of View of the Subject-Matter', *Burlington Magazine*, xcvi (August 1954), pp. 241–8.

Savigny, J. B. H. and Alexander Corréard, *Narrative of a Voyage to Senegal in 1816* (repr. London, 1968).

On Géricault in England

Fox, Celina, 'Géricault's Lithographs of the London Poor', *Print Quarterly*, vol. 1(1988), pp. 62–6.

Johnson, Lee, 'The Raft of the Medusa in Great Britain', *Burlington Magazine*, xcvi (August 1954), pp. 249–53.

—— 'Géricault and Delacroix seen by Cockerell', *Burlington Magazine*, cxiii (September 1971) pp. 547–9.

Lodge, Suzanne, 'Géricault in England', *Burlington Magazine*, cvii (December 1965), pp. 616–27.

Sells, Christopher, 'New light on Géricault, his Travels and his Friends 1816–23', *Apollo* (June 1986), pp. 390–5.

On the art of the early nineteenth century
Brookner, Anita, *Jacques-Louis David* (London, 1980).

Craske, Matthew, *Art in Europe 1700–1830* (Oxford, 1997). A sound general introduction, with full bibliography.

Eitner, Lorenz (ed.), *Neoclassicism and Romanticism 1750–1850: Sources and Documents* (London, 1971), 2 vols.

Rosenblum, Ron, *Transformations in Late Eighteenth-Century Art* (Princeton, NJ, 1967).

On English art c. 1820
English Sporting Painting 1650–1850, Hayward Gallery, London (London, 1974).

Boase, T. S. R., *English Art, 1800–1870* (London, 1959).

Deuchar, Stephen, *Sporting Art in Eighteenth-Century England* (New Haven, Ct. and London, 1988).

Edwards, Ralph and L. G. G. Ramsey (eds.), *The Regency Period* (London, 1962).

Godfrey, Richard T. *Printmaking in Britain* (Oxford, 1978).

Haydon, Benjamin, *The Diary*, ed. W. Bissell Pope (Cambridge, Mass., 1960), 5 vols.

Lister, Raymond, *British Romantic Painting* (Cambridge, 1989).

Matteson, Lynn, 'Géricault and English Street Cries', *Apollo*, October 1977.

Piper, David, *The Genius of English Painting* (London, 1975).

Twyman, Michael, *Lithography 1800–1850* (London, 1970).

Whitley, William T., *Art in England 1800–1820* and *Art in England 1821–1837* (New York, 1973).

On London, c. 1820
The Annual Register for the Year 1820 (London, 1821).

London, World City 1800–1840, Museum of London (New Haven and London, 1992). Highly recommended

Altick, Richard, *The Shows of London* (Cambridge, Mass., 1978). A scholarly and fascinating history of the exhibitions and entertainments of London, with a full account of William Bullock.

Briggs, Asa, *The Age of Improvement 1783–1867 (London, 1979)*

Darnley, Sir Charles and Marquise de Vermont, *London and Paris: Comparative Sketches* (London, 1823).

Gash, Norman, *Aristocracy and People: Britain 1815–1865* (London, 1979).

Halevy, Elie, *England in 1815* (London, 1924). Still the most illuminating general account of British society of the time.

Hibbert, Christopher, *London: the Biography of a City* (London, 1974).

Lamb, Charles, *Letters*, ed. Evans (London, 1935), vol. i.

Low, D. M., *That Sunny Dome: A Portrait of Regency Britain* (London, 1977).

Summerson, John, *Georgian London* (London, 1962).

Thompson, E. P., *The Making of the English Working Class* (Harmondsworth, 1968).

On the Cato Street conspiracy
Gattrell, V. A. C., *The Hanging Tree* (Oxford, 1994).
The Times, 2 May 1820.
Wilkinson, G. T., *An Authentic History of the Cato Street Conspiracy* (London, 1820).

On Géricault and horses
British Sporting Painting, op. cit.
Deuchar, *Sporting Art* , op. cit.
Grunchec, Philippe, *Géricault's Horses* (London, 1985).
Mortimer, Roger, *History of the Derby Stakes* (London, 1962).

CHAPTER 2 – RICHARD WAGNER, COMPOSER

On mid-Victorian England
Aslet, Clive, *The Story of Greenwich* (London, 1999).
Best, Geoffrey, *Mid Victorian Britain* (London, 1979).
Briggs, Asa, *The Age of Improvement*, op. cit.
—— *Victorian Cities* (Harmondsworth, 1968).

Dyos, H. J. and D. H. Aldcroft, *British Transport: An Economic Survey* (Leicester, 1969)

Dyos, H. J. and Michael Wolff, *The Victorian City* (London, 1973), 2 vols. A fine compendium of scholarly essays.

Kitson Clark, G., *The Making of Victorian England* (London, 1962).

Thompson, F. M. L., *The Rise of Respectable Society* (London, 1988).

Young. G. M., *Victorian England: Portrait of an Age* (London, 1953). A classic general essay on the period.

On Richard Wagner

Millington, Barry, *The Wagner Compendium* (London, 1992). A vital reference book.

—— *Wagner* (London, 1984). A recommended short critical and biographical study.

Newman, Ernest, *The Life of Richard Wagner* (London, 1933–47, repr. 1976), 4 vols.

Skelton, Geoffrey, *Richard and Cosima Wagner: Portrait of a Marriage* (London, 1982).

Spotts, Frederick, *Bayreuth: A History of the Wagner Festival* (New Haven and London, 1994).

Wagner, Cosima, *Diaries*, trans. G. Skelton, ed. M. Gregor-Dellin and D. Mack (London, 1978), vol. 1, 1869–77.

Wagner, Richard, *Mein Leben* (My Life), trans. A. Gray, and ed. A. Whittall (Cambridge, 1983).

—— *Prose Works,* trans. and ed. A. A. Ellis (London, 1892–9; repr. 1972), 8 vols.

—— *Selected Letters*, trans. and ed. B. Millington and S. Spencer (London, 1987)

On London musical life

Atwood, William G., *The Parisian Worlds of Frédéric Chopin* (New Haven, Ct. and London, 2000). Contains an interesting account of Chopin's antipathy to London.

Cairns, David, *Berlioz*, vol. 2, 'Struggle and Greatness' (London, 1999), Chapters 15 and 21.

Clark, Ronald, *The Royal Albert Hall* (London, 1958).

Ganz, A. W., *Berlioz in London* (London, 1950).

Hueffer, Francis, *Half a Century of Music in England 1837–1887* (London, 1889).

Lee Hall, Jennifer, 'The Refashioning of Fashionable Society: Opera-Going and Sociability 1821–61' (Ph.D. thesis, Yale University, 1996).

Musgrave, Michael, *The Musical Life of the Crystal Palace* (Cambridge, 1995).

Raynor, Henry, *Music in England* (London, 1980).

Reid, Charles, *The Music Monster: A Biography of James William Davison* (London, 1984).

Temperley, Nicholas (ed.) 'The Romantic Age 1800–1914', *The Blackwell History of Music in Britain*, vol. 5 (Oxford, 1988).

On Wagner and Wagnerism in London

Anonymous, 'Lyric Feuds', *Westminster Review*, July 1876, pp. 145–60.

—— 'The Wagner Festival at Bayreuth', *MacMillan's*, xxxv (November 1876–April 1877), pp. 55–63.

Dzamba Sessa, Anne, *Richard Wagner and the English* (London, 1979). Concentrates mostly on Wagner's posthumous influence on literature, music and painting.

Eliot, George, *Letters,* ed. G. Haight (New Haven, 1954–5), vol. 6, 1874–7.

Ellis, W. A., *Life of Richard Wagner* (London, 1900–8), 6 vols. Vol. 5 deals exclusively and in exhaustive detail with the London visit of 1855 and contains full texts of all the reviews.

Hueffer, Francis, *Half a Century*, op. cit.

Ionides, Luke, *Memoirs* (Paris, 1925). Contains the recollections of his sister Chariclea Dannreuther.

Spencer, Stewart, 'Wagner in London', *Wagner*, iii (1982), pp. 98–123. Contains documents relating to Wagner's dealings with the Philharmonic Society.

On London Wagnerites and anti-Wagnerites

Dibble, Jeremy, *C. Hubert H. Parry: His Life and Music* (Oxford, 1992).

Dzamba Sessa, Anne, 'At Wagner's Shrine: British and American Wagnerians', in *Wagnerism in European Culture and Politics*, ed., D. Large and W. Weber (Ithaca and London, 1984).

MacCarthy, Fiona, *William Morris* (London, 1994).

Newall, Christopher, *The Grosvenor Gallery Exhibitions* (Cambridge, 1995).

Parry, Hubert, *Diaries* (Unpublished MS, Shulbrede Priory, Surrey).

Reid, *Music Monster*, op. cit.

Shonfield, Zuzanna, *The Precariously Privileged: A Professional Family in Victorian London* (Oxford, 1987). A study of Jeannette Marshall, based on her remarkable diaries.

CHAPTER 3 – RALPH WALDO EMERSON, PHILOSOPHER

Emerson, Ralph Waldo, *The Journals and Miscellaneous Notebooks*, vol. x, 1847–8, ed. Merton M. Sealts (Cambridge, Mass. 1973).

—— *The Collected Works*, various editors; vol.3 (in two parts) 'Essays: First Series and Second Series', (Cambridge, Mass., 1983); vol.4, 'Representative Men' (Cambridge, Mass., 1987); vol.5, 'English Traits' (Cambridge, Mass., 1994).

—— *The Letters*, ed. Ralph R. Rusk; vol. 1, 1813–35; vol. 3, 1842–47; vol. 4, 1848–55 (New York, 1939).

This chapter largely draws on the above volumes and the magnificent textual scholarship they embody. To assist easy reading, Emerson's erratic spelling and punctuation in his letters and journals has occasionally been very slightly amended.

On Emerson's life

Garnett, Richard, *Life of Ralph Waldo Emerson* (London, 1888).

Porte, Joel, *Representative Man* (New York, 1979).

Richardson Jr, Robert D., *Emerson: The Mind on Fire* (Berkeley and LA, 1995).

Scudder, Townsend, *Lonely Wayfaring Man* (London and New York, 1936).

On Carlyle

Carlyle, Thomas and Jane Welsh, *Collected Letters*, Duke–Edinburgh edn.; vol. 6, October 1831–September 1833 (Durham, NC, 1977); vol. 22, July 1847–March 1848 (Durham, NC,1995); vol. 23, April 1848–March 1849 (Durham, NC, 1995).

The Correspondence of Emerson and Carlyle, ed. J. Slater (New York, 1964).

Fielding, K.J., 'The Cry from Craigenputtoch', *Times Literary Supplement*, 13 August 1999.

Holme, Thea, *The Carlyles at Home* (Oxford ,1979).

Kaplan, Fred, *Thomas Carlyle* (Cambridge, 1983).

Wilson, A. N., *God's Funeral* (London, 1999). In particular, chapter 4.

On the English in America and Americans in England

Bowen, Frank C., *A Century of Atlantic Travel* (London, 1930).

Dickens, Charles, *Dickens on America and the Americans*, ed. M. Slater (Austin, Texas, 1978).

Hitchens, Christopher, *Blood, Class and Nostalgia* (London, 1990). A critique of Anglo-American relations in the twentieth century.

Lockwood, Allison, *Passionate Pilgrims: The American Traveller in Great Britain, 1800–1914* (New York and London, 1981).

Mulvey, Christopher, *Anglo-American Landscapes* (Cambridge, 1983)

Trollope, Fanny, *Domestic Manners of the Americans*, ed. J. E. Money (Barre, Mass., 1969).

On Emerson and his impact in England

Conway, Moncure, *Emerson at Home and Abroad* (London, 1883).

Crabb Robinson, Henry, *The Diary*, ed. D. Hudson (London, 1967).

Goudes, Clarence, *American Literature in Nineteenth–Century England* (New York, 1944).

Scudder, Townsend, 'A Chronological List of Emerson's Lectures', *PMLA*, li (1936), pp. 242–8.

Sowder, William J., *Emerson's Impact on the British Isles and Canada* (Charlottesville, Va, 1966).

On Arthur Hugh Clough

Chorley, Katherine, *Arthur Hugh Clough: The Uncommitted Mind* (Oxford, 1962).

Clough, Arthur Hugh, *Correspondence*, ed. F. Mulhauser (Oxford, 1957), 2 vols.

—— *The Emerson–Clough letters*, ed. H. L. Lowry and R. L. Rusk (Cleveland, Ohio, 1934).

—— *The Oxford Diaries*, ed. A. Kenny (Oxford, 1990).

CHAPTER 4: THE PSYCHIC CLOUD: YANKEE SPIRIT-TRAPPERS

On the general history of spiritualism

Brandon, Ruth, *The Spiritualists: The Passion for the Occult in the Nineteenth and Twentieth Centuries* (London, 1983). In particular, chapters 2 and 3.

Brown, Salter, *The Heyday of Spiritualism* (New York, 1970).

Crookes, William, *Researches into the Phenomena of Modern Spiritualism* (London, 1874).

Gauld, Alan, *The Founders of Psychical Research* (London, 1968).

Howitt, William, *The History of the Supernatural* (London, 1863).

Inglis, Brian, *Natural and Supernatural* (London, 1977). An enjoyable history of the entire field.

Oppenheim, Janet, *The Other World: Spiritualism and Psychical Research in England, 1850–1914* (Cambridge, 1985). The most scholarly and fair–minded of recent accounts.

Owen, Alex, *The Darkened Room: Women, Power and Spiritualism in Late Victorian England* (London, 1989).

Pearsall, Ronald, *The Table–Rappers* (London, 1972).

Podmore, Frank, *Modern Spiritualism: A History and a Criticism* (London, 1902), 2 vols.

—— *The Newer Spiritualism* (London, 1910).

Wilson, Colin, *The Occult* (London, 1971).

On spiritualism in the USA

Brown, op. cit.

Clark, Uriah, *Plain Man's Guide to Spiritualism* (Boston, Mass., 1863)

Howitt, op. cit.

On Mesmerism

Winter, Alison, *Mesmerised: Powers of Mind in Victorian Britain* (London and Chicago, 1999).

On Daniel Home

Anonymous [Bell, Robert], 'Stranger than Fiction', *The Cornhill Magazine*, August 1860.

—— 'Home, Daniel Dunglas', in *Dictionary of National Biography*, vol. ix (Oxford, 1938).

—— 'Home, Great Home', *Punch*, 18 August 1860 (see also 9 June, 11 August, 18 August and 8 September 1860).

—— *Report on Spiritualism*, London Dialectical Society (London, 1871).

Burton, Jean, *Heyday of a Wizard: Daniel Home, the Medium* (New York, 1944).

Dingwall, Eric John, *Some Human Oddities* (London, 1947).

Dunraven, Earl of, *Experiences in Spiritualism with D. D. Home* (Glasgow, 1924).

Hall, Trevor H., *The Enigma of Daniel Home* (Buffalo, NY, 1984). A fanatically strenuous attempt to rationalise Home's powers.

Home, Daniel Dunglas, *Incidents in My Life* (London, 1863 and 1872), 2 vols.

—— *Lights and Shadows of Spiritualism* (New York, 1877).

Home, Madame, *D. D. Home: His Life and Mission*, ed. A. Conan Doyle (London, 1921).

Jenkins, Elizabeth, *The Shadow and the Light* (London, 1982). Detailed and perhaps excessively sympathetic. Chapters 23–6 contain the best account of Lyon v. Home.

Wyndham, Horace, *Mr Sludge, the Medium* (London, 1937). A cynical approach.

On Mrs Hayden
Anonymous, 'The Ghost of the Cock Lane Ghost', *Household Words*, November 1852.

On Home in France
Barthez, Dr E., *The Empress Eugénie and her Circle* (New York, 1913).

On the Davenport brothers
Brown, op. cit.

On the Brownings and spiritualism
Browning, Elizabeth Barrett, *Letters to her Sister*, ed. L. Huxley (New York, 1913).

—— *Letters of Mrs Browning*, ed. F. G. Kenyon (London, 1897), 2 vols.

Browning, Robert, *Letters*, ed. T. Hood (New Haven, Conn., 1933).

Forster, Margaret, *Elizabeth Barrett Browning* (London, 1988).

Porter, Katherine H., *Through a Glass Darkly: Spiritualism in the Browning Circle* (Lawrence, Kansas, 1958). A delightful monograph.

Taplin, Gardner B., *The Life of Elizabeth Barrett Browning* (London, 1957).

On Dickens and Home
Dickens, Charles, *Letters*, vols. ix and x, ed. G. Storey (Oxford, 1997–8).

—— 'The Martyr Medium' in *All the Year Round*, 4 April 1863.

On investigators into spiritualist phenomena
Gauld, op. cit.
Hall, Trevor, *New Light on Old Ghosts* (London, 1965).
Jenness, George A., *Maskelyne and Cooke* (Enfield, 1967).
Maskelyne, John N., *Modern Spiritualism* (London, 1875).
Pearsall, op. cit.
Podmore, op. cit.
Sitwell, Osbert, *Left Hand, Right Hand* (Boston, Mass., 1944), Appendix A.

CHAPTER 5 – AUSTRALIAN CRICKETERS

On Aborigines
Brough Smyth, R., *The Aborigines of Victoria* (London, 1878), vol. 2.
Clark, C. M. H., *A History of Australia* (Melbourne, 1978), vol. 4, 'The Earth Abideth'.
Hale, Revd. Matthew, *The Aborigines of Australia* (London, 1889).
Hughes, Robert, *The Fatal Shore* (London, 1987).
Wood, Revd J. G., *The Natural History of Man* (London, 1870), vol. 2.

On race
Barzun, Jacques, *Race: a study in modern superstition* (London, 1938).
Lively, Adam, *Masks: Blackness, Race and the Imagination* (London, 1998).

On Australian cricket
Altham, H. S. and Swanton, E. W., *A History of Cricket* (London, 1948), vol. 1.
Mangan, J. A. (ed.), *The Cultural Bond* (London, 1992). In particular, James Bradley, 'The MCC, Society and Empire'.
—— *The Games Ethic and Imperialism* (London, 1986).
Moyes, A. G., *Australian Cricket: A History* (London, 1959).
Pollard, Jack, *The Formative Years of Australian Cricket*, 1803–1893 (Sydney, 1987).

On the Aborigines' tour
Mulvaney, John and Rex Harcourt, *Cricket Walkabout* (London, 1988).

Brighton Gazette, 11 June 1868.
Eastbourne Standard, 6 October 1868.
Sheffield Telegraph, 26 May 1868.
Sporting Life, 16 May 1868.
The Times, 27 May, 15 June, 14 September 1868.
Yorkshire Gazette, 18 July 1868.

On cricket in Victorian England
Altham and Swanton, op. cit.
Bailey, Peter, *Leisure and Class in Victorian England* (London, 1978).
Birley, Derek, *Sport and the Making of Britain* (Manchester, 1983).
—— *Land of Sport and Glory* (Manchester, 1995).
Bradley, James, 'Inventing Australians and Constructing Englishness: Cricket and the Creation of National Consciousness', *Sporting Traditions*, xi.11 (May 1995).
Briggs, Asa, 'Thomas Hughes and the Public Schools' in *Victorian People* (Harmondsworth, 1965).
Holt, Richard, 'Cricket and Englishness: The Batsman as Hero', *International Journal of the History of Sport*, xiii.1 (March 1996).
Hughes, Thomas ('An Old Boy'), *Tom Brown's Schooldays* (London, 1857).
Sandiford, Keith, 'Cricket and Victorian Society', *Journal of Social History*, xvii (Winter 1983).
Scott, Patrick, 'Cricket and the Religious World in the Victorian Period', *Church Quarterly*, iii.2 (October 1970).

On London shows
Altick, op. cit
Household Words, 11 June 1853

On Spofforth and the Australian tours 1877–84
Cricket, 17 August 1882; 29 January 1903.
The Globe, 28 May 1878.
Punch, 28 May 1878; 9 September 1882.
The Times, 28 May 1878; 29, 30 August 1882.
Vanity Fair, 13 July 1878.
Anonymous, 'Recollections of Mr F R Spofforth', *Wisden's Cricketers' Almanack for 1927* (London, 1927).
—— 'An Interview with the Demon Bowler', *Pall Mall Budget*, 1886,

reprinted in *Bat and Pad: Writings on Australian Cricket*, ed. Mullins and Derriman (Melbourne, 1984).

Barker, Ralph, *Ten Great Bowlers* (London, 1967).

Cardus, Neville, *Days in the Sun* (London,1924).

Cashman, Richard, *The Demon Spofforth* (Sydney, 1990).

—— 'Symbols of Unity: Anglo Australian Cricketers', in *The Cultural Bond*, ed. J. A. Mangan (London, 1992).

Giffen, George, *With Bat and Ball* (London, 1898).

Grace, W. G., *Reminiscences* (London, 1899).

—— *Cricket* (London, 1891).

Harte, Chris, *A History of Australian Cricket* (London, 1993).

Hawke, Lord (ed.), *The Memorial Biography of Dr W. G. Grace* (London, 1919).

Mandle, W. F. , 'W. G. Grace as Victorian Hero', *Historical Studies*, lxxiix. 9 (1981).

Rae, Simon, *W. G. Grace: A Life* (London, 1998).

Spofforth, F. R., 'In the Days of my Youth', *M. A. P.* (28 November 1903).

CHAPTER 6: THE TEETOTUM SPIN: EXOTIC DANCERS

On Dame Nellie Melba

Anonymous, 'The Australian Girl', *Sketch*, 4 September 1895.

Hetherington, John, *Melba* (London, 1965).

Melba, Nellie, *Melodies and Memories* (London, 1925).

Radic, Therese, *Melba: the Voice of Australia* (Melbourne, 1986).

On Opera in late-Victorian London

Christiansen, Rupert, *Prima Donna* (London, 1995)

Glackens, Ira, *Yankee Diva: Lillian Nordica and the Golden Days of American Opera* (New York, 1963).

Rosenthal, Harold, *Two Centuries of Opera at Covent Garden* (London, 1958).

Shaw, G. B., *Shaw's Music*, ed. D. Laurence (London, 1981), 3 vols.

On Gladys de Grey

Buckle, Richard, *Diaghilev* (London, 1979).

Karsavina, Tamara, *Theatre Street* (London, 1930).

Melba, op. cit.

On women in nineteenth-century London theatre
Anonymous, 'Morals of Ballet Girls', *The Era*, 23 January 1859.
Bailey, Peter, *Leisure and Class in Victorian England* (London, 1978).
Beamish, Jonas A., *The Antitheatrical Prejudice* (Berkeley, Ca. and London, 1981).
Jackson, Russell (ed.), *Victorian Theatre* (London, 1989).
Kent, Christopher, 'Image and Reality' in *A Widening Sphere*, ed. M. Vicinus (Bloomington Ind. and London, 1997).
Richards, Sandra, *The Rise of the English Actress* (London, 1993).
Soldene, Emily, *My Theatrical and Musical Recollections* (London, 1897).

On ballet and dancing in nineteenth-century London
International Dictionary of Ballet, ed. M. Bremser (Detroit, 1993), 2 vols.
Anonymous, 'Spoken by a Dancer', *Punch*, 27 February 1864.
—— 'Curates and Ballet Girls', *London Truth*, 11 December 1879.
—— 'Stage Morality and the Ballet', *Blackwood's*, March 1869.
Beaumont, Cyril, *Complete Book of Ballets* (London, 1937).
Bedells, Phyllis, *My Dancing Days* (London, 1954).
Brinson, Peter and Peggy van Praagh, *The Choreographic Art* (London, 1963).
Crawford Flitch, J.-E., *Modern Dance and Dancing* (London, 1912).
Guest, Ivor, *The Dancer's Heritage* (London, 1960).
Holroyd, Michael, *Shaw*, vol. 1:1856–98 (London, 1988).
Jackson, Holbrook, *The Eighteen Nineties* (Harmondsworth, 1939).
Morgan, Ted, *Winston Churchill: Young Man in a Hurry* (New York, 1982).
Saint, Andrew (ed.), *Politics and the People of London* (London and Ronceverte, 1989).
St Johnston, Reginald, *A History of Dancing* (London, 1906).
Stokes, John, *In the Nineties* (Hemel Hempstead, 1989). In particular, 'Prudes on the Prowl'.
Sturgis, Matthew, *Passionate Attitudes: The English Decadence of the 1890s* (London, 1995)

On the Alhambra and Empire
Anonymous, 'Royal Visit to the Empire', *The Music Hall*, 6 July 1889.

—— 'The Shah at the Ballet', *Star*, 5 July 1889.

Guest, Ivor, *Ballet in Leicester Square* (London, 1992).

Mander, Raymond and Joe Mitcheson, *The Lost Theatres of London* (London, 1968).

Pritchard, Jane, 'The Empire in Manchester', *Dance Research* (Winter 1995), xiii.2.

Shaw, G. B., *Shaw's Music*, op. cit.

—— *Immaturity* (London, 1930).

Symons, Arthur, 'At the Alhambra', *The Savoy*, September 1896.

On Stewart Headlam

Anonymous, 'Curates and Ballet Girls', op. cit.

Bettany, F. G., *Stewart Headlam* (London, 1926).

Headlam, Stewart, *The Ballet* (London, 1894).

Richard, Ralph, 'Stewart Headlam – the Dancing Priest', *About the House* (Christmas 1984), vii.1.

On Pierina Legnani

Anonymous, 'A Chat with Signorina Legnani', *Sketch*, 26 April 1893.

—— 'Signorina Legnani', *St Paul's*, 25 August 1894.

International Dictionary of Ballet, op. cit.

Brinson and van Praagh, op. cit.

Fokine, Michael, *Memoirs of a Ballet Master*, trans. V. Fokine (London, 1961).

Karsavina, op. cit.

San-Francisco, Paul, 'Tea time with Pierina Legnani', *Dance Magazine* (11 November 1955), xxix.11.

On Kate Vaughan

Anonymous, 'A Chat with Kate Vaughan', *The Era*, 20 April 1889.

Fellom, Martie, 'Kate Vaughan', Proceedings of the Ninth Annual Conference, Society of Dance History Scholars, 1986 (Riverside, Ca. 1986).

Michel, Artur, 'Kate Vaughan or the Poetry of the Skirt Dance', *Dance*, January 1945.

On Skirt Dancing

Anonymous, 'The Dancing of the Day', *Pall Mall Budget*, 14 April 1892.

—— 'The High Priestess of Skirt Dancing', *Sketch*, 2 August 1893.

—— 'The Length of a Petticoat', *Daily Graphic*, 13 February 1891.

—— 'The Science of Skirt Dancing', *Daily Graphic*, 14 April 1892.

Crawford Flitch, J. E., op. cit.

Perugini, Mark, 'Skirt Dancing: Its Place in Dance History', *The Dancing Times*, February 1945.

On Cyrene

Anonymous, 'Cyrene, at the Alhambra', *Sketch*, 5 April 1893.

On Loie Fuller

Bishop, Emily M., *Americanised Delsarte Culture* (Washington, DC, 1892)

Booth, Michael R., *Victorian Spectacular Theatre 1850–1910* (London, 1981).

Current, Richard and Marcia, *Loie Fuller: Goddess of Light* (Boston, Mass., 1997).

Duncan, Isadora, *My Life* (London, 1928).

Fuller, Loie, *Fifteen Years of a Dancer's Life* (London, 1913).

Johnson, Paul, 'A Dumpy Girl from Chicago', *Spectator*, 23 August 1997.

Lista, Giovanni, *Loie Fuller: Danseuse de la Belle Epoque* (Paris, 1994)

Sommer, Sally R., 'The Apprenticeship of Loie Fuller', *Dance Scope* (Winter 1977–8), xii.1.

—— 'Loie Fuller', *Dance Chronicle*, (1982), iv.4.

—— 'Loie Fuller' in *International Encylopaedia of Dance*, vol. 3 (New York and Oxford, 1998).

On Isadora Duncan

Serov, Victor, *The Real Isadora* (London 1972).

Duncan, op. cit.

On Adeline Genée

Guest, Ivor, *Adeline Genée* (London, 1958).

On the Ballets Russes

Brooke, Rupert, *Selected Letters*, ed. G. Keynes (London, 1968).

Buckle, *Diaghilev*, op. cit.

Drummond, John, *Speaking of Diaghilev* (London, 1997).

Fokine, op. cit.

Garafola, Lynn, *Diaghilev's Ballets Russes* (Oxford and New York, 1989). In particular, chapter 11.

—— and N. Van Norman Bear, *The Ballets Russes and its World* (New Haven, Ct. and London, 2000)

Karsavina, op. cit.

MacDonald, Nesta, *Diaghilev Observed* (London, 1975).

Roose-Evans, James, *Experimental Theatre* (London, 1970).

Woolf, Virginia, *The Letters*, vol.1, 'The Flight of the Mind 1888–1912', ed. N. Nicolson (London, 1975).

On Nijinsky

Buckle, Richard, *Nijinsky* (London, 1971).

Drummond, op. cit.

Holroyd, Michael, *Lytton Strachey* (London, 1994).

Morrell, Ottoline, *Memoirs*, ed. J. Gathorne-Hardy (London, 1964).

Nijinsky, Vaslav, *The Diary of Vaslav Nijinsky*, trans. A. Fitzlyon and ed. J. Acocella (Paris, 1999).

On English culture and the outbreak of the First World War

Hynes, Samuel, *A War Imagined* (London, 1990).

Acknowledgements

My agent Caroline Dawnay and my editor Penelope Hoare have shown both great forbearance and encouragement in their nurturing of this book. Ilsa Yardley did a superb job of copy-editing, and Stuart Williams and Henrietta Bredin did sterling work on the picture research. Fram Dinshaw, Kenneth Glover, Suzy Hogarth, Bill and Virginia Nicholson, Jane Pritchard, Uta and Leslie Thompson, Giles Waterfield and Sarah C. Woodcock have also helped in various ways. I am grateful to them all.

I would like to thank the staff of the London Library, British Theatre Museum, Society for Psychical Research and the MCC Library at Lord's; Lady Shonfield and Caroline Miles, for permission to quote from Jeannette Marshall's diaries; and Laura Ponsonby and Kate and Ian Russell for their hospitality at Shulbrede Priory, and permission to quote from Hubert Parry's diaries.

Index